True Green

True Green

Executive Effectiveness in the U.S. Environmental Protection Agency

Edited by Gerald Andrews Emison and John Charles Morris

LEXINGTON BOOKS
Lanham • Boulder • New York • Toronto • Plymouth, UK

Published by Lexington Books
A wholly owned subsidiary of The Rowman & Littlefield Publishing Group, Inc.
4501 Forbes Boulevard, Suite 200, Lanham, Maryland 20706
www.rowman.com

Estover Road, Plymouth PL6 7PY, United Kingdom

British Library Cataloguing in Publication Information Available

Library of Congress Cataloging-in-Publication Data
True green : executive effectiveness in the U.S. Environmental Protection Agency / edited by Gerald
Andrews Emison and John C. Morris.
p. cm.
Includes bibliographical references and index.
ISBN 978-0-7391-7130-1 (cloth : alk. paper) -- ISBN 978-0-7391-7131-8 (electronic)
1. United States. Environmental Protection Agency--Evaluation. 2. United States. Environmental
Protection Agency--Management. 3. Environmental protection--United States--History. 4. Environ-
mental policy--United States--History. I. Emison, Gerald A. II. Morris, John C. (John Charles), 1959-
TD171.T78 2012
354.3'28230973--dc23
2012016593

Printed in the United States of America

This book is dedicated to the senior executives of EPA. Their knowledge and commitment to public service have yielded a cleaner environment for our nation. Their examples will serve as a beacon to those who follow.

Table of Contents

Acknowledgments

The genesis of this book was a roundtable at the Southeastern Conference on Public Administration in Wilmington, NC, October 2010. This panel brought together four remarkable individuals, all of whom had served many years as members of the Senior Executive Service. The stories they related, and the lessons they imparted to the audience that day, were fascinating. We quickly realized the collective wisdom of these public servants was too valuable to ignore, and the concept for this book took shape.

First and foremost, we thank our contributors to this volume. These men and women exemplify the very best in public service, and their collective years of public service represent a dedication to their fellow citizens that is unmatched. We also thank our editor at Lexington Books, Melissa Wilks, as well as the staff at Lexington Books, for their guidance and expertise as this book came together. We also thank Brittni McCrimmons, an MPA student at Old Dominion University, and Barrie Rhemann, an MPA student at Mississippi State University, for their help with formatting and editing. Finally, we thank our wives, Donna Kay Harrison and Elizabeth Dashiell (Betsy) Morris; their love and support made this book possible.

Preface

Today we often read about the complexity and intractability of the environmental problems facing our country and the world. Climate change is but one example. We must address not only the complex scientific nature of the issue but also the multinational economic implications of the solutions. On a national level we hear of a range of issues, from the impact of gas and oil extraction on groundwater to the health implications of low levels of ozone and particulates. Woven throughout the discussion of these issues are the economic and intergovernmental implications of possible solutions.

As I read about these types of issues and the controversy surrounding them I am reminded of my experience from the 1980s. As a political appointee of President Reagan, I was Executive Deputy Director of the Federal Emergency Management Agency in 1983 after fifteen years working in public safety agencies at the local, state and federal levels. In early 1983 I was assigned by the White House, along with three colleagues from other agencies, to provide management support and direction at the Environmental Protection Agency. What was to have been a short ninety-day detail developed into six years, the first two years as Assistant Administrator for Solid Waste and Emergency Response and the final four years as Administrator of the Agency. As I began my work at EPA, I quickly realized the complexity of the issues the Agency was charged with managing. For the next six years I worked with a broad group of dedicated environmental professionals developing policy recommendations across a broad range of issues. I relied heavily on members of the Senior Executive Service (SES) at EPA and promoted a team-based approach with both political and career professionals. We addressed a wide range of issues some of which included a growing problem with contamination of groundwater from leaking underground storage tanks; depletion of the stratospheric ozone layer from long-lived manmade chemicals; continued degradation of wetland habitat from uncontrolled development; and the cleanup of toxic waste sites at current and former manufacturing sites. As we worked together, I found the extensive experience of the career managers essential to the development of sound policy recommendations. Both their understanding of the scientific and legal basis of the issues, as well as their operations experience gave us a firm foundation for our approach. As policies were set in legislation (RCRA) or international agreements (Montreal Protocol) we worked to develop pragmatic approaches for their implementation. Many of the authors of this book worked with me during this period. Their leadership experiences and the programs they developed can provide today's environmental professionals with valuable insights into solutions for today's problems which I believe will lead to real environmental improvements.

After my career at EPA, I led an environmental engineering company and then two large manufacturing companies. From this vantage point in the private sector, I continued to see environmental managers developing and implementing practical solutions to environmental problems. Whether working with the professional managers at EPA or those in the private sector, I have seen true progress toward "green solutions." It is important that we learn from these experiences and use them as a foundation for the development of solutions to our environmental problems today.

Lee M. Thomas

Administrator

U.S. Environmental Protection Agency, 1984–1989

Introduction

John Charles Morris and Gerald Andrews Emison

The past five decades have witnessed a focused effort on the part of the national government to improve environmental quality in the U.S. In addition to creating a federal agency specifically charged with the implementation of national environmental policy, Congress has approved a series of laws designed to better protect the environment. These laws have prescribed limits on the release of environmentally dangerous compounds, regulated human exposure to specific toxic chemicals, and even provided for the direct enforcement of certain requirements. In short, a wide range of actions over the past half-century have established the national government as the preeminent force in environmental quality.

These efforts have led to a series of undeniable successes in terms of environmental quality in some settings. Toxic chemicals are no longer dumped randomly across the landscape; the use of lead-based paints has been largely eliminated (and completely eliminated in residential settings); and the smog so prevalent in many American cities in the 1960s has been significantly reduced. Rivers no longer catch fire, but have become the focus of redevelopment efforts in many cities. In spite of these successes, however, environmental matters are increasingly part of the national policy conversation. Although we have set national standards for ambient air quality (ozone and particulates, for example) and water quality (dissolved oxygen levels, nutrient loads, etc.), the attainment of many of these standards remains elusive. Acid rain continues to create significant environmental degradation in several regions of the nation, and the ubiquity of some toxins and pesticides from past practices challenges both scientists and policy makers alike (Rosenbaum 2011). Finally, while water shortages have been a fact of life in the West for many years, water supply issues are becoming more important in the Midwest and the South (Newman 2010).

A more recent phenomenon is a public (and increasingly, corporate) focus on "green behavior." Companies now advertise that their products are environmentally friendly, and consumers have shown a willingness to purchase "eco-friendly" goods. Toyota Motors Corporation touts their Prius model not only as a means to consume less fossil fuels (and thus reduce both air pollution and one's carbon footprint), but also highlights the percentage of the vehicle that contains recyclable materials. The Chevrolet Volt and Nissan Leaf are other examples of products that are sold as being "eco-friendly." Laundry soap, consumer packaging, and even Polartec™ fleece fabric are all sold as "green" products. While many of these products do have legitimate and positive environmental impacts, it becomes more difficult for both consumers and observers to distinguish between "green" consumer behavior and "green" career institutional image management.

The focus of this book is on "green behavior" as exhibited by senior career managers in the U.S. Environmental Protection Agency (EPA), the nation's premier environmental institution. Created in 1970, the EPA has been the administrative instrument through which we have sought to develop, regulate, and enforce national environmental standards. The senior managers in the EPA serve not only as the administrators responsible for successful implementation of environmental laws, they also serve a critical role as the interface between the offices and bureaus within the agency and the political leaders (both appointed and elected) above them. Such people must not only exhibit a commitment to the goals of the agency and the laws for which they have direct responsibility, they must also possess the scientific knowledge and management skills required to work effectively in the policy arena. They must also have the skills to administer these programs in what is often a complex, combative, multi-sectoral, and multi-institutional setting. This, in turn, requires the ability to balance multiple conflicting interests— individual interests, private individual and corporate interests, and the interests of nonprofit groups as well. Moreover, all of these interests must be balanced against an elusive and ill-defined notion of the public interest.

The arena in which these individuals operate presents many challenges. However, progress toward the attainment of national environmental goals requires the existence of leadership within large-scale institutions, and such leadership's success often depends upon adapting to unique and evolving settings. This volume focuses on the authentic experiences of career government professionals who have dedicated their lives to environmental protection. Written in their own words, these descriptions of the actions and philosophies exhibited by these environmental leaders provide important insight into both the challenges and successes (and, rarely, the failures) achieved over the course of their long careers. In doing so, these leaders help us fundamentally redefine "green behavior." No longer is "green behavior" simply a specific consumer activity or marketing fad, it most aptly describes the career-long commitment of competent, dedicated public servants toward the ultimate goal of a cleaner environment for both current and future generations of Americans.

In many respects, the task of a senior executive manager is similar to that of a ship's navigator. Both the executive and the manager need to know where they are, and where they want to go. Their job is to identify the best route to travel, and must constantly monitor their position to know where they are, and to ensure they are making good progress toward the destination. Both operate in an environment that can be turbulent, complex, and changing; both must be aware of these factors and plan accordingly to ensure a useful course is maintained. The contributors to this volume demonstrate vividly the turbulence and complexity of their environments, and describe how they successfully navigated the dangers.

ENVIRONMENTAL PROGRESS DEPENDS ON LARGE-SCALE INSTITUTIONS

Whether public, private or nonprofit, the roles of large scale institutions are critical to environmental progress. National and multinational corporations dominate the industrial activities that generate many environmental contaminants. Electric utilities combust fossil fuels. This combustion generates sulfur dioxide, oxides of nitrogen, and particulate matter as well as other pollutants. Chemical processing plants, through both their products and their waste streams, generate chemicals, such as volatile organic compounds and heavy metals, known to be harmful to the environment. In addition, many products integral to American life are produced by large corporations. For example, the products of the automobile industry, through the combustion of gasoline, emit a wide range of pollutants. Whether it is the environmental contaminants that are directly emitted as a residual or the product itself, large private sector organizations are inextricably tied to the need for environmental protection.

The past forty years have demonstrated that reliance upon private sector choices alone to staunch environmental pollution is unwise. The article "The Tragedy of the Commons" (Hardin 1968) identified a fundamental flaw in market behavior that prevents private actors from dealing with shared public resources in an efficient manner. As a result, the protection of the public from the consequences of self-interested utility maximization in the private sector has required government intervention. The establishment of environmental regulatory organizations at the national level and at the state and local levels has yielded large-scale governmental regulation through highly specialized bureaucracies. As a consequence government intervention, usually through regulations, has emerged as the antidote to inefficient private sector decision-making.

As these government regulatory agencies have emerged and matured, they have presented their own set of inefficient behaviors when they sought to improve the environment. We have learned that uncritical application of Leviathan government practices yields inefficiencies and ineffectiveness that can be as troubling as the problems the institutions aimed to solve. Government inability to anticipate the consequences of regulatory intervention has often resulted in a countervailing inefficiency to market shortcomings.

The importance of large-scale nonprofit institutions to environmental protection has also been demonstrated through the synergetic interaction of public and private organizations. Often public agencies develop client private sector interests so that the public agencies are captured. This results in an "iron triangle", in which legislators, government bureaucracies and private sector interests work together to their own mutually beneficial, distinct advantages in contrast to the larger public interest. As a result, many of the foundational statutes for environmental protection provide for juridical democracy exercised by nonprofit organizations as a means of muting such agency capture (Lowi 1979). Nonprofit special interest groups consequently have become essential to balance the interests at play in environmental protection. These factors contribute to the undeniable importance of attending to large organizations which marshal resources that directly or indirectly affect the environment.

LARGE-SCALE ENVIRONMENTAL INSTITUTIONS ARE COMPLEX

Executive management of large institutions, whether business, government or nonprofit, is generally acknowledged as being extraordinarily challenging due to its complexity. Such executive positions concern planning, organizing and controlling considerable resources to achieve an organization's purpose. They must ensure that the organizational structure is coherent and enables work that will achieve the organization's objectives. Organizational processes must advance communication and yield decision-making that is sound. These executives must concern themselves with individuals' organizational behaviors that accommodate motivational variability, incentives and mandates for achieving organizational results. The human resources processes to achieve these behaviors must be fair and provide equal opportunity. Further, organizational strategy, which is typically the unique responsibility of executives, must integrate activities even while an organization's environment is changing.

Executive management of large-scale environmental organizations, in particular those concerning regulatory processes such as the US Environmental Protection Agency, are even more complex. Environmental executives in these settings are called upon not only to carry out the responsibilities of routine executive management, but they must do so upon a subject that is itself extraordinarily complex. Environmental decision-making is founded upon the chemical, biological, and engineering characteristics of the physical environment as these interact with the economic, social and political consequences of such decisions. Such situations raise the complexity of executive management to an additional exponent than standard executive management.

Public decisions with high stakes, such as those involved in environmental protection regulatory decisions, attract intense political interest. As if this were not enough, these political interests are becoming more polarized, extreme and contentious. Such circumstances require adaptive management by career public service executives in order to advance effective approaches to environmental management. As a result, these public executives regularly confront complexity layered upon complexity. The executives described in this book have found ways to succeed in the face of such complexity and uncertainty.

The modern challenge of environmental protection is how to act effectively across multiple sectors within the complex and turbulent terrain of large private-sector institutions, large government institutions and the behavior of individuals who compose such institutions. In a democratic society the path lies through advancing collaboration among involved parties and sectors in order to protect the public interest. Since the 1980s an antigovernment, anti-regulatory attitude has placed an even higher premium on the ability of government executives to work successfully in such multi-sector environments. For government regulation of the environment to succeed, government administrators must possess and use collaborative skills to negotiate this rugged terrain and achieve collective, or public, goals. To achieve this, governments must act on their own accord consistent with their statutorily assigned activities. Further, regulatory agencies must act in collaboration with nongovernment organizations, state governments, local governments, and the private sector. The interaction and adaptation of these institutions determines the future effectiveness of environmental protection. Understanding the roots of effective functioning in such a rich and complex landscape is essential for continued environmental progress in the industrial and industrializing world. This book seeks to do so through the career experiences of successful EPA executives.

A TRANSCENDENT CHALLENGE: COMPLEXITY

Page (2009) has characterized complexity as the property of a system of nonperiodic patterns in which structure and function emerge. In particular, he holds that a complex system has a number of attributes. It has diverse elements, and these elements are interdependent and connected to each other. Lastly, there is adaptation and learning among the elements. Does managing environmental protection at the executive level fit the definition of such a complex system? How do the national environmental management system's diversity, interdependence, connectivity and adaptation stack up against this generic definition?

First, is managing environmental protection a diverse task? It concerns human health and ecological health. For example, particulate matter affects human respiration as well as plants abilities to photosynthesize. Water quality concerns economic consequences of public choices as in-stream aquatic organisms. Physiological functioning of mammals' lungs is altered by exposure to particulates, but such particulates can also inflict economic damage through soiling of materials.

Not only is there diversity in environmental pollution's effects, the social and institutional arrangements for altering pollution are diverse. In the United States, we frequently employ a federal approach to environmental quality management. In the command and control system the central government, through EPA, set national standards, but the implementation of the program to achieve these standards was the province of state governments, assisted in some cases by local governments. These arrangements presented a variety of institutions addressing environmental quality.

These diverse institutional actors are also connected and interdependent. The federal government in air and water quality matters frequently depends on states for primary enforcement actions, while states depend upon EPA's scientific expertise to interpret the evidence underpinning environmental standards. Such connections and interdependence extend beyond the public sector. Many pollution regulations aim to reduce emissions from private industry. The regulations depend on action by the private sector to achieve pollution reduction. And the private sector is deeply affected by the level of standards EPA sets and how state governments implement the standards. This produces a connected network of interdependence. In pesticide regulation, the federal government directly regulates industrial products in order to protect public health from exposure to pesticides.

Controls for air pollution emissions and water quality discharges are similarly interconnected. The choice of control levels depends upon interactions of economic cost, available technology, related health effects and the politics that express the values that connect all of the elements of a pollution control choice. Frequently reduction of air emissions can yield sludge that, if left unregulated, can contaminate receiving waters.

The nation's environmental quality management system requires adaptation and learning, another attribute of a complex system. The dominant paradigm for controlling pollution, the command-and-control approach, requires the government to order through regulations polluters to achieve a set standard, then government monitors compliance with that standard. Over the past ten years many critiques of this approach have arisen . As a consequence, a new approach emerged that relies less on regulatory control and more on voluntary action by pollution sources to abate pollution . Out of this new structure have emerged novel roles for government and the private sector. These roles rely less on compulsion and more on collaboration. Their success depends upon knowledge sharing to a much greater degree than the command-and-control system.

These characteristics of diverse, interdependent, connected and adapting elements suggest complex systems at work in environmental pollution management. The physical properties of environmental pollution and its controls, along with the politics inherent in such high stakes across institutional responsibilities, pose inherent challenges to executive effectiveness.

WHY EXAMINE EXECUTIVE LEADERSHIP?

By definition, our choice of members of the Senior Executive Service (SES) in EPA necessarily focuses our attention on executive leadership in the organization. There are several important benefits to this choice. First, the contributors to this volume began their careers in lower- and mid-level management. They thus have the benefit of having served at different levels within the agency. Second, their years of service in the agency means they have a firm understanding of the role of the agency in environmental management, and understand both the strengths and weaknesses of the policy instruments for which they have held been responsible. They are able to speak to the unique challenges posed by the implementation of environmental policy. Third, their positions in the SES occupy an important space between rank-and-file agency personnel and political appointees. While political appointees tend to be very transient in federal agencies, senior career managers are typically within the agency for long periods of time. Their position astride the divide between the "career employees" and the "political animals" gives them the unique ability to understand the larger policy and political landscapes, as well as issues of technical competence, organizational structure, and agency culture. It also requires them to strike a delicate balance between two groups whose motivations and goals are often at odds with one another.

Fourth, executive-level managers are, by definition, in positions to wield high-level decision-making authority in an organization. They are not only responsible for the decisions made, but for compliance with the laws (and the intent) of Congress, the smooth operation of the bureau or office for which they have responsibility and, ultimately, improvement in the environment. Finally, senior managers are necessarily in a position where they must engage directly with the panoply of environmental interests from across the broad spectrum of society. Environmental policies are often touchstones for political conflict, and senior managers must be adept at negotiating the political minefields of a contentious policy arena. They must be able to build coalitions, engage in collaborative endeavors, negotiate between radically opposed interests, and remain true to the law. In short, they provide navigation skills to help guide their agency through often troubled and complex waters. Executive-level leaders are thus worthy of our careful attention and study: the lessons and insights developed over time in this highly-charged arena not only help us understand policy formulation and implementation in environmental policy, they also provide valuable understanding of the rarified world of successful executive leadership.

The insights provided by these individuals provide important lessons into the real-world issues faced by executive-level government managers on a daily basis. Their actions are worthy of study not simply because they lead from these positions, but because to lead effectively they have insight into the actions, approaches, and techniques of high-performance management and leadership in environmental protection. Their practices merit both study and replication because they have provided measurable reduction in environmental risk in time, space, and across a range of pollution media. In short, their accomplishments are not due simply to "cookie-cutter" management theory, they are the result of years of learning and experience, coupled with a remarkable dedication to public service and the achievement of their nation's environmental goals—in short, they embody "green behavior" in the most pure sense.

A GLIMPSE OF WHAT FOLLOWS

This book seeks to capture the experiences of successful senior executives in the US Environmental Protection Agency. By looking across pollution media, across approaches to environmental control, and across geographic dimensions we hope to better understand those practical and concrete actions that enabled success in the programs that these executives managed. Doing so can allow us insight into future effectiveness.

The intentions, history and results of the civil service act of 1978 are reviewed by Thomas Kelley in chapter 1. He pays particular attention to the evolution of the Senior Executive Service from 1979 to 2003, the period in which most of the experiences discussed in this book took place.

One of the most costly, complex and effective suites of environmental regulation is air quality planning and management. In chapter 2 Jerry Emison examines these activities for lessons related to the effective implementation of the command-and-control system. In addition, individual executive characteristics for effectiveness in such a setting are discussed.

Susan Wayland discusses the regulation of pesticides application and exposure in chapter 3. In doing so she discusses both institutional and individual limitations on resources, knowledge and capacities.

The majority of EPA's regulatory programs are implemented through regional offices. These offices work closely with state environmental agencies, and in chapter 4 Stan Meiberg discusses the pitfalls and effective practices of managing collaborative environmental regulation in such an intergovernmental setting. In doing so, he gives special attention to the circumstances of the southeastern United States as a case rich with variation.

In chapter 5 Robert Wayland examines the transition from the traditional path of water quality control to that of a geographic orientation for wetlands and watersheds protection. The past twenty years have seen a shift to a place-based approach, and the skills required for executive leadership in these evolving and varied settings constitute the basis for this chapter.

The underground storage tank program departed from command-and-control system. In chapter 6 Ronald Brand discusses employing the business-based franchisor approach for relationships between the federal government and state governments. Such effort posed new challenges and opportunities for making progress on environmental protection as well as requiring a different type of executive behavior than that of the command-and-control system.

In chapter 7 Thomas Kelley discusses his experiences leading the indoor air program during a time in which it deployed an information-based approach to reduce risks to unconventional contaminants. In doing so he focuses on the characteristics of effectiveness for both programs and executives.

The Government Performance and Results Act established strategic planning and results monitoring is a key element for performance in the federal government. Chapter 8 examines EPA's experience in meeting these requirements across a disparate number of programs as experienced by David Ziegele while he led EPA's strategic planning efforts.

John Morris and Jerry Emison in chapter 9 synthesize the lessons from the preceding individual chapters' contributions. They identify key executive behaviors relevant regardless of program focus, and highlight those practices in environmental protection likely to be especially relevant for future gains through environmental management. In doing so they emphasize adaptation and tailoring of executive behavior to suit the unique circumstances and consequences of the particular environmental challenges faced.

REFERENCES

Environment for the Future. 1998. *The Environmental Protection Sysem in Transition: Toward a More Desirable Future*. Washington, DC: Center for Strategic and International Studies.
Hardin, Garrett. 1968. The Tragedy of the Commons. *Science* 162: 1243–1248.
Lowi, Theodore J. 1979. *The End of Liberalism*. New York: W.W. Norton.
National Academy of Public Administration. 1995. *Setting Priorities, Getting Results: A New Direction for EPA*. Washington, DC: NAPA Press.
National Academy of Public Administration. 1997. *Resolving the Paradox of Environmental Protection: An Agenda for Congress, EPA and the States*. Washington, DC: NAPA Press.
National Environmental Policy Institute. 1997. *Environmental Goals and Priorities: Four Building Blocks for Change*. Washington, DC: NEPI Press.
Newman, James. 2010. In Emison, G. A., and J. C. Morris, eds. *Speaking Green with a Southern Accent*. Lanham, MD, Lexington Press.
Page, S. E. 2009. *Understanding Complexity*. Chantilly, VA: Teaching Company.
Rosenbaum, Walter A. 2011. *Environmental Politics and Policy*. Washington, DC: CQ Press.

Chapter One

Call and Response

The Senior Executive Service

Thomas E. Kelly

Americans today are familiar with the civil service only as our national system for managing career federal employment. Its core principles of competence, impartiality, and protection from political whim are vital to the efficient management of a vast technocracy employing more than 2 million people. But no law of nature determines that such advanced values must prevail in government personnel administration. Throughout the first century of the American republic the "spoils system" ensured that whom you knew greatly outweighed what you knew as the most decisive criterion for both selection and retention of federal employees, especially for senior positions. As one robust account puts it:

> Throughout the nineteenth century, public contracts and public jobs were viewed as a sort of booty to be claimed by privateers who, with each election, swept in on the not particularly fat but nonetheless undefended ship of state. Patronage was the order of the day, with rotation its great principle and corruption its great result. (Huddleston and Boyer 1996, 150–151)

When its time finally came in 1883, civil service reform was the culmination of persistent efforts over several generations to ensure substantive credentials and professional standards of performance replaced cronyism and payoffs as guiding principles for federal service.

1

CIVIL SERVICE REFORM

The Pendleton Act created the Civil Service Commission, equipping it with broad powers to design and enforce rules for the hiring, training, evaluation, and reward of government employees, who henceforth could be discharged, not simply to make room for someone's well-connected pal, but only for cause. Over time Max Weber's characterization of bureaucracy as "the routinization of charisma" worked its irresistible way to ensure that formal procedures came to govern nearly all measurable aspects of federal service. In 1923 the Classification Act established a tiered structure to ensure equal pay for equal work. Under this new grade schedule, federal positions were ranked across fifteen graduated levels on the basis of differential responsibility and complexity of assigned functions. In 1949 amendments to the Classification Act crowned the pay structure with three new grades, 16 through 18, principally as a means to stem the accelerating loss of top scientific and technical professionals, many of whom were being lured away by higher salaries offered in the private sector. These "supergrade" positions were available as well to the most senior career policymakers whose skill and experience qualified them for a combination of managerial, technical, and political challenges well above the norm.

Of course, no single response to the myriad complexities of government personnel management can satisfy all needs, and the supergrade solution soon ran into problems of its own. Most of these arose from the proliferation of laws and administrative authorities that subjected different agencies to different rules, creating confusion and inequity regarding who could do what, where, and in return for how much.

> Agencies . . . were overwhelmed by the complexity of the laws conferring supergrade position authority. . . . Supergrade slots were allocated by Congress to specific agencies through a welter of discrete legislative actions. Even more problematic was the fact that agency managers had to cope with a confusing array of appointment authorities. While most senior executives were appointed under the competitive civil service, many were not. That is to say, one GS-16 position was not necessarily the same as another GS-16 position. (Huddleston 1987, 39)

Basing the unit of classification on the position itself, rather than on the credentials and experience of the individual filling that position, often thwarted the transfer of accomplished senior employees to beckoning posts, even when the transfer was preferred by management. On the advice of the Hoover Commission in 1955, President Eisenhower proposed a Senior Civil Service, which would not only centralize administration of senior career employment across all agencies but also rank employees on the basis of individual qualifications, rather than on the listed duties of their positions. This would have meant agency heads could reassign SCS members as needed. The proposal was too much too soon for its time and met with such universal hostility (for reasons as mutually contradictory as that it would either unacceptably enhance or undermine—take your pick—authority for political managers) that it never gained purchase.

The next concerted attempt at senior personnel reform emerged in 1971 under President Nixon, who proposed to supplant Supergrades with the Federal Executive Service. The FES was built on the framework of Eisenhower's SCS, but added significant new features. For instance, up to 25 percent of FES positions could be non-career, and FES members would serve under three-year renewable contracts. Members whose contracts were not renewed would either drop back to an available GS-15 position or choose to retire, if eligible. Those ineligible to retire, and who also refused the GS-15 position to which they were assigned, would find themselves in an awkward position indeed. It was principally this provision that raised the greatest obstacle to passage of the FES, as critics declaimed the opportunity it would afford the president to re-politicize the bureaucracy, although not to the same extent as the old and discredited spoils system.

The Nixon administration had come to power soon after Kennedy's inspiring call to public service and Johnson's Great Society. Political executives arriving to serve the new president in 1969 encountered a workforce they viewed as inherently hostile, as well as numerous administrative blockades to their agenda—bureaucratic "landmines" as they were termed colloquially—that had been artfully laid by departing Johnson appointees. Their view of the workforce they inherited likely anticipated that of Reagan appointees when their turn came to take up residence in Washington in 1981. A delightfully candid Reagan appointee once said to me, "You know what we call you, don't you?" I told her I didn't. "'Crats,'" she said. When I asked what the term meant, she cheerily replied, "Oh, you know, bureaucrats, Democrats, what's the difference? You're all just 'crats' to us" (Anonymous, ca 1983).

Nixon's suspicious approach to the federal workforce became an especially sensitive consideration early in his first term, especially in 1970, when certain illicit practices found their way into the national spotlight. I myself sent an unvetted letter to the deans of Schools of Public Health seeking candidates for a sensitive health policy position at the Department of Health, Education and Welfare (HEW). As the naïve management intern tasked to staff out the recruitment, I alluded in writing to what I had personally observed, that political affiliation would be an important determinant of a candidate's suitability, even for this senior career position. In my headlong plunge to get the job done, I signed and mailed the letter late on a Friday, when my supervisor was unavailable to save me from my unguarded zeal. As mistakes go, this was way up there, and its very magnitude helped me later on to be patient and encouraging with young employees as they bumped through learning challenges of their own. News of the pungent revelation quickly reached the AP wire, and Daniel Schorr reported on it gravely during a Walter Cronkite news telecast. It might easily have been the end of my bright new federal career had not my high boss, a Nixon employee himself, vouched internally for both the innocence of my intent and the accuracy of my observations. Those in the know at HEW were well aware that checks on political registration were taking place even on non-political recruitments as low as GS-13. With skepticism of the president's adherence to a politically neutral civil service already slowing action on the FES proposal, my indiscretion threw one more log on a growing fire. The ensuing Watergate scandal finally pushed the FES proposal entirely off the president's agenda.

There matters stood when President Carter took office in 1976. Carter had run his campaign as a Washington outsider arguing that "small is better" and vowing to prune and reform the civil service. While the new president may not have shared Nixon's distrust of the individual worker, he and many of his advisors viewed the federal bureaucracy itself as a metaphorical "Dead Hand" (Auerbach and Rockman 2000, 11–12). As the Carter people saw it, by its size, complexity, and organizational inertia, the executive branch was built to resist any administration's policy direction, especially to the extent that prospective change might threaten existing bureaucratic values, traditions, or procedures. Under this Dead Hand theory, the supergrade system had fostered overlong incumbencies by senior career managers, many of whom had gained leverage within the system more by virtue of technical expertise than through managerial competence and adaptability. Beyond that, senior career managers were seen to operate at one point of the classic Iron Triangle. In today's Washington, bureaucrats constitute one particularly stout corner, interest groups and their lobbyists a second, and Congressional oversight committees the third in a dynamic triangle of alternately competing and cooperating forces. The Iron Triangle was so powerful that each corner yielded only grudgingly to influence by parties outside it—including at times the president himself with respect to his authority over executive agencies. The longer a non-political manager served in a position of real power, the more predictably he or she would fall under the influence of lobbies or the Congress, and the harder the president would have to fight for the loyalty and attention of his nominal employee.

THE CIVIL SERVICE REFORM ACT OF 1978

In 1977 President Carter assembled the Federal Personnel Management Project (PMP), to be run jointly by the Civil Service Commission (CSC) and the Office of Management and Budget (OMB). CSC Chairman Alan "Scotty" Campbell chaired the PMP, while Dwight Ink, on leave from American University, took on the day-to-day role of Executive Director. The PMP quickly organized nine subject-matter task forces on separate areas of civil service reform. The project also set up a high-level work group comprising the assistant secretaries for management (or administration) in the federal agencies. Knowing that agencies had the power to make or break the initiative, PMP organizers agreed to propose nothing that did not earn the support of the multi-agency work group. The PMP recruited experts from academia, public policy institutes, and the federal agencies themselves to write position papers and draft recommendations. High among its concerns was the need to rethink and restructure the way senior federal executives would be organized and managed in a new system. Academics were aware of significant precedent in the establishment of senior executive services in other countries. In reviewing the historic rationale for introducing such systems, PMP advisors found a high consistency between the problem statement in the United States and those that had motivated the introduction of a national corps of public-sector executives in other countries. A prominent study of such systems worldwide (Schiavo-Campo and Sundaram 2001, 436–437) summarizes the most persistently recurring issues:

- Increasingly inadequate compensation for highly skilled senior staff, in comparison with the private sector; and difficulty in attracting highly qualified professionals from the private sector to government employment;
- Perceived lack of responsiveness of regular senior staff to the priorities of the political leadership; and
- Absence of a public-spirited, interagency, service-wide elite cadre.

Based on PMP recommendations, President Carter sent legislative proposals to Congress that led to fast passage of the Civil Service Reform Act of 1978. As promised, the centerpiece of the new system was the SES, designed with one eye on emulating models already in place internationally, and the other on adaptation to meet operational and cultural requirements in the United States. In setting up a new system for executive management, framers of the act sought to address needs encountered by other countries that had taken equivalent action: redesigning compensation and recruitment to retain and attract top talent; ensuring policy responsiveness by incumbents; and forming a central executive corps capable of flexible cross-government reassignment.

ELEMENTS OF THE SES

As enacted in 1978, the SES had the following statutory features:

- Uniform Executive Personnel System: Recruitment of new supergrades ended. Incumbents would be encouraged to transfer voluntarily to SES positions.
- Rank-in-Person: Job classification was abolished for SES positions. As in the military, an SES member would carry his or her rank—essentially salary and status—from position to position, thus easing executive mobility and allowing for "quick fit" allocation of executive resources.
- Redesignation of Political/Career Positions: Most SES positions were newly categorized as "general," meaning they could be filled by either a political appointee or career employee. A smaller number continued to be reserved exclusively for the career civil service. This meant that career employees could serve in sensitive positions of significant authority that had previously been filled by political managers. They could also accept political appointments while retaining eligibility to return to a career position at a later time. To restrict political intrusion into career ranks, political appointments were limited to 10 percent of SES positions across the government.
- Freedom of Assignment: To promote executive mobility and afford flexibility in response to changing agency needs over time, top managers were permitted to reassign SES members from position to position, and even from agency to agency.
- Executive Development: The SES would be built through recruitment and training. The Office of Personnel Management (OPM, which replaced the old Civil Service Commission) would enrich the pool of executive resources through a variety of career and skill development programs.
- Performance Appraisal: SES members would be evaluated annually on the basis of both personal and organizational performance. Based on consistently poor evaluations, an SES member could be bumped back to the GS-15 level.
- Pay-for-Performance: Longevity-based pay increments were eliminated. Based on performance, SES members could ascend through six graded salary ranks. The salary associated with each rank would change systematically through annual percentage adjustments requested by the president and appropriated by Congress.
- Performance Awards: SES members with high performance evaluations could expect handsome rewards. Up to 50 percent of career SES members in each agency would be eligible annually for a cash bonus of up to 20 percent of their pay.

- Special Rank Awards: The act created two classes of elite managers. On the recommendation of an agency, and with endorsement by OPM, the president could confer a special rank on up to 5 percent of executives each year. Those judged to be "Meritorious Executives" would receive a one-time award of $10,000, while "Distinguished Executives" would receive $20,000—all in addition to any performance bonus. (Huddleston and Boyer 1996, passim)

In 1996 Scotty Campbell, Carter's Civil Service Commissioner who oversaw the original design of the SES, recalled some of the major concerns from his own perspective that motivated this striking shift in federal executive management. Eighteen years after the fact it was evident that the administration's principal aim in reforming the civil service was to exact greater responsiveness from career managers to its policy objectives. Along with a need to reduce centralization in decision making, Campbell cites two other key problems the system was designed principally to correct:

> First, we saw an inadequate emphasis on performance. The system was more geared to protecting employee rights than rewarding accomplishment. There were inadequate incentives for high quality performance and an inability to respond to poor performance. . . . Next, we could see the dysfunctional effects of the career/non-career interface. Individuals work out adjustments as time moves along in an administration, but we wanted to see people work more effectively sooner—particularly important because of the short tenure of most political appointees— usually no more than two years. (Campbell 1996, 27)

The new president wanted above all to breathe new life into the "dead hand" of the bureaucracy by commanding greater responsiveness from "his" point of the Iron Triangle. In 1981, even closer to the time the reforms were instituted, Campbell wrote,

> The pivotal incentive for reform has been the White House. Every new administration feels the negative aspects of the bureaucracy's pressure for continuity. New policy makers arrive with mandates for change and find that, though they can change structures and appearances, it is very difficult to make dramatic changes in direction. (Campbell 1981, 305)

Although the Civil Service Reform Act contained many "good-government" provisions to rationalize civil service hiring, training, and compensation at all levels of government, it was the institution of the SES, with the new tools it offered to facilitate and accelerate policy change, that the administration deemed most vital to its own interests. Given the predictably slow pace of implementing such sweeping changes—enacted, as they were, fairly deep into his first term—Carter no doubt looked forward to flexing his new powers expansively throughout a second term. Instead the 1980 election ensured that the "responsiveness" features of the Civil Service Reform Act would later be ironically dubbed, "Carter's gift to Reagan." (Auerbach and Rockman 2000, 35)

CONFLICTING AIMS

As with most public programs in the United States, the SES had to appeal to a wide range of views and interests. As Huddleston describes it:

> The framers of the SES brought to the table fundamentally conflicting ideas about what an American higher civil service ought to look like—ideas that had, at turns, shaped a series of unsuccessful reform efforts for the preceding thirty years. For some, the SES was to be the reincarnation of the aborted Senior Civil Service, an elite, European-style corps of generalist civilian executives. For others, it was a second chance at a Federal Executive Service, a system that would help elected officials and their appointees get a firmer political grip on the vast federal bureaucracy. Still others saw the SES primarily as a vehicle for bringing the supposed rigor of private sector management techniques to the federal government or as a backdoor way to increase the pay and perquisites of civil servants. (Huddleston 1992, 165)

To avoid the legislative fate of its failed predecessors, the SCS and the FES, any proposal for the SES had to appeal to a wide range of divergent philosophies and political interests in the Congress, which required that its proponents gloss over any internal inconsistencies of which they might have been aware. Since the bill passed so quickly, the legislative strategy clearly succeeded, but the challenge of administering internally conflicting statutory direction lay ahead. Perhaps the most significant point of stress was the juxtaposition of the public-first values of the civil service against the profit-first ethic of the private sector. While public servants are never purely selfless (just as private entrepreneurs do not always work strictly for themselves), the underlying values and reward structures underlying the two systems run in opposite directions. When elements of both public service and private enterprise coexist in a single system, both thesis and antithesis must search uncomfortably for a satisfactory synthesis.

One stream of thought flowing into the creation of an American SES was to have it emulate the "Mandarin" model of government leadership as practiced widely in Europe and Asia. Great Britain, for one, sought out methods of administration originally developed in China and employed them first in colonial India before introducing them to England itself. Schiavo-Campo and Sundaram (2001) describe this Asian/European structure as it was designed to serve primarily public-service values:

Recruitment in the Mandarin systems, as in Japan, is competitive and merit-based, usually through a centralized agency such as a public service commission. Applicants are usually young, screened by means of both general and specialized examinations, followed by intensive interviews of shortlisted candidates and other forms of individual and group assessment. The successful applicants enter directly a particular class of service, usually on a fast track with the opportunity for advancement to senior positions within a few years. Such an SES system is a rank-in-person system, where one is hired not for a specific job but as a fungible individual suited to a variety of senior jobs. In many Commonwealth countries, the candidates are recruited into a national generalist elite service or a number of central functional services, such as accounts, revenue, and communications, and are liable to be rotated from one job to another within the service or between ministries. (Schiavo-Campo and Sundaram 2001, 437)

Countries with Mandarin systems frequently operate special training academies with high barriers to entry and rigorous curricula and practica to equip graduates for professional public service in a wide range of potential settings. While the United States Foreign Service adheres fairly closely to the Mandarin model, the SES has adopted only enough of its features to invite comparison with it. This lack of adherence to international models for such vital elements as recruitment, training, and development has fostered looseness and variability in the conception and direction of the SES over its history, as have frequent changes of political and administrative philosophy among those overseeing the system. It is perhaps instructive that we have to look back thirty years to see what the thing was actually supposed to be. For long stretches since that time it has been more fruitful to describe the SES with reference to its observed operation at the moment, rather than to its adherence to a coherent and consistent original design.

Into the classic notion of a corps of public-spirited, elite specialists trained and developed to serve where needed, the SES incorporated values and methods drawn from the competitive arena of the private sector. Ring and Perry offer a succinct summary of this mental model:

The SES was grounded in an assumption that federal programs would be most effectively managed by mobile generalist executives who could be assigned to any agency. Once assigned, agency performance would depend upon the motivation of appropriate individual performance. Because the management of the federal government was similar to management in the private sector, it would be possible to motivate federal managers by using the same kind of techniques that, it was assumed, had been successful in motivating private sector managers. The improved individual performance that resulted from increased motivation would also lead to better agency performance and, in turn, a more effective, efficient, and responsive federal government. (Ring and Perry 1983, 123)

The key to this logic is that management of the federal government is similar to management in the private sector. Quite a lot depends on the validity of that assumption. Features like pay-for-performance and bonuses for exceptional achievement appeal more to the instinct for personal enrichment than to promoting public-service goals in a collaborative atmosphere. In the public sector there are no profit-and-loss statements, no comparative sales records, by which to distinguish top performers by reasonably unambiguous criteria. Measures designed over the years to substitute for profit-and-loss benchmarks typically do little more than redesign the cloak of objectivity in which the underlying subjectivity is dressed. By imposing a reward system based on perceived differential contributions to the agency's work, incentives built into the SES set up implicit rivalries for credit and visibility among colleagues for whom cooperation might have been the more goal-appropriate attitude. There ensued a subtle competition for the plum positions that would attract the greatest recognition—those closest to the secretary, say, or with the highest public visibility, staff and dollars.

Career development and mobility also suffered as individuals balked at leaving their posts for significant periods of training, fearing their absence would place them at a competitive disadvantage upon their return. For similar reasons SES members resisted moving to a new agency to avoid penalty in a bureaucratic game of Chutes and Ladders. Moving to a new agency, where a reputation earned over years might not precede them meant their place in the SES pecking order would fall, perhaps never to rise again to the relative advantage they currently enjoyed. In the private sector executive mobility can be swift, but the SES did little to overcome organizational inertia that tended to keep top public officials in place. Lack of turnover at the top also kept the reward structure relatively static, while narrowing opportunities for quick advancement, especially for new arrivals. The idea of a mobile corps of skilled, disciplined, flexible public-sector managers recruited, developed, motivated, and rewarded for placing the country's needs ahead of their own ambitions may be ultimately irreconcilable with a system of compensation based on competition and personal reward. To force these opposing elements into the same framework in the belief they would produce something new and greater as their synthesis was a bold experiment indeed.

PUTTING THE SES TO WORK

From the beginning the new system struggled to gain traction. Recall that a major criticism of the supergrade system stemmed from its utility as the chief means to retain specialized technical expertise by granting higher pay at higher grades. However, since supergrade slots were based on rank-in-position, the pay associated with those positions typically had to be justified by expansive supervisory duties—the higher the grade the greater the managerial responsibility imposed. This created a situation in which some of the most significant federal management positions were occupied by technical specialists with neither the taste nor gift for managing people, a flaw the SES was meant to correct. However, as the very first step in implementing the new system, all current Supergrades were invited to transfer into the SES without further preparation or ceremony. When close to 95 percent agreed to the transfer, a high proportion of the available slots were occupied by spectacularly talented specialists on whom the magic dust of their new SES designation had no discernible effect. They remained world-class technical experts with neither the skill nor the disposition to manage people effectively.

It is appropriate that many executive positions are filled by people with specialized training, who are often among the most highly esteemed practitioners within their technical specialties. The public demands subject-relevant competence from those who serve, and a relevant degree and experience is all but required for an executive who must credibly lead technical staff in specialized areas. The closer one gets to the real work, where the technical competence of the decision maker is crucial for both staff morale and policy coherence, the more important it is for attorneys to be led by an attorney or scientists by a scientist. The promise of the SES was not that those with such extraordinary gifts would gradually be replaced by generalists but that managerial skills would gradually become as present and valued as technical qualifications in filling even such leadership positions as these. In fulfilling this aim the SES got off to a slow start.

At the same time, agencies fought aggressively to retain their prerogative to recruit, reward, and retain their own people. Here the Iron Triangle came into play again. As much as OPM might have intended to exert its role as central manager of a single federal system for executive development, to realize the vision of an elite national executive corps, it has never exerted strong leadership in this manner. If the old saw is true that man proposes but God disposes, OPM played the role of man, but Congress, abetted by OMB, got to play God. In the event, OPM received neither the resources nor the practical authority to wrest control of executive selection and placement from the agencies, from which both lobbyists and congressional committees required predictability and stability in their dealings. Even, as often happens, an agency's policies and actions were opposed by an oversight committee and certain private interests, there was an advantage to the committee chair in dealing with "the evil you know," instead of "the evil you don't know." Since there was incentive within the Iron Triangle to limit executive recruitment to a set of known actors, a dynamic emerged which favored stability, with transfers and promotions more likely to take place within a single agency than across multiple agencies.

Another consequence of OPM's weak role in SES management is that promised executive development programs, while endorsed rhetorically, have been offered only sporadically. When the SES began there were at least loose plans for programs of deep and formal training, intended to broaden executive experience and prepare individuals for roles outside their own agency "stovepipe." They remain the exception. There was even consideration given at one time to granting executive sabbaticals, adapted from the academic model—substantial time earned for every x number of years in the hot seat of authority to work on career-refreshing projects away from the office. However, very few senior federal executives have ever taken sabbaticals.

That is not to say that SES members do not occasionally take leave of their agencies for significant respites. But this often has less to do with executive development than with the need to seek a temporary outplacement when an executive has hit a career roadblock of some sort—perhaps a conflict with a new political manager or an adverse relationship with a powerful legislator. At such times humane agencies may enter an Interagency Personnel Agreement (IPA), which allows the executive to work away from the agency for a set period of time—as much as a year and sometimes longer. The assignment may be set in another federal or state agency or with a nonprofit organization conducting public service that is compatible with the home agency's mission. Facing difficult circumstances in the office, the executive may well be grateful for the fresh start an IPA might represent.

All considered, the goal of a centrally administered Mandarin corps of itinerant executives has not materialized. But the SES has developed organically, building strengths of its own, having created a culture within and specific to each agency. At EPA, this culture has been fostered since the mid-eighties by an annual meeting that gathers all SES members in a single place for three days of policy updates, training, and face-to-face discussion. In an agency characterized by enormous day-to-day pressure, with communication complicated by wide geographic dispersal of offices and personnel, it can be difficult to develop and sustain a sense of community at work. Since is always easier to conduct business with someone you know than with someone whose name you just had to look up, this meeting creates linkages that build *esprit de corps* and facilitate the flow of business throughout the year. In its early history, the meeting was a real grind of long work days with participants responsible to produce a draft strategic plan as the product of its three-day collaboration. Early organizers feared that, absent such a task, the gathering would be attacked as a junket (if a junket can fairly be said to take place at an airport hotel in Washington, DC). In recent years the meeting has been built around policy communication, leadership development, and community building, rather than false labor toward a false product to rebut a false accusation.

To offer a sense of the value of these gatherings, I cite my own first attendance at meeting designed for SES training and enrichment—a precursor of what later became the national meeting . It remains singularly memorable for a vignette (Anonymous, ca 1988) that typifies as well as anything I know the extraordinary pressures under which SES managers often work. The featured speaker was an outgoing congressional staffer, a man who had long been at the right hand of one of the most powerful committee chairs of that period. The chairman took delight in withering agency managers with hyperbolic attacks and eye-crossing demands for discovery. The staffer was now moving off the Hill for new employment and had agreed to discuss his work and the "inside" attitudes and impressions he and his colleagues had formed over years of working with, against, and over EPA. At one point the national director of one of the most prominent regulatory programs rose for a question. "I just want to know one thing," she began. "Why?" The staffer blinked and asked what she meant. She went on,

> I have been called before your committee numerous times over the past several years. I have been criticized, ridiculed, and attacked, mostly professionally, sometimes personally, and always in public. I work hard; I do a good job; I am proud of my program and my people. When I speak with you off the record, you seem to agree with me on that. Yet, in public hearings, the chairman accuses me of incompetence or worse, knowing I am not allowed to fight back. I care about what my family thinks, and it matters to me that this is what they read about me. I know you are feeding the Chairman his statements and questions. So my question to you is simply, why did you do this?

The staffer blinked again before he answered,

> Well, gee, I guess I never thought of it that way. On the Hill we don't really think about you. We care about the chairman and his constituents. Sometimes he needs you to look bad so he can make his point about the Administration. He needs to reassure his constituents that he is looking out for them. If you took it personally, I guess I'm sorry. And, since I'm leaving the Hill, I can promise you I won't do it again anytime soon. (Anonymous c. 1983)

You can't improve on learning like that, and I kept the lesson in mind for the several times I was called upon myself to testify before Congress.

SO, HOW HAS THE SES DONE? — A PERSONAL TOUR

A stroll through the stacks at a nearby university library suggests that a substantial literature has grown up over the years examining the theory, structure, and development of the SES. Today, as yesterday, many are calling for redesign and reform of the system, offering the topic for multiple Congressional hearings, the most recent held in March of 2011. What follows is a set of observations from the inside on the system as it appears to a federal manager who served within its ranks for nearly twenty-five years. Some of the conclusions I draw might not sit well with everyone, but they are mine nonetheless. Below, under each of the SES design elements listed above is one view from a guy who sat at the desk.

Uniform Executive Personnel System

Although the original vision has not materialized of an elite corps of itinerant executives centrally administered by OPM, the SES has become a recognizable entity spanning all but a few excepted Executive agencies and subject to government-wide standards. As the original supergrades departed federal service they were replaced under criteria that increasingly emphasized management skills for supervisory positions, including when the work to be supervised was primarily technical. Still, to combat "brain drain," the loss of top-flight technical talent to the private sector, agency managers felt continuing pressure to promote non-managerial experts into the SES where they would enjoy higher salary and prestige. In 1990 the last holdover supergrade positions were finally abolished and two new classifications created, ST for senior-level scientists and SL for other senior-level officers without substantial supervisory duties. The intent was to acknowledge and reward non-managerial employees for exceptional technical and/or policy responsibility while reserving SES positions for managers.

While individual agencies have taken substantial control of SES administration within their own walls, OPM has developed a number of tools and standards to ensure at least some cross-government consistency (www.opm.gov/ses/). Most visibly, there are now five Executive Core Qualifications (ECQs), which serve as fundamental training and recruitment criteria to ground the expectation that new SES members will arrive on the job adequately equipped to manage people and fiscal resources across a broad range of executive settings. These are listed with no discernible syntactic consistency as: 1) Leading Change, 2) Leading People, 3) Results-Driven, 4) Business Acumen, and 5) Building Coalitions (Office of Personnel Management, 2010). The ECQs form the template on which SES recruitment and training is built across the federal government. In SES recruitment the agency must certify an individual's substantive fitness for the job at hand, and OPM must independently verify the individual's eligibility for the SES through mastery of the ECQs. While EPA has launched several episodic SES candidate development programs over the years, formal channeling programs have not taken hold as the primary, or even most reliable route for middle managers to ascend to the SES. For reasons including resource constraints and the pressure of competing business, EPA, like many other agencies, has had difficulty maintaining stable, productive executive training programs to which high-quality candidates will confidently entrust their career aspirations.

Without a strong OPM to weave together the many strands of senior-executive administration across the executive branch, the SES is a corps still seeking its esprit. Group identity and solidarity is now mainly a function of sub-group relationships within individual agencies. Formal efforts to build a cohesive and self-aware SES, such as EPA's annual Senior Management Meeting, have proved irreplaceable, if inherently fragile. For instance, EPA's national meeting (discussed above) was banned for several years by a new administrator who reportedly viewed it as a frivolous exercise characterizing the misplaced values of the outgoing administration. Fairly late in this administrator's lengthy tenure, communication and coordination among regional offices and even within headquarters become so difficult that the administrator reportedly demanded a remedy, to wit, a face-to-face meeting for all senior managers. The tradition of an annual SES gathering was thereupon quickly restored.

In 1980 a group of SES members in the Department of Treasury recognized the need for an independent organization to unite the SES and represent its interest. They formed the Senior Executive Association (SEA), which since that time has offered increasingly useful membership services while actively promoting policies and legislation aimed at ensuring the SES continues to attract and retain the best qualified federal managers. Even so, SES group identity remains low, and the Association's representational work has never been rewarded with robust membership.

Rank-in-Person

The principal reasons for replacing grade-in-position with rank-in-person were to fill key vacancies quickly and flexibly and to facilitate movement of senior personnel across agencies. Retaining one's rank meant that an SES member would not sacrifice his or her salary or status, regardless of any management position to which he or she might be assigned. In my view, this is one of the real successes of the SES, because, in building a sense of personal security for the employee, it has encouraged many desirable intra-agency reassignments. Still, many barriers to mobility persist. At the individual level, an executive may resist moving from a job with high bonus potential to another with lower potential. At the organizational level, a certain bureaucratic tribalism often favors executive transfer or promotion within a sub-organization over the free flow of executives across the full organization. Having wrested substantial control of the SES from OPM, some agencies later failed to invest in consistent central management of its internal corps, leaving substantial hiring discretion to bureau chiefs. Unless OPM asserts a more dominant role, or individual agencies decide to invest in more assertive central management of their own executive resources, rank-in-grade will continue to support managerial flexibility in specific cases, but is unlikely to overcome a deep programmatic bias to promote from within the arena of the familiar.

Redesignation of Political/Career Positions

The Civil Service Reform Act opened up movement between political and general positions so that a career employee could accept a political appointment without sacrificing the right to return to career service at a later time. Political appointments were limited to 10 percent of all SES positions government-wide with up to 25 percent allowed in a given agency. Government-wide the overall percentage of political SES is currently 9 percent, but the distribution within agencies can vary widely. About 20 percent of the SES at the Department of Education are political, while at the Veterans Administration (VA) and the Department of Energy (DOE), the equivalent number is lower than 5 percent (Stier 2011, 3). Presidential "loading" of some agencies with political appointees stands at odds with the ideal of establishing a stable, professional management corps under political leadership. The sometimes uneasy relationship between political appointees and career executives requires the continuous renegotiation of a creative balance between short-term political imperative and long-term policy stability. With a 20 percent allotment of political appointees on board in a single agency, that balance may shift quickly—and even perilously so. Still, with a 10 percent cap on political SES imposed across the executive branch there is an effective brake on any tendency an administration might have either to exert zigzag policy direction or to surreptitiously revive the spoils system in the twenty-first century.

Freedom of Assignment

The central corps of government-wide executives promised by the Mandarin model has not emerged. As the framers of the legislation well knew, the proposal would never pass Congress without agency buy-in, which is why senior agency administrators helped write the new proposals on the PMP. But these officials were for the most part short-term political appointees who, after helping get the legislation through, could guarantee little about the future implementation of the program. With the new law in place it would take either draconian administration or willing cooperation by the new members of the SES to realize in practice the benefits promised in theory by the new system. When most supergrades transferred into the SES at the outset, they embraced the promise of financial reward and career flexibility, but remained wary of how the mobility provisions would be used or abused. The early exercise of this new authority would prove crucial.

At EPA supergrades with significant managerial responsibilities learned that they would be required to reapply for their current positions and then, only if selected, join the SES in order to retain the duties associated with the old position. This created a good deal of resentment, notably among regional enforcement directors, who were already smarting at the recent loss of authority to negotiate settlements with accused environmental violators in lieu of prosecution. Instead, violations would now be referred to the Department of Justice for litigation under a "file first, negotiate later" policy, which EPA enforcers believed would clog the system and reduce the measure of environmental improvements they could squeeze out by jawboning perceived violators. Despite their increasing sense of embattlement, most regional enforcement directors chose to reapply for their positions and were duly appointed to the SES to resume their current responsibilities. One senior enforcement official resigned, however, rather than continue under powers he perceived to have been whittled down unacceptably. (Mintz 1995, 29)

The subsequent geographical reassignment of two regional Water Division directors amplified underlying concerns, especially since the transfers were viewed in the ranks as little more than a symbolic flexing of authority. A few other proposed reassignments at the time were viewed as expressions of personal pique by new political management in the region involved. At least one manager resigned rather than accept transfer. In hindsight, there may have been nothing particularly sinister about any of this. A long-retired regional Water Division director told me recently that, all considered, his move from Denver to Boston had worked out very well for him. He also thought there had been a constructive basis for other proposed transfers that had raised such alarm at the time (Anonymous 2011). Fairly or not, at a crucial moment for the development of trust in the new system, suspicion grew that SES mobility provisions were being misused, and many executives dug in. As it happened, the Carter administration did not proceed with a concerted series of geographic moves at EPA. However, in 1981, Ann Gorsuch, EPA's first administrator under the Reagan administration, waited through the statutory six months hiatus after the inauguration and then directed geographic reassignment of some policy managers who were perceived as resistant to new direction. The agency's national director for environmental economics resigned rather than accept reassignment from Washington, DC to a position without policy responsibilities at an isolated research laboratory in Oklahoma.

EPA is a national organization with facilities in more than twenty separate commuting areas spread around the country. In addition to its headquarters in Washington, DC and ten regional offices, substantial portions of the

Air Quality program operate out of North Carolina and Michigan; there are research laboratories in Alabama, Nevada, Rhode Island, Ohio, Florida, Oklahoma, and Oregon, to name a few. In spite of this rich diversity of place, EPA has never adopted the practice of some agencies (Treasury comes to mind) of requiring geographic mobility as the price of organizational advancement. Stability in place is part of the culture, as is the reluctance of senior managers to force a break with this tradition. If there were ever an opportunity for change on this dimension, initiation of the SES presented it. Whether due to missteps in management or communication at the beginning, or to the insuperability of entrenched organizational culture, SES mobility remains the exception at EPA, rather than the rule.

With each agency left by OPM to chart its own course, few have ventured much further in imposing mobility requirements than has EPA, and perhaps for similar reasons. A student of federal executive policy, Patricia Ingraham, concluded, "The mobility provisions were widely perceived to be punitive and a method to get rid of unwanted personnel, rather than as tools for improved management or career-development purposes" (Ingraham 1995, 85). It seems to me that mobility, when detached from a comprehensive program of career training and development, such as a long-term, stable, and predictable candidate development program, is frequently apt to be perceived (and occasionally used) as a feared tool of punishment rather than a desirable step toward advancement.

Executive Development

As discussed above, OPM has built an effective foundation to ensure managerial and leadership competency for the SES across the government by means of Core Executive Qualifications that serve as the basis of executive certification. At the same the agency has not truly realized its intended role as central administrator of the SES, offering recruitment, training, and development services for a national executive corps in the European-Asian tradition.

Performance Appraisal

If a system of rewards rests on the assessment of merit, then assessment of merit is the key to its credibility. For an employee to be motivated to adopt intended behaviors by the prospect of pay for performance, he or she must believe the assessment will be objectively determined on the basis of actual performance. But this can never be. Subjectivity is always in play. At EPA hard work, long hours, and brilliant achievement are frequently in evidence. At risk of invoking the "Lake Wobegon" principle, the "exceptional" manager is not at all uncommon at EPA. The agency recruits talented, highly motivated people who typically do what it takes to get the job done. To be considered "fair," the appraisal system must at least occasionally acknowledge the depth and quality of that work, even if the award pool may never be big enough to compensate each high performer every year. Unfortunately, formal appraisal systems frequently run on either stated or covert quotas that hinder reviewers from rendering a just verdict. If only 10 percent of the talent pool can receive a top rating, then 90 percent will receive less than that, regardless of their relative contribution.

A recent survey by the SEA reveals some troubling attitudes and opinions across the SES. Recall that the original pillars of performance appraisal and merit-based reward were advanced on the basis that they would motivate public performance in the manner of the private sector. In that light it is useful to consider that the majority of SES respondents believe that *de facto* quotas affect the integrity of final performance ratings, and that respondents perceive discrepancies between ratings and reward. Consider, too, that SES members assert that the current system has not affected their performance or the performance of their peers. They do say, however, that it has negatively affected their morale. This view is not limited to those whose achievements have been minimized in their ratings. One SES member at the Veterans Administration told the SEA:

> I have done about as well as any executive could have asked for under performance and pay system. My pay raises and bonuses have been among the highest in the agency, but I think I see systemic flaws which are in fact demoralizing significant portions of our SES cadre and will weaken its foundations in the future." (Senior Executives Association 2006, 8).

How, then, do we explain the dedication and high performance of so many of these people? In my experience, that's the special spirit of public service. For many of these people good work is its own most significant reward, to which the opportunity for an earned bonus is merely a welcome supplement. They extend themselves to achieve excellence not because of the reward system, but in spite of it. Pay for performance as currently administered in the SES does little more than spoil the satisfaction of a job well done. One Defense Department manager had this to say:

> What a tremendous waste all of this is—wasting human capital seems to me to be the biggest sin of all. Until the day I leave I will give this work my best because I owe it to the taxpayers and to the warfighters risking their lives for our country, but I sure don't do it because of this pay for performance system. In fact this system insults me and wastes my time. (Senior Executives Association 2006, 8)

Pay for Performance

Executive-level government work is strenuous and demanding. As any current or former manager will tell you, the headaches and distractions can be enormous. It takes a special kind of talent and ambition to aspire to these jobs, and the intent of the SES to reward those willing to accept and able to succeed at such work was well-founded. In many years, however, executive-level pay adjustments have lagged behind those of the rank and file. The president requests, and Congress enacts, separate across-the-board pay adjustments for General Schedule (GS), military, and SES employees, respectively, and the SES sometimes receives relatively less than their own employees on a percentage basis.

On top of this, in 2004 SES became ineligible for locality pay. This is the increment above base pay that is federal employees receive to adjust for costs of living that vary widely from place to place. Consider it "hardship pay" for accepting a job in Chicago or San Francisco, where an apartment can cost half again as much as it might in a smaller city. To illustrate how important locality pay can be, consider the base pay on the current GS schedule for an entry-level GS-15 in a low-cost area, which is $99,628. The same GS-15 would receive 24 percent more, or $123,758, to perform the same work in Washington. At the request of President George W. Bush, Congress eliminated the locality increment for the SES on the grounds that federal executives would thereafter work harder to earn performance incentives. This action has contributed to such anomalies as that, in Washington, DC, employees at the bottom of the GS-15 scale currently earn $4,000 more annually (and even a GS-14 at Step 6 gets $1000 more) than their newly recruited SES supervisor is scheduled to receive (Carey 2011, 13). Since competition for relatively scarce performance bonuses stacks the deck against the most recently appointed executives, unless an exception is made a newly recruited SES is asked to accept far greater responsibility in return for embarrassingly lower pay than his or her senior subordinates. It may not be coincidence that aspiration by current GS-15s to enter the SES is not as fervent as it once was. On the other end of the scale, the SES pay range has not risen fast enough to create room for employees with the consistently highest ratings to receive an annual raise. Since they are "stuck at the top," their only incentive is the possibility of a bonus to supplement an unincreased salary (Partnership for Public Service 2009, 10).

Performance Awards (Bonuses)

The old supergrades must have been giddy at the prospect that up to 50 percent of newly vested SES members could expect to earn bonuses of up to 20 percent of their pay. It was a sweet dream indeed, and it did not last much past morning. Although only two agencies (Small Business Administration and National Aeronautics and Space Administration) actually delivered on that promise in the first year of the program, members of Congress quickly took to the floor decrying such lavish rewards for pampered public employees. That year's appropriation reduced the percentage of SES members eligible for a performance award (bonus) from 50 percent to 25 percent, after which new OPM guidelines reduced it still further to 20 percent. Those new rules required that bonuses at 20 percent of salary could henceforth be paid to no more than 5 percent of SES managers, with corresponding limitations on how many could receive awards at progressively lower levels. Of course, all that happened a long time ago, and most current SES members entered the service after the original, expansive promises had been withdrawn, so *caveat emptor* is fairly in place. Nowadays performance bonuses are subject to a strict dollar cap applied at the agency level. Awards are made from an annually fluctuating fund with the consequence that, while some awards are still made at 10 percent or 20 percent of salary, even those who receive a 5 percent bump consider themselves fortunate. One SES member said in a related context: "We are like chickens pecking for crumbs. . . . There is no budget to fund pay for performance, and we ought to stop the charade (Senior Executives Association 2006, 8). Today's SES bears little resemblance to the vision of a system its framers confidently asserted would emulate private-sector incentives for its top executive producers.

In practice, bonuses are rarely announced or publicly celebrated. Recipients may choose to reveal their good fortune or not at their personal discretion. I happily recall the action of my SES supervisor when I was a GS employee, who called his staff together to thank us for the work that had resulted in his bonus. That was leadership in action. Nowadays most recipients simply inform their spouses and await a pleasant bump in a future electronic bank deposit. After the dust has settled OPM issues an aseptic report with an impersonal summary of ranges of awards issued, arrayed as both agency-specific and government-wide statistics. One can assess how executives in one agency fared as a group relative to executives at another, but not whether Ellie over in Accounting got the bonus you think she deserved this year. While this may deny Ellie much deserved public acclaim, it also spares her the knowledge that someone she may think more deserving was passed over. In its own awkward way, this anonymity promotes collegiality and reduces negative competition.

Special Rank Awards

In addition to bonuses, the SES has a more generous and exclusive program of presidential rank awards. Presidential rank awards work differently from bonuses. Each year agencies are invited to nominate to OPM their best-performing senior employees over a period of several years. The Distinguished Executive Award comes with a bonus of 35 percent of salary, and no more than one percent of the SES roster may receive it in a given year. Up to 5 percent of SES members may receive the Meritorious Executive Award with an accompanying bonus of 20 percent (www.opm.gov/ses/performance/ presrankawards.asp). Recipients are prominently announced and accept the plaque at a banquet sponsored by the Senior Executives Association. They are typically honored as well at one or more public gatherings within their home agencies. At EPA, the annual Senior Management Meeting has traditionally provided the setting for this ceremony. In the outside world, news stories about deserving executives transmit positive information about federal service that counteract the negative portrayal more often advanced for public employees.

While this may sound like an unambiguously good idea, it turns out to be a good idea with ambiguities. Given the relative few who may ever become nominees, not many SES members hold a realistic hope of receiving this honor. For the typical SES member the value of the award is more symbolic than material. It is experienced in one's professional gratification that an admired colleague might be recognized in such an exceptional way. When Presidential Rank Awards are announced, many SES executives send congratulatory notes to the recipients with whom they are close, and share their satisfaction that one of their own has become a deserving winner. But this is not always how it goes. The determination of Distinction, or of Merit, is likely to be as subjective as the initial performance assessment itself, and final agency decision maker often must choose nominees second-hand, relying on well-composed narratives and advice from trusted counselors. Every year, it seems, as the list of honorees is posted, eyes roll at a name or two, as favorites are seen to be favored or old debts to be repaid. It is never clean. That said, I believe the Presidential Rank Awards program is good enough as it stands and should be retained. There is no way to guarantee that only to the utmost deserving are crowned with riches and glory, and it is too good a thing to lose, knowing that at least some of the most deserving do receive rewards at levels originally promised when the SES was still shiny and new.

A FINAL WORD ON PAY FOR PERFORMANCE

Members of the SES are what their title suggests, senior executives. To premise the compensation of senior executives in the public sector on a model designed for the compensation in the private sector is my idea of folly. Private executives pull down salaries, bonuses, and deferred compensation that often amount to 20 or 30 times the annual earnings of the average employee in their firms. By contrast, federal senior executives may sometimes earn less than their subordinates. That says it all. As long as federal executives are public employees working in what are sometimes called "political bureaucracies," they will be held to a politically-derived calculation of what level of compensation will be tolerated, regardless of what may ever have been proffered. America's hard-working people, many of whom are struggling paycheck to paycheck, and some of whom may be laid off from their jobs at any time, are understandably envious and even resentful of federal workers. They hear stories about public employees enjoying high pay, generous benefits, and job security, all in return for what they view as bungling, mangling, and decorating America's daily life with red tape. Many ordinary Americans know little and care less about the extraordinary requirements laid upon federal employees, how hard they work, how well-educated, efficient, and creative they have to be to succeed at increasingly complex tasks. People on Main Street often value only those federal programs and services that benefit themselves or their families immediately and directly. They have little regard for the people who get up early and stay late at the office to plan and deliver those programs. That is why politicians run against the federal workforce and win reelection partly on that basis. It's easy, and it works. So long as government workers are simultaneously envied and demeaned by their neighbors, there can never be a system of performance assessment and compensation for public executives that emulates that of the private sector. The public will not stand for it, and their elected representatives will either block or sabotage such a system at the first opportunity. Failure to recognize this deeply ingrained quality of American life is the deepest and most irremediable flaw in the foundational logic of the SES.

SO WHY DOES ANYONE JOIN THE SES ANYWAY?

In this somewhat jaded review, I have examined the SES against its stated goals with particular reference to its designed mechanisms. In those terms, the service has repeatedly fallen short of its aims. There's no getting around that, but it's only part of the story. Public service is a calling, and those of us who respond to the call find satisfaction in ways that the designers of the SES did not accurately assess. Though we work for the money—and who with a job does not?—we came to the government for something more, the chance to test our talents and grow our skills to improve the lives of our fellow citizens. If that sounds pie-eyed and idealistic, perhaps it is, but it is our truth nevertheless. As I see it, we who chose federal service and gradually became good enough at it to aspire to executive responsibility combine idealism with a flinty-eyed realism on the job. It's the only way you can manage your way through the contradictions.

The SES is not what it's cracked up to be. It's really much better than that. For all its flaws, it is still a great place to be if you happen to love the satisfaction of leading change and growing people, if you're results-driven, can develop and exercise business acumen, and enjoy building coalitions that turn good ideas into action—and you want to do all of that to deliver essential public service. Some of us believe that government has a crucial role to play in tandem with private enterprise in building a strong nation of healthy people enjoying clean skies and fishable, swimmable waters. For people like us government can be a great place to find the work we love, and to do it with smart people who love the work. Rising to leadership, helping to set the agenda, getting to inspire great talent to great achievements—if one cannot find reward enough in that, it's not clear to me that the flash of a bonus will make the right kind of difference.

The people who designed the SES assumed that government was not truly different from any other business, so they theorized that incentives effective in the business world would work just as well in government. They forgot that public employees are accountable to the public, and not to a corporate board. Government lacks the profit motive, so even the most entrepreneurial public managers are looking for better ways to serve people, not to outgun competitors for market share. Federal agencies succeed when their SES managers overcome systematic incentives to compete against and defeat one another, and instead work together to get vital things done. So there it is. For those who enjoy bucking the system to achieve great results in public service, the United States Senior Executive Service is the place to be.

REFERENCES

Anonymous. ca 1983. Personal communication with the author.

Anonymous. ca 1988. Public exchange witnessed by the author.

Anonymous. 2011. Personal communication with the author.

Auerbach, Joel D. and Bert A Rockman. 2000. *In the Web of Politics: Three Decades of the US Federal Executive*. Washington: Brookings Institution.

Campbell, Alan K. "The Original Vision of the SES . . . Revisited, 25 Years From The Bureaucrat to the Public Manager." *The Public Manager*, (1996): 27–28.

———. "In Norton E. Long. The SES and The Public Interest," *Public Administration Review* (1981): 305.

Carey, Maeve P. April 2011. CRS Report for Congress. *The Senior Executive Service: Background and Options for Reform*. Washington: Congressional Research Service.

Huddleston, Mark W. 1987. Background Paper, 27–87. In *Government's Managers: Report of the Twentieth Century Fund Task Force on the Senior Executive Service*. New York, NY: Priority Press.

———. 1992. To the Threshold of Reform: The Senior Executive Service and America's Search for a Higher Civil Service. In ed. Patricia W Ingraham and David H Rosenbloom, 165–197. *The Promise and Paradox of Civil Service Reform*. Pittsburg, PA: University of Pittsburg Press.

Huddleston, Mark W., and William W. Boyer. 1996. *The Higher Civil Service in the United States: Quest for Reform.* Pittsburgh: University of Pittsburgh Press.

Ingraham, Patricia W. 1995. *The Foundation of Merit: Public Service in American Democracy.* Baltimore: Johns Hopkins University Press.

Mintz, Joel A. 1995. *Enforcement at the EPA: High Stakes and Hard Choices.* Austin, TX: University of Texas Press.

Office of Personnel Management. *"Guide to Senior Executive Service Qualifications."* Last modified 2010. www.opm.gov/ses/references/guidetoSESQuals_2010.pdf

Partnership for Public Service. *Unrealized Vision: Reimagining the Senior Executive Service.* 2009. Washington.

Ring, P. S., and J. L. Perry. 1983. "Reforming the Upper Levels of the Bureaucracy: A Longitudinal Study of the Senior Executive Service." *Administration & Society.* 15 (1): 119–144.

Schiavo-Campo, Salvatore and Pachampet Sundaram. 2001. *To Serve and to Preserve: Improving Public Administration in a Competitive World.* Manila: Asian Development Bank. (pp. 436–437)

Senior Executives Association. 2006. *Lost in Translation.* Washington: SEA

Stier, Max. 2011. Testimony before Senate Subcommitte on Oversight of the Federal Workforce. Partnership for Public Service. Washington

.

Chapter Two

Managing a Conventional Path

Lessons from Air Quality Planning and Management

Gerald Andrews Emison

When I became the director of the office of air quality planning and standards, I was astonished at how complicated the job was. The position had many different moving parts, and these dynamic conditions made the position much more difficult than any engagement I had previously. I had served as a staff engineer at EPA, worked for a local county council, as well as a management consultant for a state government. Immediately before joining the air quality program, I had directed agency level program evaluations in EPA. But none of these were as difficult as the air quality job.

I was required to function simultaneously in many different roles. It became apparent that I could influence many elements of the position, but could not control these elements. The stakes were simply too high and the features too dispersed for a single actor to control events and decisions. In short, I had found myself in a truly executive position.

In the air quality program from 1984 to 1990 I dealt with a range of topics. In our major urban areas attaining ozone and particulate matter national ambient air quality standards competed with regulating air toxic pollutants that cause cancer. Using the best technology to control emissions competed with meteorological monitoring as bases for scientific control of pollution. Leading the highly trained professionals in EPA competed with managing similar professionals in state and local air pollution agencies. These activities occurred in a political setting that combined bureaucratic politics within the administration as well as the partisan politics of divided government. These aspects not only made for multiple considerations. They interacted and yielded an ever-changing landscape I had to traverse daily in order to do my job, which was to improve the nation's air quality.

This chapter seeks to draw out lessons from my experience directing the air quality program from 1984 to 1990. It does this by looking at the air quality program that employed a conventional command and control regulatory approach. This approach envisioned the government commanding, through federal regulations, the standards for polluters to achieve and using monitoring and enforcement to control such emissions. This approach has been the predominant method for government environmental protection since the early 1970s when the modern environmental era began . Even with such a conventional and seemingly straightforward approach, I found that complexity characterized almost every situation and required adaptive responses. This experience formed the policy basis that led to the core of the Clean Air Act of 1990 (PL101–549) as well as my receipt in 1988 of the senior executive service presidential rank award.

When I left the air quality program to become the deputy regional administrator of EPA's office in Seattle, I found this challenging nature was replicated in the regional office. The type of challenges changed, but the forms remained similar to those in air quality. Certainly the individuals were different, as were the issues. But the interconnected nature of the position was very similar. I was not so much on top of a hierarchy dealing with environmental issues as embedded in a network. In the regional office I found myself dealing with endangered species issues in the collision of protection for the northern spotted owl versus the economic consequences of limiting timber production. Similar environment-economy conflicts arose in cleaning up nuclear waste at the Hanford nuclear reservation and stabilizing contaminated soil at the lead smelter in Bunker Hill, Idaho. Technology, economics, management and politics collided repeatedly. These repeating traits in two EPA organizations suggested that a deeper pattern might be present across these venues. Such general properties might be worth considering as features of executive environmental management. Since the dominant attribute of these experiences was interconnection, it is from such complexity that lessons emerge for executive effectiveness. I believe recognizing this attribute of executive management is vital to effectiveness. It derived from three types of conditions I had to manage simultaneously to be effective as an air quality executive: the physical properties of air quality, the politics of air quality, and interpersonal skills. Thinking of air quality management tasks as inherently interrelated can frame lessons I learned from managing air quality. To accomplish this, we will look at the characteristics of air quality's physical features, its politics, and the executive behaviors I found closely associated with achieving air quality management success.

THE CROSS-LINKED PHYSICAL PROPERTIES OF AIR QUALITY

Early in my tenure in the air quality program I learned that the physical properties of air quality were interrelated, and to be effective, management responses needed to reflect that fundamental feature. To employ an analogy from Page (2009), the landscape of air quality's physical traits was diverse, interdependent, connected and adaptable. These characteristics existed across the physical elements of air quality: pollutants, effects, emissions, exposures, responses, and mitigation approaches.

When we consider pollutants, there was a diversity of types. Conventional pollutants under the national ambient air quality portion of the Clean Air Act (Title I of Public Law 101–549), such as ozone and particulate matter, were ubiquitous and prompted a range of health and environmental effects. They could cause a loss in lung function through ozone exposure or heightened cardiovascular disease through exposure to particulate matter. Toxic pollutants such as those regulated under Title III of the Clean Air Act had diverse and heinous effects through cancer or teratogenic effects. And controlling one category of pollutants, such as toxics, could affect other pollutants, such as hydrocarbons and oxides of nitrogen, the precursors to ozone. As a consequence, the nature of pollutants presented complexity as a regular feature. Choosing how to manage these pollutants required incorporating such complexity.

Air pollution emissions were also complex in amount and location. For example, the amount of emissions from power plant flue gas desulfurization controls was governed, in part, by the amount of bottom ash allowed. Similarly, control of sulfur emissions, which lay at the core of the acid rain program of Title IV of the Clean Air Act, could be achieved by changing from high sulfur to low sulfur coal or by employing flue gas desulfurization. The interaction among emissions was extensive. The location of emissions presented an interactive management problem. To reduce ground-level concentrations of particulate matter, higher stacks might be employed. Yet this could shift the environmental problem from a local one to a regional one as meteorological conditions dispersed the pollutants across the region. Similarly, interconnectivity was also found in ozone control. Since ozone was formed through photochemical reactions in the atmosphere, the emissions of one area were typically transported to another area where the effects were felt. Accounting for such regional ozone transport was the direct purpose of long range oxidant modeling. This modeling proved to be difficult because of the interactions of atmospheric chemistry, meteorology and sources' behaviors. This offers further evidence of the complexity of air quality emissions.

Not only was air quality complex in pollutants and emissions, the exposures and responses to such exposures to air quality pollutants were diverse, interactive and connected. The exposures that stem from benzene emissions from coke plants typically spread across the larger urban areas where steel was manufactured. But such exposures were rendered even more complex when we considered that the highest exposure to benzene from these plants typically occurred in nearby neighborhoods which were almost always low-income areas.

The mitigation of controlling air pollution was also complex. Emergence of new controls occurred when painting operations at auto assembly plants became more effective. New paints were created along with improved emission capture technology by the auto industry. These mitigations were interconnected. As refrigeration units that condense paint's hydrocarbon emissions became more efficient, the cost of using them declined even as painting application methods became more effective. A vastly reduced emissions profile from auto assembly plants resulted from such diverse and interdependent features.

Page (2009) categorizes landscapes for complexity as Mt. Fuji, rugged, or dancing. Mt. Fuji landscapes are areas in which there is a single or small number of solutions. In such cases the challenge is to find the best solution. Rugged landscapes, on the other hand, are areas in which a number of solutions are present and connected. The challenge is to find a solution that is better than other proximate ones. Finding the single best solution on such a landscape can be very costly, and satisficing rather than optimizing often is the best use of search techniques. Dancing landscapes are ones in which the elements are not only connected but which change depending on how the other elements change—they dance.

The problems of complexity arising from the physical properties of air quality provide rugged or dancing landscapes, but they masqueraded as Mt Fuji landscapes. There may be simple questions, such as what is the best level of controls on a source of particulate matter. But the answers depend on responses that recognize the complexity of diverse control methods exposures and responses, employed in an interactive manner that actually changes over time. I found that for every complex control approach there was almost always a simple answer—and that answer was almost always wrong when the diversity, interconnectivity and adaptation of the controls were considered.

Other complex challenges that I confronted when dealing with air quality were ones concerning the interaction of values and risks. Put simply, we could separately estimate control costs, effectiveness and the health-related effects of such actions. What we could not provide through analysis was how these interacted with politics in the dancing landscape that was air quality. As a consequence we could not identify through engineering alone when to cease adding further controls. This choice was fundamentally one of values concerning risks versus costs, and issues of values devolved to politics, not engineering. We were looking at systems that made estimation of costs and related effects difficult. Yet the most difficult element was the interaction between risks and costs. At some point a level of control had to be chosen and the consequences of such a choice accepted. This interaction often paralyzed political appointees. They were frozen by simple statements of purpose such as "an ample margin of safety to protect the public" contained in the hazardous air pollutant portion, Section 112, of the Clean Air Act of 1977 and the challenge of choosing a level of the standard when locations, qualities, exposures and consequences all interacted. This required choosing a risk and control level by deploying political values, at which political appointees frequently bridled.

Under these conditions, it became essential to exercise choices that considered the diversity, interconnectivity and further adaptation of the situation. It meant accepting that such choices were fundamentally estimates of risk and costs informed by the political choice between these aspects.

THE INTERRELATED PLAYING FIELDS OF POLITICAL CHOICES IN AIR QUALITY

The politics of air quality presented a landscape of diverse, interactive, connected and adaptive elements. While my position as director of the office of air quality planning and standards was a career civil service one, it most assuredly involved politics. And these politics were not straightforward. They came in three broad categories: partisan, bureaucratic and intergovernmental. Each of these was complex and nuanced within itself, and they interacted among themselves to create an ever-changing landscape for political complexity.

Partisan politics suffused all major regulatory decisions that affected national air quality during my service in the air quality program. In part this was due to a difference in values held by the political parties. Typically, Republicans placed emphasis on reducing pollution control costs to industrial sources while meeting minimum standards of emissions. Democrats were more inclined toward stringent pollution controls that did not breach acceptable cost standards. In short Republicans sought to optimize cost reduction subject to the constraint of meeting environmental standards, but the Democrats favored optimizing emission reduction subject to the constraint of cost limitations. Yet such direct differences in values were not the only aspect of partisan politics. Often a party would take positions that contrasted with the other party's views in order to distinguish one party from the other.

At the policy level for ozone control, many Democratic members of Congress pressed EPA for a more environmentally stringent interpretation of the physical concentrations of ozone. This would require tighter emission controls than currently required, raising costs to emitting industries. In one particular instance concerning Tulsa, Oklahoma, a Democratic congressman from that area had strongly criticized EPA for its alleged relaxed interpretation of such rules. He then reversed himself when his district was caught in even the looser requirements. As a result he strongly criticized EPA for being unreasonably stringent.

An example of the interaction of partisan politics occurred during development of a regulation controlling toxic benzene emissions from coke ovens. During the Reagan administration my office recommended, and the administrator chose, a control level that would reduce emissions of benzene from leaking doors and lids in a coke battery by about 95 percent. This level was chosen by rejecting an option of 98 percent emission reductions. The decision was broadly criticized by Democratic members of Congress as trading public health for cost savings to the steel industry. The criticism became so withering that EPA's political leadership withdrew the original regulation before it took effect and delayed adoption by years. Even though the public health gains from adopting a benzene standard were well documented, this controversy kept the agency from adopting benzene standards for a number of years. This action consumed so much political capital that once the benzene standards were adopted, no further hazardous air pollutant standards were established until after the act was amended with a new approach to toxics in the Clean Air Act of 1990. The interaction of interests had yielded a new landscape that was a different political condition.

Even on matters that did not involve partisan considerations, politics of a complex nature could arise from bureaucratic interests. For example, during the decision process for regulating phosgene, tangled bureaucratic politics made a simple choice quite complex.

Phosgene was well known to have dangerous health effects from its use against troops in World War I. Since it was unregulated in the United States, it presented a worthy target to reduce risks from industrial processes that used phosgene as a feedstock. To regulate such chemicals we needed clear scientific evidence of potential harm, and such studies from the 1940s to the 1950s provided in the scientific literature this evidence.

My office moved to regulate phosgene, and in doing so obtained a preliminary decision from the administrator to list phosgene as a hazardous air pollutant. This action was the initiating step in regulating such emissions.

As the formal decision document was under review at the administrator's level of EPA, the agency's office of research and development objected to using the scientific studies upon which the regulation of phosgene was based. The data upon which the scientific assessments for phosgene were based came in part from Nazi death camp exposures. Some scientists from the office of research and development raised ethical concerns about using the data. My office responded by raising ethical concerns about not using the data and thereby allowing potentially harmful emissions to go unregulated. The disagreement was quite sharp. Conflicting appeals to fundamental values within the bureaucracy ensued, with heavy lobbying on both sides. The situation was resolved only when the administrator personally chose to stop the regulatory process. This bureaucratic struggle's resolution depended upon a decision at the highest political level within the agency. Phosgene emissions remained unregulated as a consequence. In this case a simple regulatory matter was rendered complex through clashes of bureaucratic interests expressed in terms of conflicting, interacting ethical responsibilities.

Intergovernmental political clashes also complicated air quality decisions. The shared governance model of air quality management had the federal government setting national ambient air quality standards as well as the general processes to be employed for achieving ambient air quality standards. State environmental agencies were responsible for developing and implementing specific actions to implement the federal decisions. Within a state government there was often a clash between the environmental agency and economic development interests. Frequently the state environmental agency sought stringent compliance with expensive emission controls while economic development interests favored lower-cost approaches. This created considerable conflict for state environmental agency staff, and they often sought to diminish this conflict by having EPA remove their discretion and direct them to choose the stringent path.

This led to considerable intergovernmental conflict. The state environmental agency sought EPA to impose on them standards for reasonably available control technologies (RACT) in ozone nonattainment areas. Frequently these standards were beyond the levels the EPA could or would endorse. EPA viewed the choices as matters of discretion on the part of the state. The state had a range of choices it could exercise. The state environmental agency felt EPA had a responsibility to help them do the "right" thing by removing the state environmental agency's latitude and neutralizing state economic development interests. The multilayered complexity of state environmental versus state economic interest interacted with EPA's technical and political limits concerning the role of the federal government. This created a rugged landscape of intergovernmental political considerations that defied simple solutions.

Effectiveness in such settings required me to think in complex political terms even while drawing upon the initial complexity of air quality's physical properties. This placed a premium on understanding the implications in a number of simultaneous dimensions and doing so within a welter of factors to consider.

Managing the Intricacy of Personal Behavior

Managing air quality was challenging not simply due to the interlinked conditions of its physical and political attributes. It was challenging because any executive activity in government is one that takes place in a dancing landscape of personal behavior. There are traits and conditions that I encountered that drew their character from the fact that government executives get work done through others. They must depend on personal conduct for effectiveness. The behaviors, purposes and values of diverse people constantly interacted. Any successful executive needs a set of behaviors that accounts for such diverse, independent, connected and adapting individuals. To consider this I found it useful to think of these management behaviors in two groups, managing oneself and managing others.

Managing my own behavior in such a complex world required a variety of skills. Since change was a prime characteristic, I found constant adaptation to be an essential skill. This began with a well-developed sense of values. Knowing what values mattered to me was very helpful when the landscape danced. Similarly, knowing with clarity my purpose in a shifting setting enabled me to stay focused on essentials even as transition took place. Being prepared to adjust to novel circumstances drew on these skills and equipped me to adapt.

Related to these was the insight from knowing my own strengths and weaknesses. As conditions changed due to complex interactions of air quality, physical properties and politics, different skills became important. I found, for example, that I could be fairly effective planning, organizing and controlling my office's activities. This was quite valuable when developing the insights for new provisions of the clean air act. When the tasks shifted from developing to selling the ideas, I needed different strengths. In this case an unflinching understanding of my own strengths and weaknesses led me to hand the selling responsibilities to one of my staff who was gifted in the tasks of explanation and persuasion.

There was another set of skills I found invaluable in the face of multidimensional change. First, the ability to switch smoothly from topic to topic was essential. In preparing this chapter, I looked over my appointment calendars for a sample of days as director of air quality. It was an unusual day in which I had less than ten meetings, each on a separate topic. When this was combined with telephone calls and other unscheduled interruptions, it was a rare day in which even an hour could be devoted to a single topic. Similarly, the ability to recall diverse information, both conceptually and factually, was necessary to keep pace with the demands of the position. Due to the variety and number of topics I worked, a good memory became an essential tool. In short the ability to smoothly and rapidly change focus was necessary.

The next essential set of skills concerned processing information. An executive gets work done through others. In order to do this an executive must be able to communicate with clarity and economy. The ability to receive information required speedy reading of written material and focused listening during oral briefings. Similarly, the ability to speak and write with clarity and conciseness I found to be vital.

A related set of self-management skills I needed concerned time management. I had to know where my time was being demanded and choose to spend time on those activities that advanced my ultimate purpose. This required a single calendar, kept by my secretary, which I then followed and which my staff likewise used to adjust their schedules. Appointments became the action instrument for managing my time. As a result one of my most valuable assets was this time. How I allocated it determined what was advanced and what was delayed in the office.

High stresses came with this complex job. I found that the demands of an executive job directly yielded high conflict and led to personal stress. It became necessary for me to develop and adhere to a regular program of stress management. This involved adhering to proper diet, getting regular exercise and giving myself periodic opportunities to step away from the moment to moment demands of the job. Stress management was essential especially when I faced a constantly shifting environment. As a part of this stress management, I had to place special emphasis on physical, intellectual and emotional stamina. The job typically required ten to twelve hour days for six days a week, and this demand went on year-round. In order to be effective over the long run in which change was a verity, I needed stamina of a continuing nature.

A twin behavior of this stamina was the need, as a regular practice, to grow and develop professionally. Because the landscape was constantly in motion, I had to adjust my skills and approaches continually. This continuing improvement effort through reading and reflection was challenging because it competed with other time demands, yet without the immediacy of those demands. I must admit that such efforts usually were well short of what I wished. But mitigating this was the recognition that, as Deming held, it is the process of improvement rather than the goal of perfection that ultimately governs success (Walton 1986).

I learned that managing myself was but one side of the complexity of personal conduct in an executive setting. I also was managing others. This required an entire suite of interpersonal skills, but the most important was the ability to situate choices within the overall matrix of subordinates, peers and bosses in the bureaucracy as well as within the larger air quality institutional and political setting. The ability to manage up, down and laterally depended upon accurately seeing myself in that landscape. This positioning was made doubly challenging as the complexity of air quality evolved and the landscape changed resolutely.

This situating required constant assessment of interests for all the actors I faced. Regular reflection upon what others sought in these complex landscapes was essential. The initiating interest was self-awareness. I found I had to constantly assess my purposes. Otherwise I would be drawn into an emphasis on operating rather than achieving an outcome. Ongoing self reflection of my purpose and the purposes of others became necessary on almost every decision I faced, whether it concerned internal personnel matters or national air quality issues.

There were two moderating approaches I found valuable. First, it became quite important to remember that not every issue was a fight to the death. "Live to fight another day" became a motto for gauging how far to challenge policy issues, especially those heavy with political or interpersonal elements. It was very useful to remember that I could not exert influence if I took myself out of the picture through an extreme position. Moderation in response allowed adaptation to the constantly dancing landscape of air quality management.

The second moderating approach related to interpersonal skills. I had to constantly remind myself that "jerks don't get ahead." The game of air quality management was played in a wide variety of settings and with a wide variety of personalities. Presenting a demeanor that was positive and affable became vital. Most issues concerned individuals who had participated in previous issues; they involved repeat play. It was important to keep goodwill intact for the next cycle of policy debates.

These challenges of managing myself and others led me to adopt a set of professional practices. First, I found it was important to respect everyone. When dealing with contentious issues, it was very alluring to discount the capabilities and motives of adversaries. This would have been a vast mistake. I respected my subordinates because they held an immeasurable depth of technical knowledge and judgment. I respected my peers because they were facing challenges as difficult as mine, and usually did so with great adeptness. I respected my political bosses for both their innate skills and their political authority. I respected the public, for their well-being was the ultimate test of whether I had done my job properly. Also, I respected myself. This respect extended to respect for the logic of my arguments. I found the professional practice of persuading from evidence to be one of necessity. Any argument that did not stem from evidence was doomed to extinction as others challenged it.

Humans are complex. Engaging air quality issues combined complexity from physical processes, political interests and human nature. The diverse interdependent, connected and adapting landscapes that resulted suggest a number of lessons that we may draw in dealing with conventional pollution control under highly dynamic conditions.

LESSONS FROM AIR POLLUTION CONTROL

With such complexity in managing air quality, there are general lessons we can see from this experience. These compose a group of fundamental practices and mindsets that enable effectiveness in executive behavior in environmental protection. Page (2009) suggested a number of conclusions that could be drawn from studying complex systems generally. His advice resonates with the environmental challenges I faced as a director of air quality.

First, it is important to recognize that the primary challenge is to manage risks from environmental conflicts. This implies there are no permanent solutions. It is not possible to "fix" the environment so that hazards no longer appear. The best we can achieve is progress in reducing environmental risks. Economic activities, consumption patterns, corrective measures, and institutional capabilities constantly change. What serves an executive well is the persistent recognition that both problems and solutions are constantly evolving. The mindset of continuous improvement of processes and technologies is the only enduring path to improving the environment. Constant adaptability, especially through learning organizations, becomes the watchword for executives who take a pragmatic approach to environmental protection. This means having a cold-blooded willingness to abandon any practice that does not serve the ends of advancing environmental protection under current conditions. This requires an executive to be in a constant mode of self reflection concerning effectiveness. To do otherwise risks holding fast to obsolete actions. Ineffectiveness attendant to such obsolescence will be the legacy of such failure to adapt. The landscape of environmental protection is complex. It encompasses technological, political, organizational as well as individual personal changes. An effective manager recognizes that under such conditions, resolution of issues is unlikely, but improvement and advancement is quite likely through constant, reflective adaptation.

Diversity of approaches and the accompanying openness to new ideas is essential. With the environmental policy landscape dancing so much, new challenges will emerge. It is unlikely that old solutions will meet the test of effectiveness. Being open to the novel can be a practical and essential response to such conditions.

Environmental executives must guard against pressing for small efficiency gains at the risk of overlooking major structural changes that can yield large advances. As conditions evolve, the likely targets of highest payoff will come from new solutions to new problems, not further refinement of past solutions. There are powerful political and bureaucratic behavioral forces that will resist such change. Advocating for enduring change is likely to be a major test of persistence for environmental executives.

With such complexity of environmental protection, it will be necessary to simplify policy choices as much as possible even as we recognize complete simplification is unattainable. Focusing on core purposes through strategic choices can help to do this. There are multiple interests invested in further complexification. Environmental executives will be well served by seeking to diminish such complications by focusing on core activities and shedding nonessential work.

My experience in the air quality program convinced me that environmental executive management is challenging work. I found that air quality management tasks were extraordinarily interrelated, and that effectiveness stemmed, not from avoiding such complexity, but through honest acknowledgment that it exists and can be used to advance environmental quality. When I acknowledged this, I found that participating and contributing in such settings enabled real and enduring improvement in environmental quality.

REFERENCES

Page, Scott E. 2009. *Understanding Complexity.* Chantilly, VA: Teaching Company.
Rosenbaum, Walter A. 2011. *Environmental Politics and Policy.* Washington, DC: CQ Press.
U.S. Congress. 1990. *Clean Air Act.* PL 101–549 .Washington, DC.
Walton, Mary. 1986. *The Deming Management Method.* New York: Perigee Books.

Chapter Three

The Challenges of Pesticide Regulation

Reconciling Past Decisions While Forging a Better Future

Susan Wayland

It was my privilege to participate in the dramatic evolution of pesticide policy and strategies nationally and internationally over the past three decades. Today's array of pest control techniques bears only faint resemblance to those at the dawn of modern agriculture. The persistent, bioaccumulative, and risky products of the past have given way to a completely new generation of products safer for human health and the environment. Moreover, the fundamental approaches to pest control in the twenty-first century are far more sophisticated, and include biological, organic and other non-chemical tools as well as conventional products. This change did not come easily or rapidly. Perhaps most formidable of the challenges in my experience was the need concurrently to look backward and forward, with tight resource constraints, a moving target of evolving scientific knowledge, and short, even impossible, deadlines.

INTRODUCTION

The challenges in managing EPA's pesticide program are vast; in addition to the sheer volume of pesticide products on the market today, pesticide regulation touches the lives of virtually all citizens in everyday life, whether they are applying pesticides in their backyard, disinfecting their kitchens and bathrooms, being exposed through community pest control programs like mosquito abatement, or merely consuming breakfast, lunch, and dinner. Most pesticides are by their very nature toxic, designed to interfere with the success of living things, including insects, rodents, and weeds. Before discussing particular programs, it is important to review some background information.

Pesticides have been governed by federal laws longer than any toxic materials under EPA's purview. The Federal Insecticide, Fungicide, and Rodenticide Act (FIFRA) (7USC§136 et seq) of 1947 was initially focused on protecting farmers from products that did not work effectively. Pesticides include all products that claim to control or mitigate a pest. Environmental and human health concerns were far from the framers' minds. In fact, in post–World War II America, DDT and its cousin chlorinated hydrocarbons were welcomed as miraculous weapons to control pests and increase yields. The Food, Drug, and Cosmetic Act (FFDCA) (21USC§301 et seq) in the 1950s addressed foods that contained pesticides, and directed that no residues should exceed established tolerances, or allowable residue levels. By the time that pesticide hazards were being identified, starting most visibly with Rachael Carson's watershed book, *Silent Spring*, in 1962, decades of pesticide approvals and use had been sanctioned based on an incomplete understanding of potential risks. Those chickens would come home to roost during my time with EPA. Looking back over thousands of old decisions in the light of modern scientific standards would be a Herculean challenge.

It is also important to understand that pesticide regulation operates very differently from the rest of EPA's programs. For most water, air and land programs, EPA sets national standards and transfers funds through its ten regional offices to the states, which issue individual permits or take other implementation actions.

The pesticide program is, in contrast, a national licensing program. All products, and every use of every product, with accompanying labeling, must undergo national pre-market approval and registration by EPA's Office of Pesticide Programs. An EPA registration number appears on every pesticide product sold in this country. In addition, the program sets national tolerance levels for all pesticide residues on each food commodity on which the product may be used (for example, pesticide *x* applied on fruit trees will have specific residue limits on peaches, on apples, on oranges and so forth). Applications for registration must be supported by hundreds of scientific studies to define potential risk, which is determined by examining both potential exposure and toxicity data. The label is the law. Using a pesticide in a manner that is inconsistent with specified uses and restrictions is a violation of FIFRA. Regions and states have very important roles in enforcing label decisions and promoting better use practices, and the Food and Drug Administration and the Department of Agriculture (USDA) have responsibility for enforcing tolerance levels. However, the terms and conditions of use for each product are set nationally at EPA Headquarters.

In addition, Congress is organized in a way that oversees pesticide policy and actions differently than for air, water, and land. The authorizing and oversight committees in Congress for FIFRA are the agriculture committees. The oversight committees for FFDCA are focused on health rather than agriculture. Therefore, it is important background to understand that the primary congressional oversight for pesticide issues is not only vested in different committees from most of EPA; congressional jurisdiction itself creates an internal tension. This represents a challenge to environmental managers in EPA who must develop strategies and decisions that will be examined from fundamentally disparate perspectives.

RE-EVALUATING A QUARTER CENTURY OF DECISIONS—THE REREGISTRATION PROGRAM

EPA was formed in 1970, at which time the staff of the pesticide program was transferred from the U.S. Department of Agriculture. This was an abrupt transition for a cadre of dedicated professionals whose primary constituency had been farmers and other pesticide users. Then, almost before the boxes were unpacked, Congress amended FIFRA by enacting the Federal Environmental Pesticide Control Act of 1972. This was the first critical step in transforming the focus of FIFRA into a human health and environmental statute.

While enhancing EPA's powers to evaluate the risks as well as the benefits of pesticide decisions, the law mandated the Agency to *reregister* the pesticides already on the market. The law set a deadline of two years to accomplish this task. Reregistration required EPA to review the totality of available human health and environmental data on the thousands of active ingredients and tens of thousands of products currently registered; to identify those studies that were not adequate by modern standards; to identify outright gaps in data, to require registrants to conduct the studies necessary to fill those gaps; to review all the new data; and to determine whether the products could continue to be marketed as before, to require restrictions on some or all uses, or to remove the products from the market altogether. There are many lessons to be gleaned from the massive task of reregistration, and I will discuss four of them here.

Lesson 1: Set priorities to focus on the "worst first," and allocate resources accordingly.

It was important in facing a mountain of previous decisions to examine the older pesticides in a way that was most protective of public health and the environment. How could this be done by a fledgling agency still attempting to set new standards for pesticide registration under the amended statute, and without additional resources? To cut to the quick, it couldn't.

I will not spend a lot of time here discussing the myriad reasons for the slow start on reregistration. The Pesticide Program endeavored to set priorities, and began calling in new health and environmental data for pesticides that were used on food, assuming that food uses were the largest category of exposure to the most number of people.

However, environmental managers decided that the pesticide program had more compelling uses of its resources. In 1972, the Agency cancelled DDT, one of the most important and courageous decisions in EPA's history, made by its first administrator, William D. Ruckelshaus. It was important to remove this chemical from the market because there was abundant evidence that the pesticide lasted for decades in the environment, was bioaccumulating in the food chain, was a potential carcinogen, was occurring in human adipose tissue and mother's milk, and was causing adverse reproductive effects (e.g., eggshell thinning) on many avian species, including the bald eagle, the peregrine falcon and the brown pelican. It was courageous because the cancellation was vigorously opposed in a storm of protest from the pesticide producing industry, agriculture, and vector control managers. This was the real-world version of the premise of John Grisham's novel, *The Pelican Brief.*

That decision, which was challenged for years in court, was followed by cancellations of use of aldrin/dieldrin, chlordane/heptachlor, 2,4,5-T, DBCP, mirex and other highly visible pesticides that were cancelled for concerns about cancer, birth defects, and other serious health effects, and also challenged for years in administrative proceedings and in court. These were hard-fought, lengthy, and resource-intensive battles. The Agency simply could not allocate enough person-power to reregistration in light of the more compelling cancellation cases and the steady stream of new applications in the review queue. Congress amended the deadline once, providing an additional year. Even an additional decade was not enough.

Environmental managers often face such important scenarios, where the workload clearly exceeds the resource base to address the required task. It is critical in these cases to identify the full complexity of the mission, and to focus available resources in a way that will result in the greatest protection, for the greatest population (human and nontarget species), for the greatest good.

Lesson 2: When resources are inadequate, identify the shortfall, redefine the task, and set about acquiring new sources of funding.

It is important for environmental managers to not only direct resources wisely, but also to identify ways to increase funding and to transform the task to a manageable size. Reregistration of pesticides is an excellent example of this principle. Working with Congress, EPA and stakeholders got truly serious about reregistration with amendments to FIFRA in 1988. The law was amended to require the reregistration of all pesticides registered before 1984, a date that was considered consistent with modern scientific testing standards, and also very importantly allowed EPA to charge fees to the pesticide industry thus providing a new resource stream for the reregistration review.

The Agency devised a strategy to maximize the health and environmental benefits of the program in the shortest time possible. To establish priorities, the law allowed the program to develop a process consisting of five phases, and to break the universe of pesticides into four lists (A–D).

At the front end of the process, the pesticide program identified the information needed to make an informed decision. Then EPA set about to obtain that information from the pesticide manufacturers (Phases 1–4).

Over 1100 active ingredients were grouped into "cases" of like chemicals. The lists from A–D were intended to set priorities on the order of review. The Agency, as discussed above, focused on assessing the products that had the greatest potential to cause harm, i.e., to review the "worst first."

At the beginning of the reregistration program there were over 600 cases. In order to set priorities, the Agency asked itself what pesticides would be expected to pose the most exposure to the population. As mentioned above, we assumed that pesticides used on food crops had the greatest potential to expose the largest number of people so they went to the front of the queue (List A). Lists B, C, and D were developed based on potential for human exposure, including potential residues in drinking water, significance of outstanding data requirements, potential for worker exposure, and potential for exposure to non-target species.

Developing the data required for decision making is expensive. At the time I left the Agency in 2001, the pesticide manufacturing industry was estimating that it cost $10 million and took an average of ten years to bring a new product to market. For some active ingredients registered prior to 1984, filling reregistration data gaps cost almost as much as a new product registration. Therefore, pesticide registrants had to do their own analysis of whether the costs of developing new supporting data would be justified by projected future sales. At the initial stage of data call-in, the industry decided not to support 229 cases, and those pesticides were cancelled and removed from the market.

After all information was complete on a case, the pesticide program scientists and case managers conducted a full analysis of the total array of potential uses and risks associated with the product, and issued a Reregistration Eligibility Document (RED). That is an easy sentence to write, but the volume of work behind each RED was enormous, requiring a thorough review of all toxicology, environmental fate, chemistry, exposure, etc. studies and bringing the science and all other factors together for appropriate decision making.

Environmental managers often face a shortfall of resources. When the task is enormous, it is important not only to identify the resource issues, but also to refine the strategy, and to attempt to acquire a more adequate resource base.

Lesson 3: Ensure thorough peer review of the science supporting decisions.

Environmental managers must in most cases base decisions and set priorities based on the best science available. The reregistration program provides an excellent example of this premise.

Pesticide registration, reregistration, and cancellation decisions are based on a massive volume of scientific data. Pesticides are tested more thoroughly than any chemicals other than drugs. A food-use pesticide will be supported by over one hundred studies required by EPA to determine the potential of the pesticide to expose humans and non-target species, and to determine the likelihood of adverse impacts from those exposures. Examples of the types of studies required include those to determine the pesticide's potential to cause cancer, birth defects, acute poisoning, impacts on birds, fish, and other non-target creatures, longevity in the environment, and potential to reach surface and ground water. These studies are specified in guidelines published in the *Federal Register* through a public process. Thus, the manufacturers, the public, and all other stakeholders have an opportunity to participate, and at the end, all parties know what is expected.

For reregistration, EPA began issuing hundreds of data call-in notices, based on modern guidelines, to pesticide manufacturers, who, under the law, must conduct the studies needed to evaluate the potential risks of their products. And in order to do that, the program had to review the databases of every chemical group to determine if there were outright data gaps, or data that were inadequate by modern standards.

A key component of the reregistration process was the assurance of full scientific peer review, particularly when new data indicated a cause for concern for human or nontarget species health, or environmental impact. The reregistration process could lead to continuation of uses, albeit often with additional restrictions, or lead to removal of the entire product line from the market. Pesticides whose risks were deemed unacceptable compared to their benefits were taken off the reregistration path and put on an even more closely scrutinized track known as Special Review. Special Review often leads to cancellation of some or all uses of the pesticide. While I will not discuss the Special Review or cancellation process further in this chapter, it should be noted that the administrative and judicial remedies afforded registrants are many and usually time and resource-consuming for both EPA and the appellants. Stakes are especially high.

The underlying science supporting reregistration decisions had to be sound. Initial risk assessment reviews were (and are today) conducted by pesticide program scientists, including toxicologists, chemists, biologists, microbiologists, wildlife biologists, hydrologists, and environmental fate experts. Pesticide program economists and usage experts assess the benefits of the products, including consultation with the USDA when impacts for agriculture were likely. Science reviews were and are made available to the public. For pesticides whose risks appeared to the Agency to be unacceptable, that is, cancellation was a likely outcome, the underlying science was presented to an independent entity for peer review.

That entity is known as the Scientific Advisory Panel (SAP). It was created in statute when FIFRA was amended in 1975. This panel is separate from the Science Advisory Board used by the rest of the Agency for peer review, but its purpose is similar—to review the underlying scientific foundation of decisions being considered by EPA. The SAP was born from concerns that EPA was moving too quickly to take pesticides off the market without adequate review of the supporting science. It was a time in which extrapolation of human risks from animal studies was viewed with great skepticism. Pesticide manufacturers not only defended their products in EPA's administrative processes and in court, but also in appeals to the agriculture committees to rein in EPA.

Initially, there were concerns that the Agency's science would be put to a "political science" test rather than an honest review of the data and risk assessments. Fortunately, those concerns proved to be unfounded. The SAP became one of the most valuable and respected independent peer review committees in EPA's domain. Its meetings are conducted in public, and provide opportunities for public input. Members are nominated by the National Science Foundation and the National Institutes of Health and screened for potential conflict-of-interest issues. Public comment is allowed on the nominees before appointment.

Environmental managers must typically base decisions on a wide spectrum of scientific information. The supporting science is never absolute, is typically based on animal and exposure studies, and must be interpreted by scientists based on best practices, then extrapolated to estimate human, non-target species, and environmental risks. Peer review is essential to sound public policy and decisions. It can identify gaps in the environmental manager's risk assessment case, suggest additional sources of information to bring to bear, provide additional confidence in and ultimate acceptance of final decisions, and buttress decisions that are contested in administrative procedures or in court.

Lesson 4: Involve critical stakeholders at key junctures of the decision-making process.

Environmental decisions are never made in a vacuum. There is a potentially vast array of constituencies affected by decisions made by environmental managers. Involving those stakeholders is essential to making fully informed and most effective decisions.

Pesticide issues are an example of an environmental area affecting a very diverse and active constituent base. The directly regulated constituency includes pesticide manufacturers and marketers. Basic manufacturers are often large, multi-national chemical and pharmaceutical companies, and there are thousands of formulators and distributors of pesticide products. Other profoundly affected stakeholders include farmers, commercial pest control operators, home and garden product merchandisers, the food processing and grocery industry, public interest groups, and wildlife advocates. These stakeholders have very different worldviews.

Examining stakeholders for individual pesticide actions as well as overall policy issues illustrate this dynamic. Basic manufacturers are often represented by CropLife America (formerly the National Agricultural Chemicals Association). Formulators and smaller companies often speak through the Chemical Producers and Distributors Association, and the Chemical Specialties Manufacturers Association. Pesticide users have strong voices as well. Farmers often speak through the Farm Bureau and commodity associations, such as the National Corn Growers Association, the National Cotton Council and the National Soybean Association. Commercial pest control operators such as Orkin and Terminix weigh in on issues affecting commercially applied and household pesticides, as does the trade association representing commercial applicators, the National Pest Management Association. Those in the food production and distribution industry are front and center when food-use products are under review, and the National Grocery Manufacturers Association is an active player. Public interest groups are intensely involved, notably the National Resources Defense Council (NRDC), the Environmental Defense Fund (EDF), the Sierra Club, the Environmental Working Group, and Beyond Pesticides (formerly the National Coalition Against the Misuse of Pesticides). Advocates for wildlife protection such as the Audubon Society, the American Bird Conservancy and the National Wildlife Federation are critical *dramatis personae*. Agencies and activists interested in maintaining pesticide tools in the public health sector play an important role when a pesticide used for vector control is under review (vectors include pests such as mosquitoes or rodents that may carry serious disease such as malaria and plague to humans). Advocates for farm worker safety such as the Farmworker Justice Fund are clearly involved when dealing with the potential human health impacts on this highly exposed population. Constituencies that focus on the risk of pesticides and those which focus on the benefits are equally forceful. Those who focus on risks point out the ubiquitous and toxic nature of most pesticides. Those on the benefits side of the coin point to the health value of an abundant, affordable food supply. EPA needs to consider all such consequences.

Spokespersons for the public interest sector often disagree. An example of the divergent opinions within this community is the testing regimen to determine chemical risks. Using animal studies to predict human risk is a now well-established component of risk assessment, though there are many efforts now underway to reduce the need for animal testing. But even the animal testing concept is not fully accepted by advocacy groups. While most public interest advocates encourage more and better testing, the People for the Ethical Treatment of Animals (PETA) are intensely opposed to animal testing, period. I remember so well when then Vice President Albert Gore was campaigning for the presidency. At each campaign stop, a person in a large bunny suit would be there to protest EPA's stand on animal studies. While the program at issue was under my purview, it focused on high-volume industrial chemicals testing rather than pesticides and did not involve the testing of rabbits. However, I'm sure that a bunny was more effective in the protest than would have been a person in a rat suit. I relate this vignette simply to point out that you can never take anything for granted, and that unexpected curveballs can come at any time. Even a presidential election can provide a forum for debate of programs that were not heretofore on the national stage.

In addition to advocacy groups, EPA values, and has established, mechanisms for input from a wide variety of more formal advisory groups, as well as consultation with the U.S. Department of Agriculture and the Department of Health and Human Services.

All Registration Eligibility Documents (REDs) were provided through the *Federal Register* for formal comment. However, that did not constitute adequate public participation. During the reregistration years, some formal groups consulted, not necessarily on reregistration activities *per se,* included the Pesticide Program Dialog Committee (PPDC), the State FIFRA Research and Evaluation Group (SFIREG), the Food Safety Advisory Committee (FSAC), the Endocrine Disruptors Screening and Testing Advisory Committee (EDSTAC), the Tolerance Reassessment Advisory Committee (TRAC) and the Committee to Advise on Reassessment and Transition (CARAT) (the latter four explained later, and having fulfilled their function, are no longer active).

The input of committees representing a wide spectrum of affected parties is invaluable in understanding the complexities of real-world impacts of policy actions, and in discovering ways to reach an objective the most effective way possible. And all of these voices deserve to be heard and respected. Though they seldom agree with one another, or many times with EPA's final decisions, they are representing legitimate health, economic, and environmental points of view. As the old Bob Dylan song "One Too Many Mornings" (Dylan 1964) goes, "you're right from your side, and I'm right from mine."

Broad-spectrum advisory committees are essential, but it is also important to interact with affected parties face-to-face in more informal meetings, conferences, or on their own turf. Executive leadership is not sitting behind a desk and making judgments. You need to get out of the office to understand your constituencies. This is important not just to making good decisions, but to have your decisions understood if not totally embraced by affected parties.

For example, I've mentioned that farmers are critically affected by pesticide decisions. Their lobbyists will comment on *Federal Register* notices, but farmers are far too busy to read the Code of Federal Regulations. I spent a lot of time getting to know them and to have them understand EPA better. I've tramped through cotton fields, fruit orchards, and corn and soybean fields. I've visited food processing plants and dairy farms. I've flown with crop dusters. Many times, I've been introduced by my name, followed by "She's from EEEEE-PEEEE-AAAA," with the same inflection that would be used introducing Darth Vader, the *Star Wars* movie villain. It was important to get the message from the program out to those affected, and to dispel rumors or untruths that seem to run rampant. On more than one visit, I departed hearing the words, "You're not so bad after all." That was high praise indeed!

Effective environmental managers must ensure open communication with all parties affected by their decisions. This needs to be done face-to-face, in formal advisory mechanisms, in conferences and meetings, and through the established public comment process such as proposals in the *Federal Register*. Managers must identify the communities most affected by decisions, and actively solicit their opinions and input in order to reach the most fully informed and effective decisions.

RETROSPECTIVE ANALYSIS REDUX—TOLERANCE REASSESSMENT

Imagine a freight train rolling down the tracks toward its destination. You are the engineer, your cars are loaded and you know where you are going. Then imagine that the tracks start undulating, taking more complex shapes, and branching off to points unknown. That is the nature of science, and the constant underlying challenge for the pesticide program—advances in scientific understanding compel revisiting previous decisions in light of up-to-date knowledge.

Even before reregistration was completed, Congress, working with EPA and stakeholders, enacted landmark new legislation during the Clinton administration to address advances in scientific knowledge and risk assessment. The Food Quality Protection Act of 1996 (FQPA) (Public Law No. 104–170) was the most comprehensive overhaul of pesticide law in decades. It amended FFDCA and FIFRA in momentous fashion. Like the reregistration program, it focused on reviewing older decisions. The law required EPA to reevaluate all 9,700 current tolerance decisions over a ten-year period. There are six important lessons learned through the implementation of the FQPA.

Lesson 1: Scientific knowledge will continually advance, with increasingly complex and sophisticated risk concerns identified.

Environmental managers must stay abreast of an always-changing and evolving scientific landscape. Pesticide regulation is a perfect example of how the evolution of science and risk assessment challenges the environmental manager's ability to stay current.

To begin with, the technology for detecting pesticide residues in the environment and on food has advanced exponentially. When FIFRA and FFDCA were initially enacted, the state of the art permitted detection of pesticide residues in parts-per-million. Then it became parts-per-billion. Now it's parts-per-trillion. The advances in analytical chemistry can detect exposures at ever-increasing sophistication, but does it outpace our ability to determine risks from more miniscule exposure?

Secondly, there are new technologies and new research that question whether we are adequately assessing potential risks. Managers must make decisions based on the information available at the time they are made. When DDT was first registered, the managers making that decision believed that they were doing right by society. Likewise, over the years, scientists and decision makers did the very best they could with the information before them. But time marches on, and so does technology.

There are new concerns that were not even contemplated when reregistration was mandated. Now, there is a whole new technology of genetically modified organisms (GMOs). For example, seeds of corn and soybeans are being genetically modified to resist certain herbicides, so crops can be sprayed to control weeds without destroying the primary commodity. To some, this is a godsend for global food production and elimination of world hunger. To others, it's "Frankenfood." Seeds that are pest-resistant are governed by FIFRA, and tolerance exemptions under FFDCA are required, so the pesticide program is right in the thick of the GMO debates.

In the past several decades, there has been much more focus on risks to children. Do residues of pesticides on food actually pose more of a risk to children, who weigh less than the average adult on whom risk assessments have been conducted in the past? In addition, does the fact that children's cells are growing and rapidly dividing put them at greater risk from pesticide exposure? If one doesn't have the risk assessment tools to answer those questions, what does the environmental manager do? Furthermore, there is a growing body of scientific data raising concerns about endocrine disruptors, chemicals that can mimic human hormones in the environment. Is this a significant new risk component for humans and wildlife? How can we tell and how do we manage it?

Exposure questions are also more complex. There is the question of cumulative exposures. Individuals may be exposed to pesticides through multiple routes in any one day (e.g., water, food, and direct application). How do you account for such scenarios? Aggregate exposure, that is, exposures from different pesticides that have a common mechanism of action, is also a concern; if you only consider the impact of each individual exposure from individual chemicals, you are missing the holistic impact of exposures from multiple chemicals that have the same mode of toxicological action on the body.

Environmental managers must stay abreast of the evolution of scientific knowledge, and prepare to consider environmental risks in increasingly difficult and complex ways. This requires continuous interaction with the scientific community, and, in organizations like EPA with the ability to either perform or fund scientific research, direct resources to areas of emerging environmental concerns.

Lesson 2: Focus on evolving concerns with additional caution in risk assessments while providing leadership in forging new risk assessment tools.

Managers of environmental programs must step up to the challenges posed by the evolution of scientific knowledge. The implementation of FQPA illustrates this concept in several ways.

One especially significant change embodied in the FQPA is the modification of the statutory standard for establishing tolerances for food-use chemicals. The new standard is "reasonable certainty of no harm" which is a health-based standard. This was an important departure from the risk/benefit standard that had governed the majority of pesticide decisions under FIFRA for decades. In fact, the law prohibits consideration of benefits except in very narrow circumstances.

Among key provisions was the requirement to add an extra ten-fold safety factor to protect children's health unless there was good reason not to. Risks to children were addressed specifically in the 1993 National Academy of Science's report, *Pesticides in the Diets of Infants and Children* in which the committee found that infants and children differ significantly from adults in their exposure to pesticide residues in foods

The pesticide program already used a hundred-fold safety factor when extrapolating from animal studies to humans (after identifying the lowest level where adverse effects were not detected, one ten-fold safety factor was added to account for the potential that humans are more sensitive then animals, and another ten-fold to account for varying degrees of sensitivity among humans). Since the science was imperfect in addressing children's risks more explicitly, the answer was to be more protective by adding an additional ten-fold safety factor. Furthermore, pesticide scientists were called upon to develop more sophisticated risk assessment tools to incorporate consideration of aggregate risk and cumulative risk in determining the suitability of a chemical's registered uses. This required developing a new paradigm in determining multiple routes of exposure and comparing those to health effects data, resulting in the concept of a "risk cup" that could not be exceeded in considering all likely exposures to pesticides with similar modes of action. Before passage of FQPA, EPA considered the risks of each individual use of each individual pesticide to determine the product's acceptability (imagine multiple measuring cups displaying "acceptable risk" for each organophosphate pesticide separately for example); after FQPA, EPA began to consider all the potential risks from active ingredients having the same mode of action (imagine then *one* measuring cup displaying all the uses of all organophosphate pesticides that act on the nervous system; each individual use had to fit into an acceptable limit in consideration of the totality of uses and consequent exposures).

One of the most significant challenges was the requirement that EPA establish new testing requirements for endocrine disruptors, and require testing of pesticides that posed a potential for endocrine disruption. FQPA required that a testing program be established in two years and implemented in three years. The mandate applied to the pesticide program and EPA's drinking water program. This timeline was not possible, since even the most basic testing regimen had to be developed and subjected to rigorous scientific and public scrutiny. At the end of my time with EPA, the Agency was still in the process of defining the proper protocols for testing. An important part of any protocol development is not just how to perform testing, but how the Agency would consider and use the test results. This is uncharted territory, and must be developed with scientific integrity, despite external deadlines.

EPA scientists were and are a big part of developing an appropriate testing regimen. The Agency also established an Endocrine Disruptors Screening and Testing Advisory Committee, a committee of outside experts in the field. Developing screening and testing requirements was a groundbreaking task. It was not until 1998 that a screening battery was proposed. It was not until 2009 that the first test orders were issued, long after I had left the Agency. This time was well spent in developing a sound approach to a very new and emerging area of concern that could affect environmental and human risk assessment for decades to come. Environmental managers must meet the challenges posed by evolving science and new areas of concern head-on, and develop new risk assessment tools while providing margins of safety that take scientific uncertainty into account.

Lesson 3: Extrapolate the lessons of the past to the present.

Today's environmental manager needs to be cognizant of lessons learned from similar programs in order to find the pathways toward success. This does not mean that new approaches should be ignored, but it is only reasonable to apply successful past strategies to current challenges.

The implementation of FQPA, for example, owed much of its strategic approaches to the lessons learned from the reregistration program. Let me explain.

EPA was required by FQPA to reassess all approximately 9,700 existing food tolerances on a ten-year schedule in light of the law's new requirements. The first third were to be reassessed by 1999, the second third by 2002, and the final third by 2006.

Once again, the Agency took a monumental task and divided it into logical parts. Again, the principle of "worst first" was used, and pesticide classes were identified for the three groups to be reevaluated. With focus, teamwork, and intense scrutiny—including sound science and public participation principles established as the working culture of the reregistration program—99 percent of the 9,000-plus tolerances were reviewed within the statutorily mandated timeframes, with the remaining 1 percent shortly thereafter.

Another lesson from the reregistration program was that new tasks require new resources, and EPA worked with Congress to acquire the staff needed to reevaluate tolerances. An aggressive hiring program brought a cadre of new scientists and other personnel. Not only did this give the Agency a fighting chance to accomplish the reevaluations in the timeframe mandated, it also provided an opportunity to achieve more ethnic and cultural diversity in the workforce.

Leadership in implementing the new law required establishing goals, and ensuring that resources were directed at priority areas at the right time. In the interests of good management, accountability, and transparency, the pesticides program issued an "FQPA Implementation Plan" in 1996 that provided a very specific road map on how it would go about implementing the complex and groundbreaking requirements of the new law. The Agency clearly and explicitly outlined how it would go about each task, in what order and in what timeframe.

In keeping with the ethos of seeking outside advice and counsel, the program established the Food Safety Advisory Committee, a large and diverse array of stakeholders, including public interest and food safety advocates, pesticide manufacturers and formulators, the agricultural community (including conventional farming and organic farming interests), and the food producing and marketing industry. It was co-chaired by EPA's Deputy Administrator and the Deputy Secretary of USDA, and worked from September through December of 1996, to assist in ensuring that our first steps in implementing the new law were sound.

While the initial advisory committee (FSAC) was invaluable in the early months of developing approaches to FQPA implementation, another advisory committee representing the full spectrum of interests, first named the Tolerance Reassessment Advisory Committee (TRAC), then later transitioned to the Committee to Advise on Reassessment and Transition (CARAT), was established by EPA and USDA in June of 2000. Its purpose was to interact with the two agencies on implementing the full gamut of FQPA responsibilities. Once again, the value of interacting with affected parties was recognized and embraced.

Therefore, the effective environmental manager will take the lessons of the past, both positive and negative, and apply them to similar programs. While prior successful templates cannot address every issue or problem, many winning principles and behaviors should be considered in order to jump start new endeavors, while always remaining open-minded to new approaches that may be even more effective.

Lesson 4: The dynamic between government and advocacy groups has changed, with non-governmental entities providing more proactive leadership.

This chapter has discussed the importance for environmental managers to embrace participation from those most affected by their decisions. This lesson is a somewhat different one. It is not only that affected parties will offer valuable input to decision makers, but also that they will take on a more proactive role that can in turn affect the course of the environmental manager's strategic approaches.

An example of this type of non-governmental advocacy is illustrated in the tolerance reassessment program. Since the focus of the program was pesticide residues on food, the food industry had a critical role to play, and not just in providing input to the Agency. Industry advocates were not sitting on their hands while EPA deliberated. The Grocery Manufacturer's Association and individual companies often take stands on issues even before they are decided by the Agency. Environmental and public interest groups can be very effective in communicating issues within their communities and the national media. When EPA expresses a risk concern with an active ingredient, there is often a private corporate decision that follows. For example, while the tolerance reassessment program was underway, Gerber Foods took steps to specify what pesticide residues were not acceptable in commodities purchased for baby food.

Such private action undoubtedly has its roots in the very public debate on the pesticide Alar, a product that was registered for and applied to apples. EPA had expressed concerns about potential health effects of the product, but was proceeding in its usual deliberate way, going through peer review with the Scientific Advisory Panel, etc. But in 1989 the National Resources Defense Council began a vocal campaign to outlaw the pesticide. Hollywood intervened, with the well-known actor Meryl Streep testifying before Congress. CBS's *60 Minutes* devoted a segment to the controversy. Mothers all over the country began calling, distressed that they might be exposing their children to serious risks through apple juice. The apple-producing industry suffered significant economic loss, as the image of their product turned from the supreme health food to the Snow White poisoned fruit. Private lawsuits followed against NRDC and CBS, with industry claiming that they suffered $100 million in economic impacts. The lawsuits did not go the industry's way. In the midst of EPA's cancellation process, the manufacturer voluntarily withdrew the registration in the face of intense public and media scrutiny. In the post-Alar world, the food-producing industry, as well as the pesticide manufacturing industry, became far more sensitive to the court of public opinion, and more willing to take steps to protect its image ahead of government action. While this can lead to public confusion, it can also avoid the resource burden of a lengthy cancellation process.

Thus, environmental managers must be prepared to address the actions taken by an increasingly vocal and decisive industry and public, which can pose communications challenges, but can also influence the ultimate disposition of resources and afford protections ahead of a traditional timetable.

Lesson 5: Prevent the recurrence of problems of the past.

Today's environmental managers must not only learn from successful (and unsuccessful) techniques from the past, they must also identify ways to prevent problems from repeating themselves. Having gone through review of the decisions of the past not once but twice, the pesticide program was keenly aware that future regulators should be spared those experiences again.

The pesticide reregistration program and the tolerance reassessment program were massive undertakings because EPA had to tackle decades of prior decisions in the light of new data. Therefore, in a look to the future, the FQPA requires the re-evaluation of pesticide registration decisions every fifteen years. This is intended to avoid the enormous challenges faced by EPA in the reregistration and tolerance reassessment programs, and ensure ongoing public and environmental protection.

Thus, environmental managers facing the issues of today must not only address current problem solving, they must also determine ways that history will not repeat itself, and set processes in motion to assure that outcome.

Lesson 6: Work with Congress to effect strong public policy.

While not all environmental managers are subject to congressional oversight and activity, almost all managers operate in a world where they are subject to scrutiny by a variety of key legislative entities, whether they be local, state or federal.

The course of the reregistration and tolerance assessment programs would not have been determined without congressional involvement and changes to existing laws. It was therefore critical to work with all appropriate legislative committees. EPA had a major stake and a major voice in informing congressional staff and members of the issues to be addressed and the practical terms of implementing various provisions. While EPA cannot lobby for legislation, it may and must inform Congress about issues central to the development of legislative solutions.

In my experience, working with the legislative branch was essential to the development of sound policy and remedies for environmental issues. This may date my experiences, but I remember so well the days when the environment was not a partisan issue, and both sides of the aisle were willing to seek common ground and reach compromise solutions. EPA now seems to be the focus of intense polarization between Democrats and Republicans, with attacks on EPA regulations and the Agency itself becoming more intense and misguided. This bodes ill for sound public policy solutions for the future, for it is important to seek compromises and common ground as much as possible to achieve sound public policy.

Thus, environmental managers today must cultivate the ability to work in a larger context of legislative and political realities, and attempt to turn problems into opportunities for better policies and environmental protections.

In summary, the retrospective analyses of reregistration and tolerance review were massive and complex undertakings. Reregistration was completed with the final RED being issued in 2008. The Tolerance Reassessment process was completed in 2007. Through these programs, hundreds of the riskiest pesticide uses were eliminated from commerce. Thousands of new scientific studies were required and analyzed. The most dangerous organochlorine/chlorinated hydrocarbon pesticides were removed from the market even before reregistration began in earnest. Reregistration resulted in the cancellation of hundreds of additional products (from the voluntary cancellation of 229 cases at the beginning of the process and twenty later through REDS). Many organophosphate (OP) pesticides, which posed acute risk concerns through attacking the nervous system, and others posing risk concerns to adults and children were phased out during the tolerance review process, including azinphos-methyl, benomyl, cyanazine, ethion, ethyl parathion fenamiphos, fenthion, lindane, mevinphos, molinate and zineb. Carbofuran, atrazine and aldicarb were eliminated or restricted because of dietary concerns, both food and drinking water. In examination of residential risks, EPA eliminated pesticide uses or imposed new use restrictions for many of the organophosphates including chloripyrofos, and cancellation of most residential uses and mitigation of other uses of acephate, bensulide disulfoton, DDVP, ODM, tetrachlorvinphos and trichtorfon. In addition, many uses of organophosphate pesticides were eliminated or severely restricted in order to protect farm workers and others exposed occupationally. Cancellation and revocation of tolerances were pursued for carbofuran due to concerns about dietary, worker and ecological risks; moreover, cancellations or use restrictions were imposed on aldicarb, atrazine, azinphos-methyl, diazinon, ethyl parathion, fenthion, methamidophos, methyl parathion, phorate and terbufos because of ecological concerns. In short, the conclusion of the reregistration and tolerance reassessment process marked an enormous milestone in U.S. food safety and human and ecological health protection.

A FUTURE VISION

So far, I've focused primarily on the tasks and challenges in revisiting older decisions, and trying to keep pace with an ever-evolving body of scientific discovery.

Reassessment of prior decisions in light of new standards is immensely important to protect the public and the environment from unintended adverse results. However, that is only half of this tale. In addition to bringing the decisions of the past into modern times, sound leadership and environmental management requires looking to the future to ensure a safer and better world.

There are many lessons learned for establishing a vision for a better future; I will discuss six of them here.

Lesson 1: Clearly articulate what criteria will be used to determine the "better mousetrap" for the future.

Environmental managers need to identify and articulate the goals to be achieved in the future. It is essential to not only identify problems, but to identify the other side of the coin—the vision of success. An example of this in the pesticide arena was expressing the criteria that would constitute preferable pesticide products from an environmental and health standpoint. Pesticide manufacturers were not putting the future on hold while they met the Agency's requirements for reassessments of the past. They were developing new products to submit for registration for the first time to replace products "lost" through reregistration, to be safer or more effective than competitors' products, or to meet new needs as pests and farming methods evolved. The pesticide program acts on approximately 10,000 actions a year. Some twenty to twenty-four totally new products are scrutinized. EPA wants these products to be superior from a health and environmental standpoint to their predecessors.

In 1993, the pesticide program issued a "Reduced Risk" policy. This document articulated criteria that would be used in the pre-market review to identify those products that would be considered an improvement over past products. These included products that work with a natural active ingredient, for example bacillus thuringiensis (a bacteria that works to attack certain pests), products whose supporting data demonstrated a low potential for ground water contamination, lower use rates, low pest resistance potential and compatibility with Integrated Pest Management (IPM) programs. FQPA endorsed this approach, identifying safer pesticides as those that could (1) reduce pesticide risks to human health, (2) reduce risk to non-target organisms, (3) reduce potential for contamination of valued, environmental resources, or (4) broaden the adoption of Integrated Pest Management (IPM) or could make IPM programs more effective.

Environmental managers in any field should set the mark for the future, and clearly identify the goals for success. Managers need to know where they are going, and determine how objectives will be measured and realized.

Lesson 2: Provide market incentives to reach your goal(s).

After clearly articulating future goals, environmental managers need to consider ways to provide incentives to achieve those goals. Not every environmental manager will have a regulatory tool available, nor will regulatory tools alone be the most effective way to achieve success in many cases. Using the example of "reduced risk" or "safer" pesticide products, the incentive offered was to put applications for qualifying products on a fast track for registration decisions. In 1995, the average time to register a new conventional pesticide was thirty-eight months. For a reduced risk product, the review time was a dramatically shorter fourteen months. As the old saying goes, time is money. Therefore, environmental managers need to consider what incentives they have the ability to offer, and reward the behaviors that lead toward the overarching objectives.

Lesson 3: Understand how your decisions will impact the rest of the world, and work for international results as well as domestic outcomes.

Environmental managers in the United States must take into account how actions in this country will affect the rest of the world. Especially in light of the fact that many pollutants know no boundaries, and in consideration of today's global economy, rarely will a decision stand in isolation.

Pesticides are a good example of this dynamic. Decisions made under FIFRA pertain to all products used in the United States However, the law does not prohibit the export of pesticides banned in this country. This gave rise to a fundamental concern about a "circle of poison," where banned substances could be exported and then reimported as residues on foreign crops unless caught at the border by FDA. Another concern was the futility of banning persistent organic pollutants (POPS) in this country when the same substances used overseas could be transported across boundaries through air and water. Also, from an economic standpoint, it is difficult for U.S. manufacturers to attempt to comply with a patchwork of global requirements and standards, while it is frustrating for U.S. farmers to be denied the use of products that are, for example, used across the border in Canada.

International relations could take up a chapter in itself, but briefly some lessons learned include:

First, work with international bodies to harmonize requirements, in this case pesticide testing protocols and standards. My office worked closely with the United Nations Environment Program (UNEP) in Nairobi, the Organization for Economic Co-operation and Development (OECD) in Paris, the Food and Agriculture Organization (FAO) in Rome, the World Health Organization (WHO) in Geneva, the Codex Alimentarius Commission (a joint

FAO/WHO venture on harmonizing food tolerances), among others to work toward standard testing regimens and tolerances to encourage global safety and facilitate trade in food.

Second, even if the law permits the export of banned substances, ensure that the importing country understands that the product is not allowed in the US and why. This was accomplished through a system, incorporated into FIFRA, known as Prior Informed Consent (PIC). Manufacturers of cancelled pesticides must issue notices to importing countries, and an official of the importing country must acknowledge receipt. On a global level, the Rotterdam Convention on the Prior Informed Consent Procedure for Certain Hazardous Chemicals and Pesticides in International Trade, which became effective in 2004, covers 35 substances and has 140 participating parties (the United States is not as of this writing an official party, but FIFRA PIC procedures apply to all banned pesticides).

Third, work with other nations to achieve agreements including treaties to control substances of particular concern. In the case of pesticides, POPS is an excellent example. Persistent Organic Pollutants such as DDT, aldrin/dieldrin, mirex, and chlordane/heptachlor were cancelled by EPA in this country as discussed earlier. A multi-year and multi-nation process, lead by the State Department and EPA, resulted in a treaty signed in Stockholm that calls for global action on affected substances. This treaty was completed and opened for signature in May of 2001, and came into force in February 2004. The EPA Administrator signed for the United States. As of the end of 2010, 140 nations had become signatories. The U.S. Congress has not ratified the treaty, but EPA has taken action on virtually all the compounds listed. Seventy-three percent of the compounds listed in the Rotterdam Convention and 70 percent of the Stockholm Convention are pesticides, thus resulting in an improved global strategy for dealing with the most problematic chemicals. It is ironic that even though the United States led the effort on both the PIC and POPS treaties, and the executive branch signed on both, the Congress has not ratified either agreement, leaving the United States as an observer rather than active participant in the implementation process.

Therefore, the environmental manager today must determine how actions taken in this country will likely impact the rest of the world and vice-versa. Steps should be taken to share information routinely and aggressively, and harmonize policies and actions across the globe whenever possible. The standards should be implemented through U.S. law or policy even before international action, especially if the Congress must ratify the agreement.

Lesson 4: Use non-regulatory tools and the power of persuasion to achieve objectives and increased environmental protection.

Environmental managers often have regulatory tools at their disposal to effect change. However, managers also need to adopt measures that will achieve environmental goals through voluntary action. A good example of this type of approach in the pesticides world is advocacy for Integrated Pest Management (IPM). This is both an environment- and farmer-friendly strategy for pest control. Integrated Pest Management is a system that strives to encourage sustainable practices and minimize pesticide applications by targeting use only when needed and in amounts only as needed. IPM programs involve the careful monitoring of pest populations in the field, through, for example, trapping devices, and treating only when pests reach a specific economic threshold. It strives to maximize use of biological pesticides, natural predators (for example, certain wasps that attack other insects), and confusants such as pheromones. Conventional pesticides are also part of an IPM program when needed. IPM serves both to reduce the total environmental burden of pesticides in the environment, and saves farmers money.

EPA does not mandate IPM, but it can certainly advocate for it. Encouraging IPM was a specific policy goal of the Clinton administration. In the early 1990s, EPA joined with USDA to begin a new program, the Pesticide Environmental Stewardship Program (PESP). That program encouraged the reduction of pesticide use and risk through voluntary partnerships with pesticide user groups, both agricultural and non-agricultural. Staff was assigned to work with each PESP partner. There were over sixty partners at the time I left EPA (today there are more than two hundred).

FQPA required USDA, in cooperation with EPA, to conduct research and education programs to support the adoption of IPM, and also directed Federal agencies to use IPM techniques in pest control operations, and to promote IPM through procurement and regulatory policies and other activities. EPA provided small incentive and implementation grants to the PESP partners to encourage more adoption of IMP approaches. USDA is actively working to facilitate adoption of IMP techniques, and has issued an "IPM Roadmap" to describe its efforts.

This is a good example of EPA using voluntary action in addition to the traditional "command and control" approach to environmental protection. During the Clinton administration, there was a renewed emphasis on pollution prevention and voluntary programs. Rather than taking an adversarial approach toward one another, EPA and USDA joined forces to work for a common goal. It was a breath of fresh air to work as colleagues rather than combatants.

In cooperating with USDA, in working with user groups, in providing grants, in working with states and land-grant universities, the message is being sent that pesticide exposure can be reduced and money saved by using IPM approaches. Environmental managers must therefore identify non-traditional ways to achieve environmental results, and seek voluntary partnerships with other agencies and the private sector to achieve environmental goals. Pollution prevention approaches can achieve results and provide economic incentives at the same time.

Lesson 5: Empower the public with information.

One of the most important advances in the late twentieth century and early twenty-first century is the ability to communicate widely and instantly to millions of people through the use of the Internet. This is a double-edged sword, of course, as not all the information on the Internet is correct. However, one of the lessons learned from my time at EPA is that the public is interested in understanding risks from many sources, and in making choices based on greater knowledge.

Of course, without labeling, it is virtually impossible to look at the produce section in the grocery store and know what level of pesticides is present. However, the pesticides program at EPA has gone to great lengths to create sites on the World Wide Web that are chocked full of information on individual pesticides, as well as policies and programs to protect public health and the environment. All individual product labeling lists the active ingredient(s), and information on each is available through www.epa.gov. I was often asked why EPA did not aggressively advocate organic produce. The laws administered by the pesticide program direct the Agency to ensure the safety of pesticide products on the market. The mandate to establish criteria for organic products rests with the U.S. Department of Agriculture. USDA has established the ground rules for what may be called "organic" in the marketplace. The point is, however, that in response to consumer demand, many grocery outlets now devote sections to "organic" as well as conventionally grown food. Citizens have the opportunity to make choices depending on their own judgment, and the marketplace adjusts to consumer demands.

Environmental managers need to understand the power of information, and in using information as another tool to achieve their programs' goals. The public will trust you more if you offer information, make your decision-making transparent, and provide individuals the knowledge to enable personal judgments.

Lesson 6: Prevent the introduction of new problems.

Environmental managers in many cases have the authority to prevent problems by using regulatory tools. An example for the pesticide program is using the pre-market clearance process to deny the introduction of problematic products. In order to achieve the goal of a safer future, EPA leadership can send a message about what it will *not* allow on the market. During my tenure, a pesticide known as "Pirate" was submitted for registration to control the beet armyworm in cotton. The scientific data showed that it had a long half-life in the environment, and could adversely affect non-target species. Specifically, data demonstrated that the active ingredient in Pirate caused avian species to lay a reduced number of eggs, and caused reduced viable embryo and hatchling survival. Residues in food items were well in excess of levels that could produce adverse effects on bird reproduction, and furthermore birds are in cotton fields and surrounding habitats when the pesticide would be applied. There were also concerns about impacts on fish when the pesticide reached water. The half-life was more than a year, and residue levels were expected to exceed the original application rate by two and a half times in just a few years.

EPA initiated a full and public airing of these serious concerns, including two peer review sessions with the Scientific Advisory Panel and consultation with the U.S. Fish and Wildlife Service (FWS). Both the panel and the FWS advised that EPA was fully justified in its conclusions, and in fact could even be underestimating the risks.

However, during this time, the manufacturer was making its case for registration on Capitol Hill. I was called to several sessions on the Hill to explain why we were not granting approval of this chemical. Because the staff had done its work thoroughly, because we had subjected our risk assessments to full and comprehensive peer review, and because we had conducted all this business in the full light of day, I was able to explain convincingly why we were not in a position to rule favorably.

The considerable political pressure to allow the use of the chemical notwithstanding, the Agency held its ground. The Administrator backed my decision to deny registration, and we published our denial in the *Federal Register*, at which time the applicant withdrew the application. This was an internal message to the staff that management would back sound science, and an external message to the world at large that we did not intend to permit this type of old-style (i.e., persistent, accumulative, and hazardous to wildlife reproduction) pesticide in the future.

Thus, environmental managers, when they have the authority, must act to prevent future problems, based on sound science and the mandate of the law.

CONCLUSION

This chapter has identified many lessons learned from one specific program dealing with an important area of environmental management. I have highlighted what I hope are the most positive aspects of pesticide policy and strategy evolution. This does not mean that the work is complete or that there is a national consensus on the effectiveness of pesticide control. There are many in the environmental and public interest sector who maintain that EPA does not move quickly or aggressively enough on pesticide risks. The manufacturing and user communities on the other hand often charge that EPA is moving too quickly and aggressively. Both sides initiate litigation against EPA and voice criticism through print, visual and electronic media. In our open society, that is how it should be. There is always room to improve, continuously review prior decisions in light of new knowledge, and address areas of emerging risk concerns.

Environmental managers face many challenges in achieving environmental progress, and most of this chapter has been devoted to exploring those for the pesticide program. But managers face general management issues that would apply to almost any field of endeavor. It is not enough to be intelligent, or committed. One needs to be able to manage people and complex issues. Among the general management lessons that I learned at EPA were:

- Provide vision. If you don't know where you are heading, you'll never get there. Publish your goals explicitly, and make them the centerpiece of internal and external communications.
- Establish the internal organizational structures and the market incentives to reach your goals. This includes resource deployment, hiring the right mix of disciplines for the tasks, and determining external incentives.
- Measure results. While I haven't dwelt on this aspect of leadership in this chapter, it is critical to know whether your program and your decisions are effective, and resulting in improved health and safety. Establish measures or surrogate measures of success.
- Reach out to all stakeholders. Do it in person as much as possible for maximum communication. Your decisions will be much better as a result. Communicate, communicate, communicate, both inside and outside your organization.
- Involve your staff, and treat them with respect. I relished large meetings where the staff could interact with me directly; not only could I hear their views and acknowledge their work, they were able to see the big picture into which their piece would fit.

- Look for opportunities to partner with other agencies, states, tribes, logical private entities, and the international community. In dealing with complex and far-reaching issues, there is a compelling case for joining forces and bringing multiple sources of resources to bear.
- Celebrate successes. That can take many forms—ceremonies to recognize special efforts, informal gatherings, even phone calls to key staff members when an action is completed. These should be immediate if possible.
- Do the right thing. Positions in the SES are often in the hot seat, with competing constituencies and political pressure bearing down from all sides. Remain calm and deliberate. Follow the science and do what is right under the law. While Shakespeare said this better centuries ago with "to thine own self be true" (Hamlet), it is critical for senior executives to behave at all times with integrity and respect for the facts. Everyone will know if you don't.
- Remember for whom you are working. For federal officials, this means the American public. The interests of the public come first. And treat them with the respect they deserve as your boss. It is important for federal executives to show the way by demonstrating respect in tone and demeanor, and counseling employees who take an arrogant attitude with the public. You may have power, but keep it in check. Everyone can be replaced.
- Retain your perspective and sense of humor. The work of the environmental manager is important and serious. However, in the full context of organizational effectiveness, you can be serious and also recognize the human side of management. Camaraderie and a sense of teamwork enhance the effectiveness of your efforts. Your peers, your superiors, and your staff want to be around a positive colleague who exudes confidence, listens well, and is not afraid to laugh at appropriate times. And try for the right balance in your professional and personal lives; that way you will succeed at both.

In conclusion, environmental managers confront a multitude of complex scientific, management, and political issues on a daily basis. This chapter has illustrated many of the facets of environmental management and has suggested lessons for future environmental managers. These professionals must be able to take seemingly overwhelming tasks and parse them into manageable and effective programs. They must develop strategies to provide the most protection for humans and the environment in the most efficient, timely manner. Resources are never adequate, so they must seek different sources of revenue, and form partnerships to merge resource bases to achieve mutually supportive goals. Clear vision, the ability to communicate and involve all stakeholders, and providing leadership and accessibility to staff and different constituencies are essential. Economic and human and environmental impacts of decisions must be carefully considered, and those most affected must be included in seeking solutions. Since most environmental issues know no geographic boundaries, it is critical to involve global as well as domestic allies. With the increasingly fast pace of technological discoveries, it is mandatory to stay abreast of new knowledge, and ensure that decisions are based on sound, peer-reviewed scientific information. Environmental managers can now harness the power of information as never before, with the Internet and other electronic media, thus empowering citizens with the ability to make many of their own choices. The characteristics of the best environmental managers include the ability to understand the big picture, the determination of how specific programs fit into the larger context, and the ability to implement multi-faceted agendas to achieve real-world results. It is challenging to do all these things simultaneously, especially in the context of a fast-paced, often hostile international stage. However, the results are critical for the future of the planet and its citizens, and the environmental manager can take pride in making a difference that means so much to so many.

Many environmental managers choose their profession just so they *can* make a difference, so I close with an example and a parable on this topic. I began early in this chapter discussing one of the first defining moments of the pesticide program, the cancellation of DDT in 1972. The results of that action, in combination with the measures taken under the Endangered Species Act, would not pay off for decades. But what a great achievement it was when the U.S. Fish and Wildlife Service removed the peregrine falcon, the brown pelican and the bald eagle from the Endangered Species List due to population recovery in a series of actions in the late 1990s and early 2000s. I celebrated this institutional success with an all-hands communication, though many of the staff were too young to have been working at the time of the cancellation. This victory illustrates the need for patience and taking the long view, and teaches us that we may not always be able to attain immediate results.

The parable I leave you with is the one about the starfish stranded on the beach. There are several versions that can be found on the Internet, some of which attribute its origin to Loren Eiseley. It goes like this:

"While walking along a beach, an elderly gentleman saw someone in the distance leaning down, picking something up and throwing it into the ocean.

As he got closer, he noticed that the figure was that of a young man, picking up starfish one by one and tossing each one gently back into the water.

He came closer still and called out, "Good morning! May I ask what it is that you are doing?"

The young man paused, looked up, and replied, "Throwing starfish into the ocean."

The old man smiled, and said, "I must ask, then, why are you throwing starfish into the ocean?"

To this, the young man replied, "The sun is up and the tide is going out. If I don't throw them in, they'll die."

Upon hearing this, the elderly observer commented, "But young man, do you not realize that there are miles and miles of beach and there are starfish all along every mile? You can't possibly make a difference!"

The young man listened politely. Then he bent down, picked up another starfish, threw it back into the ocean past the breaking waves and said, "It made a difference for *that* one."

I, and my former colleagues in the EPA pesticides program, have seen the world of pest control evolve from blunt, environmentally harmful instruments to more sophisticated, safer, and more environmentally friendly techniques. We like to think that we all played a part in making a difference in this evolution, and I salute all the environmental managers who are, or will be, making a contribution in their own way to protect natural resources, human health, and wildlife for now and future generations.

REFERENCES

Dylan, Bob. "One Too Many Mornings." Copyright © 1964, 1966 by Warner Bros. Inc.; renewed 1992, 1994 by Special Rider Music.

Gerber Foods. *Safety and Research.* Retrieved 2/5/12 from the World Wide Web: www.gerber.com/AllStages/About/Research_Safety.aspx.

National Academy of Sciences. 1993. *Pesticides in the Diets of Infants and Children.* Washington: NAP.

Public Law 92–156: Federal Environmental Pesticide Control Act of 1972 (FEPCA). 7 USC§136–136y.

Public Law 85–929: Food Additives Amendment of 1958 to the Federal Food, Drug and Cosmetic Act (FFDCA). 21USC§301 et seq.

Public Law 80–104: Federal Insecticide, Fungicide, and Rodenticide Act (FIFRA). 7USC§136 et seq.

Public Law 104–170: Food Quality Protection Act of 1996 (FQPA). 110 Stat 1489, codified in scattered sections of FIFRA and FFDCA.

Rotterdam Convention. December 2011. *PIC Circular XXXIV.* Retrieved 2/5/12 from the World Wide Web: www.pic.int.

Shakespeare, William. *Hamlet,* Act 1, scene 3, 78–82.

Eiseley, Loren. *The Starfish Story,* adapted from *The Star Thrower.* Retrieved 2/5/12 from the World Wide Web: www.muttcats.com/starfish.htm.

U.S. Department of Agriculture. *Integrated Pest Management.* Washington, DC. Retrieved 2/5/12 from the World Wide Web: www.nifa.usda.gov/integratedpestmanagement.cfm.

U.S. Environmental Protection Agency. 2000. *Chlorfenapyr (Pirate): Decision and Company Withdrawal.* 65 FR 30112.

———. 1993. Pesticide Regulation (PR) Notice 93-9. *Voluntary Reduced Risk Pesticides Initiative.* Washington, DC. Retrieved 2/5/12 from the World Wide Web: www.epa.gov/PR_Notices/pr93-9.pdf.

———. 1989. *Daminozide (Alar) Pesticide Canceled for Food Uses.* Retrieved February 2, 2012, from the World Wide Web: www.epa.gov/history/topics/food/02.html.

———. 1972. *Consolidated DDT Hearings, Opinion and Order of the Administrator.* Washington, DC. Retrieved from the World Wide Web: www.epa.gov/aboutepa/history/topics/ddt/DDT-Ruckelshaus.pdf.

———. 1997. *1996 Food Quality Protection Act Implementation Plan*. Washington, D.C. Retrieved 2/5/12 from the World Wide Web: www.epa.gov/opp00001/regulating/laws/fqpa/impplan.pdf.

———. *Pesticide Environmental Stewardship Program*. Washington, DC. Retrieved 2/5/12 from the World Wide Web: www.epa.gov.pesp/pesp/index.html.

———. *Pesticide Tolerance Reassessment and Reregistration*. Washington, DC. Retrieved from the World Wide Web 2/5/12: www.epa.gov.oppsrrd1/reregistration/.

———. *Integrated Pest Management (IPM) Principles*. Washington, D.C. Retrieved 2/5/12 from the World Wide Web: www.epa.gov/pesticides/factsheets/ipm.htm.

———. 1989. *Daminozide (Alar) Pesticide canceled for Food Uses*. Washington, DC. Retrieved 2/5/12 from the World Wide Web: www.epa.gov/history/topics/food/02.html.

U.S. Fish and Wildlife Service. August 26, 1998. *Endangered and Threatened Wildlife & Plants; Proposed Rule to Remove the Peregrine Falcon in North America from the List of Endangered and Threatened Wildlife*. 63 FR 45446.

———. August 25, 1999. *Endangered and Threatened Wildlife and Plants; Final Rule To Remove the American Peregrine Falcon From the Federal List of Endangered and Threatened Wildlife, and To Remove the Similarity of Appearance Provision for Free-Flying Peregrines in the Conterminous United States; Final Rule*. 64 FR 46543.

———. February 20, 2008. *Endangered and Threatened Wildlife and Plants; 12-Month Petition Finding and Proposed Rule To Remove the Brown Pelican (Pelecanus occidentalis) From the Federal List of Endangered and Threatened Wildlife*. 73 FR 9408.

———. November 17, 2009. *Endangered and Threatened Wildlife and Plants; Removal of the Brown Pelican (Pelecanus occidentalis) From the Federal List of Endangered and Threatened Wildlife final rule*. 74 FR 59444.

———. July 6, 1999. *Endangered and Threatened Wildlife and Plants; Proposed Rule To Remove the Bald Eagle in the Lower 48 States From the List of Endangered and Threatened Wildlife*. 64 FR 36454.

———. July 9, 2009. *Endangered and Threatened Wildlife and Plants; Removing the Bald Eagle in the Lower 48 States From the List of Endangered and Threatened Wildlife Final Rule*. 72 FR 37346.

US POPs Watch. *The POPs Treaty*. Retrieved 2/5/12 from the World Wide Web: www.uspopswatch.org.

Chapter Four

Leading at the Intergovernmental Boundary[1]

EPA's Regional Offices

A. Stanley Meiburg

In 1997, the National Academy of Public Administration published a report entitled, "The Paradox of Environmental Protection" (NAPA 1997). The paradox is: how do you achieve consistency in the national implementation of federal environmental law, while also providing for the flexibility to adopt solutions to different environmental problems whose characteristics vary from place to place, or even to recognize that effective solutions to similar environmental problems may vary depending on the circumstances in which the problem occurs?

Regional offices in the Environmental Protection Agency are an attempt to implement a governance structure that resolves this paradox. The tension between national consistency and local flexibility is central to how regions work, and affects policy, operations, and relationships—what Malcolm Sparrow refers to as "the regulatory craft". (Sparrow, 2000) Notwithstanding the vast array of statues, regulations and guidance that surround EPA, there is no formula that prescribes how to address the inevitable conflicts that come from these two imperatives. The tension can be creative, promoting new solutions to vexing environmental problems, or it can be destructive, generating conflicts that last for years and fruitlessly consume scarce resources without producing meaningful environmental results. EPA's ability to achieve its mission turns on the ability of regional offices to manage this paradox and use it to protect public health and the environment.

WHAT ARE REGIONS?

EPA's regions are organized along geographic and political boundary lines. EPA has ten regional offices located in the standard federal region cities around the country (a map can be found at www.epa.gov/aboutepa/). The regional offices vary in size from about 1200 full-time equivalent staff (FTE) in Region 5 (Chicago) to about 550 FTE in Region 7 (Kansas City). Of EPA's total staff of approximately 17,000 employees, about 47 percent are located in regional offices. The number of states and territories for which each region is responsible varies from four to eight.

Each regional office is headed by a regional administrator, a political appointee approved by the president who serves at the pleasure of the administrator. Each region has a career deputy regional administrator and a subordinate division structure that reflects the major program responsibilities of EPA (air, water, hazardous waste, Superfund, enforcement) and basic administration and support functions, but details vary from region to region. In the early days of EPA, regional offices had relatively uniform structures, but in the 1990s the Agency allowed broader organizational variations among the regions and that pattern continues today.

Different EPA national programs have different degrees of regional presence. For example, among the principal EPA programs, 70 percent or more of EPA's enforcement, water, hazardous waste and Superfund staff are located in regional offices. About half of EPA's air staff are in regions, but less than 20 percent of staff in the pesticides and toxic substances control programs are in regions. These differences reflect differences in underlying philosophy among the major environmental statutes, and cultures that have evolved over time within the Agency. The precise balances within programs shift slightly over time, depending upon the management philosophy of administrators or assistant administrators, but this overall pattern has been stable in EPA for decades.

EPA's regional offices have a broad range of responsibilities, such as:

- Disseminating national rules and guidance on all aspects of environmental protection to states, local governments, regulated entities, and citizens.
- Providing technical assistance to state and local authorities.
- Reviewing (and in some cases, affirmatively approving) transactions delegated to state agencies under federal law. These include such things as water pollution discharge permits, state implementation plans under the Clean Air Act, operating permits under the Clean Air Act, and state permits for the treatment, storage and disposal of hazardous waste.

- Issuing permits required by federal statutes which are not delegable to states, or where states have not requested or received delegated authority pursuant to federal law.
- Administering over $1 billion per year in federal operating grants to state environmental agencies. This includes both fiscal management and program oversight.
- Giving and overseeing capitalization grants to states for waste water and drinking water revolving loan programs. In recent years the amount of this assistance has ranged between $1.9 and $3.9 billion per year (not including an additional $6 billion for this purpose made available through the American Recovery and Reinvestment Act of 2009).
- Conducting investigations and inspections of pollution sources.
- Conducting field investigations and environmental sampling and monitoring.
- Taking either administrative or judicial enforcement actions against violators of pollution laws.
- Responding to emergencies involving the release of pollution into the environment, whether accidental releases or consequences of natural disasters.
- Conducting cleanups of abandoned hazardous sites under CERCLA (Superfund), either directly using funds available through the Hazardous Substances Response Trust Fund or by overseeing actions taken by responsible parties under the terms of administrative or judicial orders and consent agreements.
- Reviewing environmental assessments and impact statements prepared by other federal agencies on major federal actions pursuant to the National Environmental Policy Act.
- Implementing federal law directly on tribal lands under principles of government-to-government relationships.

EPA'S REGIONS DIFFER FROM THOSE OF OTHER FEDERAL AGENCIES

While EPA is not alone among federal agencies in having a regional structure, EPA's regions have a unique combination of attributes. For one thing, EPA has a relatively large regional staff, over 8000 strong, far larger than other regulatory agencies such as the Occupational Safety and Health Administration or the Food and Drug Administration. Natural resource agencies, such as the Park Service, the Fish and Wildlife Service, the Forest Service, the Natural Resources Conservation Service, or the Civil Works Directorate of the Army Corps of Engineers, may have more staff within similar regional boundaries, but their personnel are dispersed throughout their territory, in parks, refuges, or local district offices. In contrast, with the exception of applied science laboratories and field investigators, EPA regional staff are almost all stationed in the regional office city.

The concentration of EPA's field staff in large regional offices is a function of the era in which EPA was created. The federal resource agencies mentioned above were either established as part of the New Deal or were transformed by it. The very essence of the New Deal (and its Johnson administration successor, the Great Society) was direct action by the federal government on behalf of individual citizens. Federal agencies that were created or expanded during the New Deal had field offices and staff who were caseworkers for individual citizens and their problems. The civil rights movement of the 1960s and its dependence on direct federal intervention in the South was perhaps the most extensive illustration of this philosophy, but direct federal actions were in evidence from Park Service, Fish and Wildlife, and Forest Rangers, to Agricultural Extension Service Agents and soil conservation specialists, to Social Security caseworkers, to FBI agents and officers with the Bureau of Alcohol, Tobacco and Firearms.

The Nixon administration's "New Federalism" stressed greater support for and deference to state officials, policies and authorities. Notwithstanding the current belief of conservatives that environmental programs exemplify the overreach of federal authority, the Clean Air, Clean Water, and Resource Conservation and Recovery Acts of the 1970s reflected a view that states were to be the lead implementers of environmental programs. The mechanism for this lead was to be the delegation of federal authorities to states. To be sure, delegations were contingent upon a demonstration (subject to approval by EPA) that states had adequate resources and authority to act effectively, and federal environmental legislation of the 1970s transformed standard setting by giving vast new authorities to EPA. But the central role of states in implementing national environmental protection was present from EPA's very beginning.

The first regional offices were created by consolidating staff from EPA's predecessor agencies (with the Interior Department's Federal Water Pollution Control Agency being the largest contributor). While the new statutes gave extraordinary new authorities to EPA, these new regions were to carry out new programs themselves only until they could be delegated to states, at which time regions would shift to an oversight role. Unlike agencies such as the Centers for Disease Control and Prevention that routinely station federal officials in state or local departments of public health, there was never much interest in placing EPA staff in state or local offices except for training and assistance purposes, and that only temporarily.

While it took many years for states to expand their own environmental programs and for delegations to take full effect, by the early 1990s most delegable EPA authorities had been granted to states, and with some exceptions (notably the Superfund program), EPA's role shifted to reviewing actions taken by states rather than being a primary decision maker. Though this may seem a distinction without a difference, the dynamics of decisions are quite different when a state decides first and EPA responds. For one thing, as a reviewer, EPA must figure out what it will do if a state does not act exactly as EPA would have done. Statutory review deadlines and the need to respond to citizen suits—distinctive features of environmental legislation passed between 1969 and 1990—create action-forcing events which compel EPA to define the lines that states cannot cross. This choice requires judgment and can involve very delicate negotiating both within the Agency and between EPA and states as EPA struggles to answer the question of how good is good enough. [2]

SOURCES OF CONFLICT IN EPA REGIONS

No matter how specific environmental laws and regulations are, it is not possible to outline precise responses to every possible situation. For example, decisions about whether to object to a particular permit may require professional judgments about such things as the effectiveness of proposed control technologies, types and frequency of monitoring requirements, and the extent to which public participation was conducted in accordance with law. Disagreements among experts are bound to arise. Regions face both ways—toward states that want additional flexibility to use their own processes, and toward headquarters offices that push for national consistency. It is the job of regional officials to mediate such conflicts, but this is neither simple nor easy.

It takes significant time and staff for EPA regions to manage and mediate these conflicts while maintaining an active oversight role. Even after the delegation of permitting and program activities, EPA's extensive statutory authorities give the agency coercive power that other agencies do not have. While EPA's authority will always exceed its capability, regional offices have many tools. The question is how to use them wisely and effectively.

In addressing any particular environmental problem, regions must deal with many actors and circumstances. It is beyond the scope of this chapter to discuss all of them in detail, but the following examples illustrate just how complex this problem-solving work can be.

EPA Headquarters

As keepers of national consistency, headquarters staff examine particular cases and intervene with regions in cases that are big enough to merit national attention or appear to place consistency at risk. National press attention increases the likelihood that headquarters offices will monitor situations more closely or seek to intervene.

Other EPA Regions

Regions communicate with and watch each other. EPA staff use both formal and informal mechanisms for exchanging information among regions, and no charge will get a quicker reaction than that one of the regions is acting on a permit or an enforcement action in a way that will undermine another region working on a similar issue. Moreover, direct conflicts among regions can also occur when a discharge from a source in one region affects an airshed or watershed in another region.

For example, offshore oil and gas exploration and production activities occur in four EPA regions. The geographic dispersion of these activities and differences in attitudes about them has created different levels of conflict with the regulated community. The most active area for offshore oil and gas exploration and production has historically been off the coast of Louisiana and Texas, and the political cultures of these two states favored such activities. In contrast, Florida for many years opposed oil and gas exploration and production off of its coasts, fearing that a spill would adversely affect the tourism so important to Florida's economy. This led to differences in approach between Region 4 and Region 6 on both air and water discharges. In recent years drilling off the northern coast of Alaska has generated great controversy, and oil companies have complained that EPA's Pacific Northwest regional office unnecessarily delayed air permits by requiring analyses not done in other regions. Similar dynamics have occurred among regions involved in creating and enforcing water pollution discharge limits from surface coal mining in the Appalachian Mountains.

States

Even though most authorities are delegated, great tension can result if a region concludes that a state is not properly exercising its authority. For example, the ability to veto any one individual permit must be weighed against the impact that such a step will have on the ability of the region to influence other permits that contribute to meeting overall environmental goals.

Adding to the complexity are the vast differences that exist among states. Environmental agencies in large states such as California, New York, Florida and Texas generally have technical resources that rival or exceed those of EPA, and financially, EPA grants are only a small portion of the resources available to these states. By contrast, smaller states depend heavily on EPA grants for basic operations and rely more on EPA expertise and capabilities.

Local Communities

For reasons that can include politics, resource allocation, and personal relationships, the interests of states and communities within that state may not coincide. For example, communities which face requirements to upgrade sewage treatment infrastructure may seek financial assistance from states, while governors who campaigned on lowering tax rates may be unsympathetic to such requests. EPA has brought enforcement actions against many municipalities, sometimes in collaboration with states, but other times when states were unwilling or unable to take such actions.

Large cities and some local communities develop direct relationships with regional offices. This can be very productive, but such relationships must be managed with care lest state officials come to believe that their authorities, or at least their prerogatives, are being violated

Non-Governmental Organizations

Both public and private sector interest groups seek to intervene with regional offices to mold and shape decisions. These relationships can be quite complex. Prescriptive statutory deadlines and broad citizen suit provisions in the various environmental laws give groups significant potential leverage in shaping decisions. Regional offices must sometimes choose between settling litigation for the best deal you can get, or by defending legally vulnerable positions.[3]

Like states and communities, NGO's come in many shapes and sizes, ranging from informal neighborhood associations to highly sophisticated national organizations. National groups may seek to bring specific matters to the attention of the administrator or other EPA officials in Washington, and while headquarters staff are generally leery of forum-shopping and support regional decisions, this can create conflict or at least cause delay while regional decisions are reviewed.

Citizens

While regional offices are not local for most citizens, they are closer than Washington, and regional staff usually (though not always) interact with individuals more than most headquarters staff do. Whether on a permit matter, an enforcement case, or a Superfund cleanup, a determined individual can find a regional person to work with, and effective individuals can shape decisions more than is generally believed.

In addition to these various actors, there are policy, political, and philosophical cross currents that shape regional activities.

Political vs. Career Perspectives

Regional administrators are political appointees. It can take up to a year and a half following an election for a new regional administrator to be appointed, and many have tenures of no longer than three years. This inevitably leads regional administrators to focus on actions that can produce immediate results, and contrasts with career perspectives that look at longer time frames. In addition, career staff members develop relationships over time with individual state officials, interest group members, and professional colleagues. Such relationships can be very useful to the skilled political appointee in achieving their policy objectives and understanding the origins, processes and values of EPA.

This writer's experience does not support the belief that regional administrators are particularly prone to making agreements based solely on short-term political considerations. Nevertheless, political sensitivity is one of the attributes that regional administrators are supposed to bring to their position, and these sensitivities shape the way solutions to particular disputes are developed and framed. For example, given the contentious nature of disputes, one of the most important policy choices in a contentious matter may be who EPA would rather be sued by, and this decision can be shaped by political dynamics.

New Initiatives vs. Ongoing Activities

Each new administration, and administrator, wants to demonstrate how they represent a change from their predecessors. Regions are affected by this desire. Tensions can rise if regional staff members see new initiatives as undermining ongoing activities, especially activities in which they have made substantial personal and professional investment over time. Conversely, leadership can build support within a region by reviving or reemphasizing programs that may have been neglected by previous administrators but which still have residual staff support.

Programs vs. Places

EPA's organizational structure is built on competing logic models that embody the paradox of environmental protection. EPA's statutory mandates, and most of its headquarters structure, are built on one of two program models. One model is built around various environmental media (clean air, clean water, solid and hazardous waste, pesticides and toxic substances), while the other is based on specific functions (research and development, enforcement, policy, information management, budget and finance).[4]

Regions are built on a geographic model, with all of the above activities applied in specific locations. This inevitably produces different perspectives on what constitutes success in environmental protection. For example, staff members who focus on reducing air emissions from coal-fired electric utilities will tend to support the installation of flue gas desulfurization (FGD) equipment that reduces loadings of sulfur oxides and mercury into the atmosphere. Water program staff members, on the other hand, are concerned that the metals captured by the FGD will be stored in an impoundment that could potentially discharge these same pollutants into waters of the United States.

Another example of this difference arises when EPA focuses its attention on industrial activity in a particular location. From a program perspective, if the activity in question is in compliance with all applicable regulations, the agency has done its job. However, members of communities may feel that compliance with applicable regulations is insufficient to address community concerns that are beyond the reach of EPA standards, including such things as land use, traffic, noise levels, perceived health effects, and aesthetics.

Science vs. Policy

Former EPA Administrator Douglas Costle summarized this tension in a 1995 interview.

> Every time we had to recalibrate a standard or set a new one, we faced this. You can't be in [the environmental] business and not be aware of the uncertainties and ambiguities in the science. People tend to think science is hard and numerical and precise. It's not, particularly in the environmental area. But there is one way, and only one way, to deal with that, and that is just to be absolutely open and honest about the gray areas. Anyway you cut it, we're making judgments, social policy judgment calls . . .[5]

Most regional administrators arrive at EPA with some experience in environmental policy, either as head of a state or local environmental agency, as a professor in an environmental field, as an attorney engaged in environmental practice, or as a leader of a non-governmental organization. But there is no requirement that this be so, and even the most experienced regional administrators experience conflicts between what they hear from their technical staff and the perceived political imperatives of particular situations. The most successful regional administrators use such conflicts as learning opportunities, and press to know about the limits of what is held to be "science."

Nationalism and Regionalism

Large organizations, including many multinational corporations, tend to prefer uniform rules across the country. Such rules increase certainty and reduce transaction costs for firms with a multijurisdictional presence. This can be at odds with the desire of an individual state to tailor its activities to meet its own particular environmental challenges or political culture. For example, for many years, due to a special exemption in the Clean Air Act, California was able to adopt its own emissions standards for new cars sold in California, much to the chagrin of automobile manufacturers. Worse (for the manufacturers), in the 1990s a movement developed for other states to adopt the California standards, a movement that gained even more force when California adopted tailpipe standards for greenhouse gases. Ultimately, in 2009 this led to a negotiated agreement whereby automobile manufacturers agreed to tighter national standards for all cars, in exchange for an agreement by California to accept national standards and not promulgate their own. [6]

Regions occupy the middle space in this debate, generally displaying a "consistency" face to the states and a "flexibility" face to EPA headquarters. Given the different perspectives involved, differences of opinion within EPA on particular matters are inevitable. Even where regional and headquarters offices are in agreement, there are obvious nuances involved in this kind of communication, and this can result in difficult moments, especially if a state or a regulated entity believes it can get a different answer depending upon whom it asks. This belief can lead to forum shopping, and avoiding such outcomes requires extremely close and clear communication within EPA. Inevitably, given the pressures of time and multiple issues, misunderstandings can arise under the best of circumstances. [7]

THE POWER OF RELATIONSHIPS

It should be apparent after looking at all of these considerations that the policy environment in which regions operate is in constant motion. Maintaining essential consistency in administering federal law, while being mindful of the different contexts in which that law is applied and utilizing appropriate flexibility in achieving EPA's mission, requires skill, subtlety, and a certain tolerance for ambiguity. Paradox is not too strong a word.

The paradox cannot be resolved by institutional arrangements alone. Outside observers can fail to fully appreciate the importance of relationships in the conduct of EPA's activities. By "relationships" I mean the networks of personal connections that exist between regional office staff and other individuals within EPA, in other federal agencies, in state and local governments, with the regulated community, with nongovernmental organizations, and even with individual citizens. These relationships can be influenced by many factors.

Professional Subcultures

Many regional staff form affinities with staff in state agencies, counterparts in the private sector parties and members of non-governmental organizations based on common membership in particular professional subcultures. While this occurs among groups such as engineers, wildlife biologists, emergency responders and law enforcement officers, it seems especially true for attorneys. A common career path for attorneys is to come to EPA directly from law school or early in their careers, then leave to join the private environmental bar. Another pattern is for attorneys to join EPA after having started their careers working for an NGO. Finally, some attorneys begin work with EPA, leave the Agency, then return as a political appointee. While personal relationships can exacerbate conflict if individual grudges or philosophical conflicts are carried over into working relationships, a more common outcome seems to be that the associations formed among attorneys facilitate the resolution of enforcement cases and litigation over statutory deadlines, almost all of which are resolved by settlements rather than trials. Environmental bar associations promote both the exchange of information and the development of personal camaraderie.

Educational Backgrounds

Regional offices tend to recruit from the geographic area where they are located. This produces affinities based on where staff went to undergraduate or graduate school. This is not to suggest, that conflicts can be resolved based solely on old school ties, but these can be another factor in promoting a common frame of reference based on common experiences.

Past Experiences

Many regional offices deal with issues or experiences that affect the entire staff to such a degree that they create defining moments for the organization and build relationships that last for years beyond the particular event. Disasters can be effective team-building exercises. For example, in Regions 4 and 6, the responses to Hurricane Katrina in 2005 and and the Deepwater Horizon oil spill in 2010 involved a large percentage of the regional staff and promoted collaboration across the usual organizational boundaries. On a smaller scale, work on other projects that require collaborative efforts over extended periods of time helps build relationship networks that carry over even when the particular project is completed.

Common Enemies

Few things can so unite regional staff as a common enemy, whether it be a particularly recalcitrant regulated entity, a litigious NGO, an obstructionist Governor, or even EPA headquarters! This last example is the source of much discussion within the Agency, and is evidence of the challenge posed by the competing demands of flexibility and consistency. In this writer's experience, outside observers tend to overstate the importance of this dynamic, yet it is undeniable that conflicts arise and, indeed, are built in to the very structure of EPA. If enough regions are convinced that a particular course of action proposed by a national program manager is ill-advised, they can exert significant pressure within the agency to change it. Occasionally this can backfire on individual regions. If a particular region is seen as an outlier among the others, they can be subject to considerable peer pressure to conform to the accepted norm.

Personal Affinities and Temperament

Finally, many relationships are built on natural affinities among individuals both inside and outside EPA. Like all federal employees, EPA's regional staff work under an ethical obligation to be impartial in their dealings with all parties, and most regional staff take this very seriously. That said, it is inevitable that differences in temperament, past experience and personal trust can help or hinder effective working relationships.

Relationships, Networks, and the Future of Regional Offices

Relationships are important at all levels in regional offices, but especially at senior levels as these relationships set the tone for the entire organization. Leaders who take such relationships seriously and work to maintain them increase their effectiveness.

This does not prevent issues, for example with states, from being driven by interests, and political considerations are drivers on many matters. But strong personal networks and mutual respect matter, especially with state environmental commissioners. Good relationships keep small problems from turning into big ones. They keep inevitable miscommunications from being over-interpreted. They facilitate the use of interest-based bargaining approaches to resolving conflicts. They enable parties to distinguish between conflicts of interests and conflicts of politics. Their value to regions cannot be overestimated, and the ability to develop these relationships by being in proximity to geographic areas of responsibility is one off the chief strategic advantages that regional offices enjoy.

There is also an advantage conferred by diversity in the makeup of regional office staff. No one person has access to all networks, and the more diverse the staff, the more likely it is that communication connections can be formed with communities of interest that may start out with a latent distrust of federal authority in general or EPA in particular.

Not all conflicts can be solved if people just learn to "get along." Relationships alone do not resolve conflicts when basic economic or political interests are not aligned. Administrative and judicial mechanisms remain essential alternatives for conflict resolution between EPA and other parties. Within EPA, ultimately the administrator (or in highly unusual cases, the president) must set the Agency's overall policy and direction.

But the issues and conflicts that can be resolved through the courts, or by high level executive leaders, are necessarily limited by available time and by the sheer scope of the responsibilities that federal law gives to EPA. Regional administrators or other regional officials, let alone the administrator, cannot pay attention to everything, and senior officials must rely on their staff to resolve most conflicts. Effective regional administrators expect their staff to work with their state/local and headquarters counterparts to properly frame matters to be decided, and to bring forward only those essential conflicts that cannot be resolved any other way.

This is what high quality relationships enable regional staff to do. The fixed geography of a region provides a focal point and some limits on the types of issues that are most important. While there are significant intra-regional differences in issues and political culture (compare, for example, Florida and Kentucky in Region 4), they are not as great as the differences between the Southeast and New England, the Intermountain West, or the Pacific Coast.

Relationships exist at all levels—between technical experts, mid-level managers, and senior career leaders. When they work well they promote horizontal, cross-boundary communication and problem-solving. When leadership properly empowers staff to engage in these kinds of behaviors, and supports the creation and continual strengthening of relationship networks, they enable the kind of behaviors that find resolutions to the paradoxes of environmental protection.[8]

Because their scope is not as broad as the national office, and because regions are more likely to speak the basic "language" of the area of the country in which they are located, they have significant advantages in efforts to resolve the paradox of environmental protection. Even EPA's lack of a state-by-state organizational structure helps, as it provides for enough proximity but not too much; familiarity, but some distance too. While program

stovepipes exist in regional offices as they do in headquarters, the countervailing principle of geographic focus (and smaller size) render them more
permeable. Historically it is more common to find regional staff with multi-
program experience than it is in headquarters.

That is not to disparage either role. EPA needs a strong national standard
setting capability, and experts in particular media areas. But the delivery of
services in specific places is enabled by regional staff who understand the
places they live in and have a more concrete understanding of the impacts of
EPA's regulatory activities on regulated entities and communities.

THE ROAD AHEAD

EPA's regional offices represent an innovative experiment in regulatory
governance, an effort to accommodate both flexibility and consistency in
support of EPA's mission to protect public health and the environment in the
context of a largely decentralized and delegated legislative structure. The
growth of state environmental agencies and America's environmental improvements over the last forty years would seem to suggest that the experiment on the whole has been a successful one.

But the experiment faces serious challenges. One is cuts in funding for
state environmental programs. Whether driven by the economic challenges
or political ideology, the current round of cuts in budgets of state environmental agencies threaten their ability to hold up their end of the decentraliza-
tion deal. This is an existential threat to the ability of regions to maintain a
somewhat detached level of engagement within individual states. Regions
can argue with states about how well federal laws are being implemented; it
is a rather different question if they are not being implemented at all.

A second threat is, ironically, the information age. It is easier than it has
ever been for headquarters officials to stay constantly in touch with local
news stories, developments, interest groups and individual citizens in each of
the regions. Absent experience, strong self-discipline or a clear management
philosophy, the temptation to micro-manage can be overpowering. If EPA
regions become simply instrumentalities for carrying out headquarters directives, their ability to be creative problem solvers will be diminished as well.
In an era where resistance to federal mandates seems to be on the rise, this
would not bode well for EPA's ability to address the challenges of a new
generation of environmental protection.

A final threat is impatience with the time it takes to achieve environmental results. Regional governance is complicated, and it is always tempting to
skip this step, to avoid deal with the messy business of decentralized implementation by using single-size, nationally applicable rules. Such rules have

contributed to the great achievements of environmental protection over the last forty years, and new ones may be needed to meet new challenges. But even with new rules, when it comes to implementation, one size rarely fits all, and to get the proper fit can take time, patience, knowledge, understanding, and relationships.

It is hard to imagine an EPA without regional offices. It would certainly be a very different agency without them. The challenges of flexibility and consistency seem likely to always be a part of the Agency's life. Regions are especially well suited to build relationships with communities and stakeholders, to find ways to work together with others to bring new insights and resources on problems that do not fit neatly into EPA's historic statutory mandates, but nonetheless bear on EPA's mission of protecting public health and the environment. To the extent that the environmental problems of the future do not lend themselves to regulatory solutions, state agencies face resource reductions, and voluntary activities become essential to EPA achieving its missions, EPA's regional offices will become even more important in the environmental protection of the future.

REFERENCES

Costle, Douglas M. 2001. *Douglas M. Costle: Oral History Interview.* Interview conducted by Dr. Dennis Williams on August 4–5, 1996, at the Ritz-Carlton Hotel, McLean, Virginia, and at Douglas M. Costle's home in Vermont. www.epa.gov/aboutepa/history/publications/print/costle.html.

Landy, M.K., M.J. Roberts, and S.R. Thomas. 1990. *The Environmental Protection Agency: Asking the Wrong Questions.* New York: Oxford University Press.

Melnick, R.S., 1983. *Regulation and the Courts: The Case of the Clean Air Act.* Washington: Brookings.

National Academy of Public Administration. 1997. *Resolving the Paradox of Environmental Protection: An Agenda for Congress, EPA and the States.* Washington: NAPA.

Sparrow, M. K. 2000. *The Regulatory Craft: Controlling Risks, Solving Problems, and Managing Compliance.* Washington: Brookings.

NOTES

1. This article is written by the author in his personal capacity only and not as part of his official duty. The views expressed are his own and not necessarily those of the United States Environmental Protection Agency or the United States Government.

2. These negotiations are made especially interesting by the unspoken reality that while in theory EPA can withdraw delegations, in practice EPA has only very limited capability to actually take programs back.

3. It is sometimes argued that it is to EPA's advantage to lose a case, and be forced to carry out a mandate, than to appear to affirmatively endorse litigation efforts by NGOs.

4. The Ash Council that recommended the creation of EPA favored a functional organization, and EPA's original organizational structure was set up to promote this. However, the combination of separate environmental statutes for media programs, and the (related) division of jurisdiction among various Congressional committees, soon drove the Agency to adopt an organizational structure that gives more significance to media programs (Landy et al. 1990, pp. 30–33).

5. Costle, 2001, accessed at http://epa.gov/aboutepa/history/publications/print/costle.html.

6. "Obama to Toughen Rules on Emissions and Mileage," *New York Times*, May 18, 2009. Corporations are not the only entities with interests in limiting regional flexibility. Historically, national environmental groups have tended to see flexibility as an opportunity for regional interests to undermine the hard fought gains achieved in stringent national standards, and have been as fearful as corporations about what regional flexibility could mean. An example of this was a debate between 2004 and 2008 over the used of a device known as the "Early Action Compact" to address nonattainment with the 1997 ozone standards. Many national environmental groups have judged that it was easier to fight about environmental policy in a central location, in Washington, rather than engage ten regional offices around the country, let alone fifty states. Of course, dissatisfaction with national environmental policy can make a regional strategy more attractive.

National and regional strategies need not be mutually exclusive, either for corporations or for environmental groups, as they tend to be fought in different arenas. National strategies focus on fights over rulemaking or national guidance. Regional strategies use challenges and objections to individual permits or citizen suits to bring enforcement actions (Melnick 1983).

7. This was exemplified in a recent letter from Governor Steve Beshear of Kentucky to President Obama concerning the controversial area of Appalachian surface coal mining. In his letter, Governor Beshear claimed that headquarters had undermined an agreement that the State had reached with EPA Region 4 on how to regulate water discharges from surface coal mines. Governor Steven L. Beshear to The Honorable Barack H. Obama, President of the United States, September 27, 2011.

8. Empowerment does not mean license. Effective empowerment includes the establishment of clear boundaries that are not within the discretion of individual staff to exceed. But even within those boundaries, there are many opportunities for creative problem solving as long as parties are clear about their interests and boundary conditions. Interest-based bargaining approaches can be useful in pursuing such solutions. The challenge for EPA is to train staff and leaders, used to traditional command and control regulatory mechanisms, in considering and using different frameworks for problem solving.

Chapter Five

The Tortuous Road to "No Net Loss" of Wetlands

Robert Wayland

Wetlands—swamps, marshes, bogs, fens, muskegs, potholes, etc.—were reviled for centuries as nuisances. The foreboding habitat of *Beowulf*'s fearsome Grendel as well as tiny malaria-carrying mosquitoes, wetlands were places to be avoided or "reclaimed," first for pastures and farming and more recently for outlet malls and airports. This country encouraged and subsidized the destruction of wetlands for decades until their importance for natural flood and storm surge attenuation, as nurseries and refuges for commercially important fish and shellfish, the nesting and feeding grounds for waterfowl, and other important physical and biological "functions and values" came to be appreciated by naturalists, then the broader public, and Congress. By the time this change in view took hold and public policy changed, half of the wetlands that once existed in the lower forty-eight United States had been destroyed (US Environmental Protection Agency 1995). By the 1970s less than 10 percent of the historical wetlands remained in several large states, including Ohio and California. Wetlands policy has zig-zagged over the past four decades and has been beset with controversy. Currently, many wetlands enjoy a significant degree of protection. EPA has been at the center of, and a cause of, many of these gyrations in policy. This chapter reviews the key events in wetlands protection from the creation of EPA through the early part of this decade. I was Deputy Assistant Administrator for Water from 1989 until I became Director of the Office of Wetlands, Oceans and Watersheds in 1991, the position from which I retired in 2003. The wetlands story illustrates several important lessons for successful environmental management:

- The value of a clear, measurable, environmental goal

- The importance of knocking down false characterizations forcefully and rapidly
- The benefits of supplementing regulatory approaches with non-regulatory approaches
- The value of collaboration among agencies
- The importance of involving stakeholders in strategy development
- Innovative implementation can enhance program effectiveness

INTRODUCTION

At EPA's creation in 1970, the Department of the Interior operated a national wildlife refuge system and protected large areas of wetlands, primarily waterfowl habitat, through ownership, easement, and management. The Department of Agriculture was encouraging wetland conversion to cropland. Ditches and subsurface drain tiles turned productive wetlands into productive corn and soybean fields (also assisted by the addition of staggering amounts of commercial fertilizer). In 1970, the U.S. Army Corps of Engineers was regulating the disposal of dredged and fill material under the 1899 Rivers and Harbors Act, issuing permits in conjunction with its mission to keep navigable waters clear of obstructions. The Corps was itself a major navigational dredger and builder of levees, seawalls and other structures which were placed in wetlands or impaired or destroyed them by disrupting their hydrology.

In 1972 the Federal Water Pollution Control Act Amendments, (33 U.S.C. §1251 et seq.) brought about major changes in governmental roles and wetlands policy. This law, known popularly as the Clean Water Act, prohibited the unpermitted discharge of pollutants to "waters of the United States" from "point sources" unless authorized by permit issued by EPA, or, in the case of dredged or fill material, by the Corps of Engineers pursuant to section 404 of the CWA. Under the new law Corps-issued permits were required to be consistent with guidelines issued by EPA. Corps permits were also subject to "veto" by the EPA Administrator under section 404(c).

Not everyone was fully comfortable with these changes, including the Corps of Engineers. The new arrangement, in which a military organization created in 1775 would be "guided" by the two-year old EPA and could have its decisions second-guessed undoubtedly rankled the Army unit.

The authors of the '72 Act expressly stated their intent "that the term 'navigable waters' be given the broadest possible constitutional interpretation" because "through narrow interpretation of the definition of interstate waters the implementation [of the] 1965 Act was severely limited. Water moves in hydrological cycles and it is essential that discharge of pollutants be controlled at the source" (Conference Report on S. 2770 1972).

Initially, Army declined to enlarge the geographic scope of its permit program. Two environmental groups sued, and in March 1975, the Federal District Court for the District of Columbia "hereby declared [the Army Secretary and the commander of the Corps] to have acted unlawfully and in derogation of their responsibilities under Section 404 of the Water Act" (Natural Resources Defense Council 1974). The Corps was ordered to change its regulations such that the permit program would apply in "waters of the United States." However, upon revising its rules to comply with the mandate of the Court, the Corps issued an incendiary press release warning of the possible regulation of "every farm or stock pond." This was widely seen as an effort to prompt Congressional action to reduce jurisdiction, remove EPA from the program, or both. It nearly succeeded. In 1977, Congress was considering "interim improvements within the existing framework" of the Clean Water Act. Amendments were introduced in both Houses to limit the definition of "waters of the United States" to navigable waters and adjacent wetlands. Ultimately, the effort to return to more limited Clean Water Act jurisdiction was turned aside, but to placate its proponents several revisions to the CWA dredge and fill provisions were made. These included authorizing general permits for categories of similar activities, exempting ongoing, normal farming and forestry activities from regulation, and providing for states to assume the federal program if the administrator determined they had equivalent authority and capability. These amendments also first introduced the word "wetlands" into the text of the CWA (33 U.S.C. §1251 et seq.).

The Corps' new authority for issuing general permits was limited to "any category of activities which are similar in nature, will cause only minimal environmental effects when performed separately, and will have only minimal cumulative adverse impact on the environment" (33 U.S.C. § 1344(e)). However, the Corps was enthusiastic in applying this labor-saving mechanism and used it to permit dozens of types of specified activities as well as for *any* activities in some "categories of waters." In headwaters streams and adjacent wetlands, up to ten acres could be destroyed without the need to notify the Corps. The EPA–Army program was criticized by environmental groups as insufficiently protective.

Tens of thousands of acres of duck-producing "prairie potholes" in the upper Midwest were vulnerable to destruction simply by being plowed and planted. Concern about loss of this nesting habitat for waterfowl led to successful efforts by the National Wildlife Federation and others to persuade Congress to revise farm policy vis-à-vis wetlands. The 1985 "Swampbuster" provision of the Food Security Act did not make it illegal for a farmer or rancher to convert wetlands to agricultural use, but it did make that farmer ineligible for financial assistance from USDA. USDA identified areas subject to Swampbuster using aerial maps.

EPA Headquarters received eight recommendations from regional administrators for 404(c) actions during the tenure of Administrator Lee Thomas (1984–1991). Although the recommendations of his regional administrators were upheld in every instance, Thomas felt that vetoes, after positions had hardened and significant investments had been made, pointed to the need for better decisions earlier in the process, before matters escalated to Washington, DC. As these decisions headed for EPA headquarters, governors, senators, and congressmen lined up on one side or the other. Thomas decided to convene a diverse, high-level, panel to make recommendations on how to make the wetlands protection more effective and perhaps less controversial.

THE NATIONAL WETLANDS POLICY FORUM AND "NO NET LOSS"

The National Wetlands Policy Forum was convened at Thomas's behest in 1988 by the Conservation Foundation, then headed by William K. Reilly. The Forum was chaired by New Jersey governor Thomas Kean and comprised two additional governors, mayors, agricultural and environmental leaders, and representatives of other interests. Federal departments and agencies participated *ex officio*. The assistant secretary of the army who oversaw the Corps at the time, Robert Page, was very interested in having the Corps do a good job in protecting natural resources. The Forum made numerous recommendations for program improvements and modifications and urged that the goal of private and governmental efforts be to achieve "no net loss of wetlands" in the short run with the ultimate goal of "increasing the quality and quantity" of the nation's wetland resources. This two-part goal was commonly short-handed to "no net loss."

To follow-up on the Forum, Thomas consolidated all EPA wetlands activities operating in several different organizational units into a Wetlands Office, except for enforcement functions. Enforcement responsibilities for all EPA programs at that time were located in an Office of Enforcement. David G. Davis, a career SES manager was named director of the Wetlands Office. Thomas also emphasized his keen interest in assisting states to assume the program, as had been authorized by the 1977 amendments. Michigan had assumed implementation of the program from EPA in 1984, and was the only state to have done so. Several states had begun to pursue assumption but given up, but others were still trying. Davis and his staff pursued implementation of many Forum recommendations, in close cooperation with Page's assistant for regulatory affairs, David Barrow.

THE MITIGATION MOA

EPA and Army completed a Memorandum of Agreement on Mitigation (Hanmer and Page) in February 1990 to clarify that a sequential approach should be followed in evaluating individual permit applications: avoidance, minimization, and compensation. Step one in the sequence was to determine whether wetlands impacts could be avoided—was there a practicable alternative to conducting the activity in wetlands? In the absence of a practicable alternative, the project should be configured to minimize impacts to waters of the United States. Finally, compensatory mitigation—the creation of wetlands or enhancement of degraded wetlands—would be required in the permit to offset any unavoidable impacts. While recognizing that "no net loss" might not be achievable in some circumstances or in every permit, the sequence was intended to take the 404 program toward no net loss overall. The Forum and federal agencies understood that wetlands would be lost due to unregulated activities and natural processes and that achieving the short and long term goals recommended by the Forum would depend on enhancing degraded wetlands and restoring former wetlands. The Interior Department's Partners for Fish and Wildlife program, begun in 1987, provided funds for wetlands restoration and other habitat improvements. Interior's National Wildlife Refuge System also acquired degraded and former wetlands and restored them.

WETLAND DELINEATION MANUAL

The Forum noted that there were sometimes different "calls" between the Corps, EPA and the Soil Conservation Service as to whether a particular site was a wetland. The Forum urged consistency and clarification. The agencies began work on an "interagency delineation manual," which would provide a common field method for the Corps, EPA, and the Department of Agriculture Department to identify wetlands.

With a large field presence to manage the permit program, the Corps had developed a delineation manual in 1987. EPA had not "signed on" to that manual, but had entered into an agreement with the Corps intended to reduce potential disagreements on geographic determinations. The Soil Conservation Service made "determinations" about the applicability of Swampbuster to farms primarily by examining aerial photographs, but sometimes under-took site visits where imagery was unclear or where a landowner disagreed with an initial determination. The development of a common manual was viewed by the agencies as largely a technical exercise and key tasks were entrusted to a large team of scientists. They addressed three key elements of determining wetlands: soils, vegetation, and hydrology. With regard to vege-tation, they provided for the first time that plants that thrived in either moist or dry soils, "facultative neutral" flora, would "count" in determining if a preponderance of vegetation on a site was adapted to wetland conditions. Additionally, they made provision for delineations based solely on hydrology and soils where vegetation had been disturbed. Developers had been remov-ing vegetation from wetlands—an activity not clearly subject to regulation—before seeking a 404 jurisdictional determination in order to avoid the need for a 404 permit. But farmed wetlands, lawfully drained to make them suit-able for cultivation before the Swampbuster amendment, also were captured by this change. In addition, government scientists tweaked the hydrology factor. The Corps had required indications of water at the surface but the Interagency Manual required inundation or saturation at the root zone. While this latter change may not have actually resulted in additional areas becom-ing jurisdictional, it did make it more difficult for a layperson to differentiate regulated from non-regulated areas. Taken together, these elements literally brought millions of acres of farmed wetlands under regulation that had not been regulated previously under the 1987 Corps manual, and made it harder to identify jurisdictional wetlands. Agency managers did not appreciate that what their staffs portrayed as the application of good science would provoke a severe backlash. The Mitigation MOA and Interagency Manual were adopted just as the Reagan administration was coming to a close and George H. W. Bush was assuming office.

In his presidential campaign, George H. W. Bush vowed he would be "the environmental president" and embraced the no net loss of wetlands goal. Bush selected William K. Reilly, who had been the chair of the Conservation Fund and involved in the Wetlands Forum, to be his EPA Administrator. Robert Page continued as Assistant Secretary of the Army for the first year of the Bush administration and was later succeeded by Nancy Dorn, who also was committed to improving wetlands protection. Her key advisor, a former EPA staffer, Michael Davis, enjoyed an excellent collaborative relationship with EPA wetland managers and staff. The Corps and EPA began to collabo-rate on several additional initiatives to realize the Forum's—and President Bush's—wetland goal.

The presidential pledge to achieve no net loss and the appointment of an EPA Administrator who had been employed by an environmental group put the regulated community on high alert. Within a year, an EPA enforcement initiative, the 1989 Interagency Delineation Manual, more rigorous scrutiny of 404 permit applications by the Corps, and the EPA–Army Memorandum of Agreement on Mitigation seemed to bear out their concerns and ignited a conflagration which threatened to immolate federal wetland protection. Farmers from Maryland's Eastern Shore descended in large numbers on Bill Reilly's office to protest the expansion of jurisdiction. A movement arguing for protection of property rights emerged and found editorial support for what they characterized as abuses by EPA and the Corps. A "National Wetlands Coalition" surfaced arguing for increased protection of *true* wetlands, a vastly decreased portion of the waters being protected under the CWA, and streamlining government by transferring much of EPA's authority to the Corps of Engineers. Legislation was introduced to implement the Wetlands Coalition goals, including removing EPA's seldom used veto power. These developments put EPA and the lately greener Corps of Engineers on the defensive through much of the George H. W. Bush administration.

PROPERTY RIGHTS

Increased efforts to protect flora and fauna under the Endangered Species Act, along with an EPA wetlands enforcement initiative, combined with wariness about the implications of President Bush's commitment to no net loss of wetlands were the impetus for the formation of a Fairness to Landowners Committee (FLOC) in 1991. The criminal conviction and jail sentence of William Ellen for extensive dredging and filling in waters of the United States to create a "duck heaven" attracted national attention. Ellen was hired to do the work on the 3,000+ acre farm in Dorchester County, Maryland, owned by Wall Street commodities trader and hedge fund manager, Paul Tudor Jones. Jones pleaded guilty to CWA violations and paid $2 million in fines and restitution. Prosecutors asserted that while the Jones relied primarily on Ellen's expertise in pursuing the project, Ellen's familiarity with permitting requirements and his failure to comply with multiple warnings and violation notices justified his incarceration (Horton 1993).

Margret Ann Riegle, also a Maryland Eastern Shore resident, distributed information about the Ellen case and several other wetlands "horror stories" on behalf of a "Fairness to Landowners Committee (FLOC)." Riegle, a former finance official for the *New York Daily News*, claimed FLOC had 25,000 members and 500 affiliated organizations. EPA and Army energized a network of field staff to marshal the facts about these stories. The agencies were able to speedily distribute "Rumor and Reality" fact sheets, which made clear that many of the "horror stories" were exaggerations and some were outright fabrications.

The National Wetlands Coalition (NWC), on the other hand, was a classic "K Street" phenomenon. It was incorporated in 1989. Its executive director, Robert Szabo, was a partner in a large DC law firm and former aide to Louisiana senator J. Bennett Johnston. NWC's board comprised Louisiana and Alaska petroleum interests, large landholding Fortune 500s, like Georgia Pacific, as well as the American Farm Bureau Federation and the National Homebuilders Association (Environmental Working Group 1996). The Coalition advanced an extensive list of suggested changes to the Clean Water Act. As the Deputy Assistant Administrator for Water, I was invited to join Bill Reilly for a meeting in the his office with Leighton Stewart, NWC Chair, and CEO of the Louisiana Land and Exploration Company, a major natural gas producer. I was told that Stewart had been helpful to the administrator on the climate change issue. Stewart described the need to save Louisiana's coastal wetlands, which were being lost at a staggering rate due to compaction of the sediments which had built the "Sportsmen's Paradise," sea level rise, and other factors. No one would dispute that these coastal wetlands were wetlands, and little of the losses in these very wet marshes and swamps were caused by activities subject to CWA regulation. Stewart argued that "not all wetlands were created equal" and that wetland regulation should be tailored to the importance of the resource. Reilly later pushed EPA staff to formulate a classification and mapping system that could guide 404 permitting. Separately, senior state officials in Louisiana were urging EPA to engage more effectively in an interagency process to protect and restore its coastal wetlands. And environmental groups had petitioned EPA to take action to reduce a large hypoxic area, or Dead Zone, in the Gulf. The Dead Zone was being fed by nutrients, largely from agricultural operations in the Midwest and which drained to the Mississippi and Atchafalaya rivers.

EPA had no personnel stationed in Louisiana. Activities there were staffed from our Dallas Region VI office. Sensing a potentially exploitable contradiction in widespread Louisiana concern about protection of its coastal wetlands and the Dead Zone, on one hand, and "reform" of the 404 program on the other, I quietly began an effort to have EPA engage much more actively on these issues in the State. We relocated an employee to Baton Rouge to coordinate with the State Coastal office and environmental department. I travelled frequently to the state and developed a positive relationship with the large and respected Corps District. Dallas EPA personnel became very active in the Task Force established by the Coastal Wetlands Planning Protection and Restoration Act (CWPPRA, or the Breaux Act) and chaired by the Corps. We hired several university coastal scientists in the summer months through the National Estuary Program. This program of engagement seemed to be effective in dispelling a lot of antipathy that had built toward EPA in Louisiana. Bill Reilly had also agreed to increase funding for a fledgling Gulf of Mexico program office, which a Sunbelt caucus of Gulf legislators clearly hoped would lead to increases in grants for their universities and state agencies. The Louisiana congressmen were regarded as having particular credibility on wetlands matters. As Mr. Tauzin (R-LA) deadpanned at a hearing during my testimony, "I'm from Louisiana . . . that's where half the state is underwater and the other half is under indictment."

THE ALASKA-LOUISIANA AXIS

But before these efforts had fully paid off, Louisiana Congressman Jimmy Hayes (R), the former college roommate of the Wetlands Coalition's Bob Szabo, stepped forward to become the point person for a legislative attack on wetlands protection. With fellow Louisianan Billy Tauzin, Hayes introduced HR 1330 on March 7, 1991. The legislation proclaimed its purpose as a bill "to amend the Federal Water Pollution Control Act to establish a comprehensive program for conserving and managing wetlands in the United States, and for other purposes." Hayes and Tauzin recruited 173 co-sponsors for the bill, which would have reduced EPA to a role of consultation with the Army Secretary, in whom all operational and policy authority would reside. Drainage and excavation of some wetlands would be explicitly subject to permitting. However, HR 1330 required a three-tiered classification system in which only "class A" wetlands would retain full protection. It also excluded prior converted cropland from jurisdiction. Wetlands in any state which had lost less than one percent of its historic wetlands (Alaska) would be unprotected, as recommended by the National Wetlands Coalition. Alaska's sole member of the House, Don Young, became an enthusiastic champion of the legislation. Hearings to build support for this legislation featured many of the horror stories of regulatory excess which we had become adept at knocking down. Showing solidarity and mutual support, EPA and Army always presented joint testimony and tag teamed responses to the hostile questions.

With almost half the House of Representatives supporting draconian changes to wetlands law, EPA's Assistant Administrator for Water, LaJuana Wilcher, directed that work commence on a new Delineation Manual that she said should be straight-forward enough for her Uncle Dennis to understand it (the period of saturation or inundation would be increased, water would need to be at the soil surface, and "facultative neutral" plants [those that could live in either wet or drier conditions] would be excluded in evaluating prevalence of plant species adapted to life in wet conditions). In November 1992, at the direction of the White House, EPA proposed an "Alaska 1 percent rule." The proposal would have to exempted wetland permit actions in Alaska from the usual sequence of avoiding, then minimizing wetlands impacts of a project and finally compensating for unavoidable impacts by creating or restoring wetlands. In Alaska, only minimization would be required until one percent of the State's wetlands had been developed. The day after the Alaska rule was proposed, America went to the polls and George H. W. Bush, the environmental president, was denied a second term.

WETLANDS AND WATERSHEDS

The Wetlands Forum had recommended better coordination of federal, state, and local programs affecting wetlands. That recommendation, along with the brouhaha that had erupted, and the realization that progress on reducing nonpoint sources of pollution was stalled, prompted senior career officials in EPA's Office of Water to consider new ways to reduce the wetlands controversy and improve the effectiveness of aquatic resource protection. By shifting separate permit programs that operated on a discharger-by-discharger and industry-sector basis to a more integrated approach, the senior executives felt that local governments, grassroots citizen groups, and non-traditional partners could be enlisted in a more effective effort. They saw the watershed, or catchment, an area of land that drains water to a single stream, river, or lake, as the logical framework for this integrated, holistic approach. The U.S. Geological Survey had mapped 2264 watersheds of the United States (Seaber 2007).

When the EPA Office of Water was reorganized in 1991, the wetlands and coastal protection offices and units which managed monitoring, and nonpoint source control, were combined to create an Office of Wetlands, Oceans, and Watersheds (OWOW), and I was designated to be its director. My management team and I set out to advance watershed management as a core objective of the new office. The watershed protection concept had been piloted to a degree in the National Estuary Program, authorized by 1987 amendment to the Clean Water Act. Additionally, North Carolina had shifted its Clean Water monitoring and permitting programs to a "rotating basin" approach, which they asserted was much more efficient than the first-come-first-served, permit-by-permit approach they had previously employed. With these challenges and regulatory innovations in mind, EPA's Water leadership at headquarters and the regional offices committed to use the flexibility in the Clean Water Act to promote a fundamental shift to integrated, holistic, watershed protection and restoration. In rallying the personnel of the new OWOW and its regional counterparts, my deputy Dave Davis and I pledged to vigorously purse this strategic change as well as to emphasize *environmental* protection, which had been virtually eclipsed by public health concerns at EPA, and to advance the science and practice of habitat restoration, to complement regulatory protections, as called for in the goal of the Clean Water Act.

EPA invited senior executives from several other agencies to join the Agency in a Federal Watershed Coordinating Committee. The Corps, National Oceanographic and Atmospheric Administration, Agriculture's Forest Service and Natural Resource Conservation Service, Interior's Park Service and Fish and Wildlife Service, Transportation Department, and the Tennessee Valley Authority all participated and expressed high interest and good support for the watershed approach. Moreover, they were very receptive to EPA's proposal for conducting a major national conference to advance the idea, timed so that it would be very appealing to incoming political appointees following the 1992 presidential election.

President Clinton appointed Carol Browner, a former staffer to Senator Al Gore and then head of Florida's Department of Environmental Protection (DEP) to be his EPA Administrator. Under Browner DEP had operated a strong wetland protection program. Florida was home to the Everglades, celebrated in Marjory Stoneman Douglas' *River of Grass*. The state was also known for marina developments blasted through mangroves and unscrupulous developers who sold submerged lots sight unseen to Midwesterners. But Florida had been atoning for its past despoliation. Browner's DEP had undertaken an in-depth look at compensatory mitigation and had found a high failure rate due to poor siting, design, construction and maintenance. Florida also had a system of water management districts which were established on a hydrological basis. In one of her first meetings with Water Office senior staff, Browner accepted the keynote spot for the national conference entitled Watershed '93, which had 600 registered presenters and attendees, and said she "got" and liked the concept of watershed protection as the organizing and integrating framework for implementing the Clean Water Act.

EPA CABINET STATUS

Bill Clinton had pledged to elevate EPA to cabinet status if elected. Efforts to implement that pledge began soon after Browner took her oath of office. In its search for champions and votes for the cabinet bill, the White House was told by Louisiana Senator John Breaux that the wetlands issue was a very serious potential obstacle. Breaux was assured that the White House would convene a high-level interagency working group to address concerns about fairness and flexibility.

A number of interests were concerned about a potentially more powerful EPA, though in reality, cabinet status would not have changed the Agency's authorities, which were spelled out in more than a dozen separate laws overseen by numerous congressional committees. Nevertheless, a variety of EPA horror stories began to appear in congressional floor statements and press releases. Working with other agencies, states, and EPA regions, we were able to quickly expand on the model that had been used to rebut the wetlands horror stories. The new round of horror stories included tall tales of regulatory excess involving pesticides, wastewater treatment issues and some of the old wetlands canards. EPA developed one-page "rumor and reality" fact sheets, following the model we had previously developed for rebutting the wetland horror stories. In those pre-email days, I found fax numbers for all members of Congress and was able to send our fact sheets to all members of Congress within forty-eight hours. The fax list came from the University of Michigan, and because we had no fax machines capable of doing so, the faxes were sent from my Macintosh computer at home. We did not want to fall victim to the adage that a lie travels around the block while the truth is still putting on its shoes!

Our strategy was evidently effective because a complaint was made to the EPA Inspector General that EPA was engaging in illegal lobbying! Having worked on the Hill and begun my EPA career in the Congressional Affairs Office, I was well familiar with what was and wasn't permissible under the Anti-Lobbying Act. An investigator for the Inspector General showed me his badge and interrogated me about how I had acquired the fax list, why I was using my personal computer, etc. A day or two later I had a chance meeting with the administrator who said, "Bob, you did nothing wrong. What you did was exactly right!" As was typical, the IG's office never notified me that they determined that there had been no wrong-doing.

Although EPA countered the horror stories, many members of Congress saw the cabinet bill as the vehicle to weaken some of the core protections embodied in statutes and regulations developed over EPA's first two decades. A risk assessment provision would have layered on new requirements that would have made additional regulations to protect public health almost impossible to adopt. When the Republicans took the control of the House of Representatives in 1995, the EPA cabinet initiative was quietly abandoned.

The Interagency Wetlands Workgroup

Meanwhile, in June 1993, the Interagency Wetlands Workgroup began an intensive effort to formulate actions that could take heat off the federal programs and improve wetlands protection. Keith Laughlin of the Council on Environmental Quality facilitated meetings of career SES representatives of a dozen or so departments and agencies that had wetland authorities. Several staff teams worked on groups of related ideas: addressing agricultural concerns, delineation issues, mitigation, Alaska, alternatives to categorization, coordination with state and local programs, restoration, etc. There was a high degree of cooperation among those working on the task. Most of the presidentially-appointed assistant secretaries or assistant administrators had not been confirmed, consequently there was little involvement from political levels of the Agencies. As EPA's representative, I was very ably supported by managers and staff of the Wetland's Division. This Division was comprised of fewer than thirty employees but they were highly motivated and very talented. The other agency with a lot on the line was the Army. Michael Davis was its Workgroup representative but the Corps' Regulatory Branch in DC was even smaller than the EPA's Wetlands Division and Davis relied on EPA to do much of the "homework" for the Workgroup assignments he accepted.

As the effort progressed, the Workgroup held meetings to listen to the views of various stakeholder groups. One session was convened to receive congressional input. The career workgroup members were expecting Hill staffers at the session in the White House Conference Center on Lafayette Park. It was somewhat startling to see Alaska's senior senator, Ted Stevens, stride into the room with seven other Congressmen and Senators. Stevens, ranking Republican on the powerful Appropriations Committee politely pressed for the promulgation of EPA's proposed 1 percent Rule.

The Interagency Wetlands Workgroup issued its report on August 24, 1993. Some of the forty actions laid out were completed on August 23 while others were promised for a year or longer in the future. The report outlined five principles for federal wetlands policy, which, right off the bat, affirmed a commitment to the short and long-term goals expressed previously by the National Wetlands Policy Forum:

1. The Clinton administration supports the interim goal of no overall net loss of the nation's remaining wetlands, and the long-term goal of increasing the quality and quantity of the nation's wetlands resource base;
2. Regulatory programs must be efficient, fair, flexible, and predictable, and must be administered in a manner that avoids unnecessary impacts upon private property and the regulated public, and minimizes those effects that cannot be avoided, while providing effective protection for wetlands. Duplication among regulatory agencies must be avoided and the public must have a clear understanding of regulatory requirements and various agency roles;

3. Non-regulatory programs, such as advance planning; wetlands restoration, inventory, and research; and public/private cooperative efforts must be encouraged to reduce the federal government's reliance upon regulatory programs as the primary means to protect wetlands resources and to accomplish long-term wetlands gains;
4. The federal government should expand partnerships with state, tribal, and local governments, the private sector and individual citizens and approach wetlands protection and restoration in an ecosystem/watershed context; and
5. Federal wetlands policy should be based upon the best scientific information available.

The "White House Plan," as it was known, met with generally favorable reactions. There were several actions taken to address the fairness issue and diffuse some of the criticisms of the Wetlands Coalition and Fairness to Landowners Committee. The 1987 Corps Manual (which required inundation or saturation at the soil surface) was adopted for use by all agencies. An administrative appeals process for permit denials would be instituted. Prior converted croplands were excluded from jurisdiction, on the basis that they had been lawfully converted and after multiple growing seasons and had long ceased to provide wetland services. The Corps and EPA committed to develop an Alaska Strategy, and withdrew the proposed the 1 percent rule. A nationwide permit authorizing single-family homes would be developed. Mitigation banking was endorsed as a way to make it easier for permit holders to satisfy compensatory mitigation requirements. Several of these commitments were also expected to improve effectiveness in protecting wetlands. Mitigation banking was expected to be more reliable because bankers had every reason make sure their mitigation "worked" and could undertake large scale restoration to serve multiple projects that otherwise would be attempting to create or restore very small wetlands. Mitigation banks were also expected to use more skill and care in citing, constructing, and maintaining wetlands than small developers would or could.

Other important elements of the White House Plan were undertaken primarily to improve the effectiveness of wetlands programs. Nationwide Permit 26, which authorized projects that would destroy up to ten acres of "headwaters" streams or adjacent wetlands without notifying the Corps was to be "regionalized" (i.e., phased out in favor of activity based permits generally authorizing much smaller impacts). The Corps and EPA issued a rule stating that ditching wetlands to drain them necessarily entailed the incidental redeposit of excavated (dredged) material and thus required a 404 permit (the Tulloch Rule). Categorization, as called for by the NWC and HR 1330 (the Tauzin-Hayes bill) was expressly rejected, for, among several reasons, having no scientific basis. EPA and Army did, however, issue guidance to field staffs emphasizing the flexibility to consider the size of impacts and functions and values of wetlands being impacted during permit evaluation. The administration pledged to support increased funding for the Wetland Reserve Program, which provided money and technical assistance to farmers who take land out of production and restore wetland functions. The plan promised technical assistance and agency support for state and local governments to undertake planning for wetland protection on a watershed basis. EPA and Army agreed that more state and local regulatory action could be recognized through "Programmatic General Permits," a less cumbersome way than "assumption," as provided in the 1977 amendments to the Clean Water Act, to assure protection of wetlands while reducing duplication.

The many future actions the plan called for presented a heavy agenda for the small cadre of Corps, EPA, Agriculture, Fish and Wildlife Service and NOAA wetland experts. But it was very important to demonstrate that the plan was not a set of empty promises. EPA and Army both detailed field personnel to headquarters to staff workgroups and staff from other agencies turned the wheel on aspects that weren't always key issues for their agencies.

EPA worked tirelessly to facilitate assumption by Maryland and New Jersey, only to see Maryland's effort abandoned after the defeat of necessary legislation by Maryland legislators concerned that wetlands would receive less protection. I had testified before the Maryland House of Delegates in favor of the assumption proposal. When it was defeated, Governor William Donald Shafer wrote to me expressing his frustration at "the stupid positions" sometimes taken by Maryland's legislature. After a mighty struggle with field personnel of Interior and NOAA, whose authority to object to individual permits under the Endangered Species Act would be terminated by assumption, New Jersey's program was approved for assumption. Timely delivery on the many commitments in the plan began to take the air out of the opposition.

While the White House Plan was under development, EPA had simultaneously been preparing a series of legislative recommendations to strengthen the Clean Water Act. The resulting "Green Book" sought new authorities to improve control of nonpoint sources of water pollution, to facilitate and support watershed management at the state and local levels and make numerous technical changes to respond to litigation and needs identified as implementation had continued. It had been more than twenty years since passage of the Clean Water Act and six years since Congress had adopted significant amendments. Bills based primarily on the EPA recommendations were introduced in the House and Senate, and hearings were held on the bills.

In the 1994 elections the president's party lost many seats in the House and control of that body passed to the Republican Party. Georgia Representative Newt Gingrich, who had been an environmental moderate, became speaker and he and his colleagues quickly moved to enact a "Contract With

America." One of its elements was a "Job Creation and Wage Enhancement Act," which included several provisions that would require additional analyses of regulatory actions. Another would have established a requirement that if an agency action reduced a property's value by 10 percent or greater, the property owner would be entitled to compensation—a very different proposition from the well settled legal standard of "takings." The Supreme Court had determined previously that property was "taken" when virtually all use was foreclosed by federal action. The Contract also promised to streamline the committee structure in the House. The Merchant Marine and Fisheries Committee, which had jurisdiction over the National Environmental Policy Act and was "green-leaning" on both sides of the partisan aisle, was terminated.

The Republicans had not controlled the House for four decades, and its new GOP Committee Chairmen were embraced their new power enthusiastically. Several hearings to explore regulatory excesses by EPA and in the wetlands program were scheduled. Once again, EPA and Army appeared together, and delivered joint testimony emphasizing the elements of the White House Plan. One memorable exchange involved Alaska's Don Young, Chair of the Water Resources Subcommittee, who worked himself into a high dudgeon as he described the unreasonable delays and denials of permits in Alaska. When he asked our reactions, I calmly read him results of a satisfaction survey Army had provided to all applicants that showed a substantial majority of respondents were satisfied or very satisfied with how they were handled. Young was furious and bolted from the room.

The House Public Works and Transportation Committee recommended legislation to the full House, HR 961, that contained elements of HR 1330, the takings provisions and "regulatory reform" features of the Contract with America and a variety of "fixes" to deal with litigation which had been decided against industrial dischargers. Administrator Carol Browner labeled HR 961 "A Dirty Water Bill" and this moniker was picked up and widely reported in the media. Whether the leadership simply wished to avert further criticism or became distracted by other issues, HR 961 was never brought to the House floor for a vote.

EPA's Louisiana strategy was paying dividends. The National Wetlands Coalition began to meet with EPA to suggest how some elements of the White House Plan should be implemented. Recognizing that the knock-out punch wasn't going to be landed by Congress they started working to influence EPA. Some of the larger members of the coalition (Georgia Pacific and the City of Los Angeles) dropped out. With the issuance of Mitigation Banking Guidance, an industry began to emerge that had an interest in strict wetlands regulation and in making compensatory mitigation successful. In August 1995, EPA and Army reported that the number of mitigation banks had doubled from 100 to 200. These entrepreneurs were effective witnesses in the waning number of Congressional hearings. The end to the short-lived regulation of farmed wetlands took much of the heat out of the opposition from the farm lobby. Large-scale projects to ditch and drain wetlands for commercial development and housing projects had been on the rise before the Tulloch rule and virtually came to a halt after it was promulgated. The sum of the changes embodied in the White House Plan began to significantly reduce wetland losses from regulated activities, and mitigation and restoration efforts increased and became more effective. Opposition to the 404 program quieted noticeably.

THE CLEAN WATER ACTION PLAN AND NET GAIN OF WETLANDS

The Clinton administration recognized that the Republican-controlled House and the Democrat-controlled Senate were unlikely to send legislation to strengthen the Clean Water Act to the President's desk. However, as the twenty-fifth anniversary of the '72 Act approached, they decided to capture the high ground. The vice president made an announcement in the White House on that anniversary: he was directing EPA and the Agriculture Department to convene a task force to find ways step up the effort to realize the goal of the Clean Water Act to "protect and restore the chemical, physical, and biological integrity of the nation's waters." Mr. Gore also directed that the initiative was to focus on three goals: enhanced protection from public health threats posed by water pollution, more effective control of polluted runoff, and promotion of water quality protection on a watershed basis. He called for a report and actions in 120 days (USEPA/USDA 1997). It only became evident later that in addition to the laudable goal of enhancing protection of water resources, the initiative, and Mr. Gore's role in it, were setting up a stark contrast between the putative 2000 Democratic presidential nominee and the Republican.

"DIRTY WATER HOUSE OF REPRESENTATIVES"

The Clean Water Action Plan was completed on schedule and announced on February 19, 1998, at an event at Baltimore's Inner Harbor with the president, vice president, EPA administrator, cabinet secretaries and others present. It was both a broad and specific plan, over 100 pages in length with commitments to take over 100 actions, many addressing polluted runoff and emphasizing use of a watershed approach to aquatic resource protection and restoration. Implementation was to be fueled by a 35 percent increase, or $568M, in spending in FY 1999 over FY 1998. In a display of confidence that the opposition to wetlands regulation had been effectively neutralized, the action plan called for a coordinated strategy to achieve a net gain of as many as 100,000 acres of wetlands annually by the year 2005. At the time the wetlands loss rate had declined, but was estimated to be 80,000 to 120,000 acres annually. The plan called for a 50 percent increase in wetlands restored and enhanced by the Corps of Engineers and increased enrollment of acres for wetlands restoration under USDA conservation programs.

George W. Bush and Wetlands Protection

The initial George W. Bush leadership at EPA, former New Jersey Governor Christine Todd Whitman and former Michigan water official G. Tracy Mehan (from the two states with assumed wetlands programs), was sympathetic to the importance of protecting wetlands and both had some personal experience with the resource. New Jersey had assumed the 404 program and Whitman was an avid kayaker. Mehan had served a previous stint at EPA in a political capacity and had directed Michigan's Great Lakes Office. But the long period of excellent relations between EPA and the Corps was in real trouble. Former Mississippi Congressman Mike Parker, the newly appointed Assistant Secretary of the Army for Civil Works, told Mehan and me at our initial meeting with him at the Pentagon that EPA was out of control and creating the Agency was the "worst mistake Richard Nixon ever made." Just five months after his appointment, he was fired by the White House after he publically took issue with President Bush's budget for activities in his portfolio. Parker's successor, J. P. Woodley, Jr., restored good rapport and collaboration with EPA.

In December 2002, on the release of new EPA-Army-NOAA-Interior-USDA-DOT guidance on mitigation, six assistant administrators/secretaries stated "the Bush administration affirms its commitment to the goal of no net loss of the nation's wetlands. The Administration is hopeful of achieving that goal and in the near future to begin increasing the overall functions and values of our wetlands." On Earth Day, April 23 2004, on a visit to a restored coastal wetland President Bush himself said that it was time for the nation to move beyond a "no net loss" of wetlands goal and he went on to say he would "work toward a goal of increasing wetlands by at least three million acres over five years" (Environmental News Service 2004).

Danger in the Courts

In 2006, Michigan developer John Rapanos appealed his conviction for filling wetlands on a property he wished to develop on the grounds that they were not subject to regulation under the Clean Water Act because they were separated from traditionally navigable waters by a man-made berm. Notwithstanding unified state and Bush administration arguments against further restricting the geographic scope of the Clean Water Act, a majority of the Supreme Court agreed with Rapanos. They disagreed, however, on what would be a sufficient "nexus" to navigable waters to permit regulation. EPA and Army have twice issued clarifying guidance in the wake of the *Rapanos* decision.

RESULTS: TWENTY-ONE YEARS AFTER THE FORUM'S GOALS

This chapter has described the ebb and flow of wetlands policy, law, and accompanying controversy. The National Wetlands Policy Forum articulated clear short- and long-range goals for wetlands protection and restoration. In October 2011, the U.S. Fish and Wildlife Service (USFWS) issued its latest Wetlands Status and Trends Report, covering the period 2004–2009 (see figure 1). Among its key findings:

> There were an estimated 110.1 million acres of wetlands in the conterminous U.S. in 2009. Wetlands composed 5.5 percent of the surface area of the U. S. An estimated 95 percent of all wetlands were freshwater and five percent were in the marine or estuarine (saltwater) systems. There were an estimated 104.3 million acres of freshwater wetland and 5.8 million acres of intertidal (saltwater) wetlands.
>
> *The difference in the national estimates of wetland acreage between 2004 and 2009 was not statistically significant* (emphasis added). Wetland area declined by an estimated 62,300 acres between 2004 and 2009. This equated to an average annual loss of 13,800 acres during the 4.5 year time interval of this study. There were notable losses that occurred to intertidal estuarine emergent wetlands (salt marsh) and freshwater forested wetlands. The loss rate of intertidal emergent wetland increased to three times the previous loss rate between 1998 and 2004. Losses of estuarine emergent (salt marsh) and changes in marine and estuarine non-vegetated wetlands reflected the impacts of coastal storms and relative sea level rise along the coastlines of the Atlantic and Gulf of Mexico. The majority (99 percent) of all estuarine emergent losses were associated with processes related to the marine environment such as saltwater inundation and/or coastal storm events.
>
> Between 2004 and 2009, 489,600 acres of former upland were re-classified as wetland. These increases were attributed to wetland reestablishment and creation on agricultural lands and other uplands with undetermined land use including undeveloped land, lands in conservation programs or idle lands. The rate of wetland reestablishment increased by an estimated 17 percent from the previous study period (1998 and 2004).

Whether the progress made since the Forum laid out goals and means for wetlands protection can be maintained is in some doubt. The erosion of Clean Water Act jurisdiction by the Supreme Court could be a game changer.

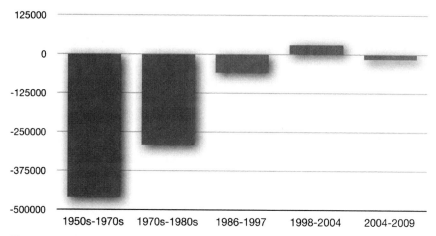

Figure 5.1.   Wetlands Loss, 1950s to 2004. Source: USFWS National Wetlands Inventory, 2009.

Additionally, the drumbeat of "job-killing environmental regulations" in the 2012 Republican presidential campaign is a worrisome sign as is the potential reduction or elimination of conservation spending in the Farm Bill. It is also the case that public awareness of the value of wetlands has improved, private conservation initiatives are expanding, mitigation and restoration science and practice has advanced, and state and local government programs have grown.

IMPORTANT LESSONS

This chapter has described a rapid revolution in U.S. wetlands policy. In less than a generation, the country moved from encouraging wetlands destruction to implementing numerous programs to protect wetlands. While the future remains uncertain, the policy of protection and restoration has been reasonably well settled for more than a decade. The story offers some lessons for other areas of environmental management.

A Clear, Measureable Goal Is Invaluable

The National Wetlands Policy Forum brought a heightened level of attention to the importance of wetlands and suggested specific actions to improve protection. But its articulation of an overarching short- and long-term goal was its greatest lasting achievement. The breadth of interests represented and the high level of the participants gave credibility to the Forum and made it more realistic to expect that presidential candidates would respond to questions about whether they would pursue the goal if elected. The simplicity and clarity of the goal was a great advantage. The availability of a large-scale, technically sound method for tracking progress, the Fish and Wildlife Service's *Status and Trends* reports, provided a credible measuring stick for progress, or lack of it, in reaching the goal. The lack of a simple, *measurable,* goal is probably why the 1995 recommendations of the National Forum on Nonpoint Source Pollution, which was chaired by three governors, and had CEO level participation, did not gain the traction the Wetlands Forum did. Difficulty in measuring nonpoint source pollution and reductions or increases, rather than inability to reach consensus, frustrated the Nonpoint Source Forum.

Knock Down False Charges Forcefully and Rapidly

Both the wetlands program and EPA more generally were criticized in sensational ways with horror stories. The Agency pushed back speedily and forcefully and the horror stories were discredited.

Supplement Regulatory Approaches with Non Regulatory Approaches Where Possible

The White House Plan emphasized cooperative and voluntary approaches to complement regulatory actions. In addition to projecting a friendlier side of regulatory agencies, like police athletic leagues, these techniques were a way to accomplish some protections that could not be achieved through regulation. Large-scale incentive programs such as the Conservation Reserve and Wetlands Reserve paid farmers for restoring and protecting wetlands. EPA developed a small wetland restoration grant program dubbed 5-Star, that clarified that states could use their nonpoint source grants for aquatic habitat restoration, and initiated a cooperative program with the Wildlife Habitat Council, an industry group supporting enhancement and management of corporate lands as habitat, to place emphasis on wetland restoration and protection. Skiing venues and golf courses use large quantities of water for snowmaking and irrigation, respectively. Developing or redeveloping these facilities can involve considerable manipulation of land and waterscapes. EPA undertook cooperative projects with the ski industry and golf courses to encourage them to reduce water and chemical use, and in the case of golf courses, incorporate restored wetlands as well as ponds and lakes hazards.

Collaboration Among Agencies Is Very Valuable

The strong cooperation built between EPA's leadership and the Corps' civilian leadership resulted in strengthened regulations and a unified front in the face of Congressional criticism. It also allowed each agency to better complement the activities of others and avoid conflicts and duplication of effort. The collaborations in the Interagency Wetlands Workgroup, Federal Watershed Leadership Team and Clean Water Action Plan Task Force brought new ideas and experiences to the table. These groups fostered a sense of teamwork to challenging tasks that needed to be accomplished in short time frames. These groups were led by career SES personnel, except the CWAP Task Force which had an assistant secretary level steering committee co-chaired by EPA and Agriculture. EPA certainly nurtured these relationships. Of course, the best efforts to build alliances can be frustrated by an unwilling or antagonistic partner, like Mike Parker, but it is certainly worth the effort to meet potential allies more than half way.

Include Stakeholders in Strategy Development

Broad participation by diverse interests enriched the discussion in formulating the Forum Report, the Clean Water Action Plan, and the report-out from Watershed '93 and '96. This raised the general trust level in the follow-up efforts. However, the effort of a federal advisory committee to build consensus on how to move the TMDL program forward, was unsuccessful. Sharply opposing positions had been solidified before the consultation process was initiated and ultimately, the committee agreed to disagree.

Innovative Implementation Can Enhance Program Effectiveness

The initial strategy for implementing the Clean Water Act was pragmatic and appropriate for the task as it then stood. EPA needed to get thousands of industrial and municipal dischargers under permit, had to develop effluent guidelines for industrial categories as a basis to move from limits based on "best professional judgment" to "best available control technology," and to move grants to hundreds of publically owned sewage treatment plants to enable them to reach "secondary treatment." But the Clean Water Act didn't specify an implementation strategy. As sources of industrial effluent discharges came under permit and the construction grants program was replaced with block grants to capitalize infrastructure revolving funds, other concerns came to the fore. Control of storm water, reduction of nonpoint source pollution, and habitat protection became more urgent concerns. The initial focus of implementation was not well suited to these challenges. Believing that a different approach would be more successful, career managers in the Office of Water set out to make a sea change. One key tenet of the new strategy was to better integrate the somewhat separate resource-based programs and organizations—wetlands and coastal and ocean waters—with other programs and tools to knit a holistic aquatic resource protection and restoration fabric. The interagency wetlands plan incorporated this philosophy as did the Clean Water Action Plan. New allies were found and empowered. Grants, technical assistance, guidance, publications, testimony, and major conferences were developed to support this implementation framework. The Clean Water Act didn't mandate these things, nor did it prohibit them. Innovative leaders charted a new course. The watershed approach was well received by states, and the effort to enlist new partners to the effort to protect aquatic resources has borne fruit. Watershed protection was embraced by successive EPA administrators and by Presidents Clinton and George H. W. Bush.

THE FUTURE

Significant progress in protecting aquatic resources has been made in almost four decades of implementing the Clean Water Act. After many years of conflict, EPA and the Corps developed an effective partnership in implementing the provisions of section 404. That partnership was guided in significant part by the recommendations and goal of the National Wetlands Policy Forum. The concepts of "no net loss" and "eventual increase in quantity and quality of the nation's wetlands" together with the National Wetlands Inventory provide a fairly clear way to evaluate progress in wetlands protection and restoration. The large-scale protection and restoration programs incorporated into farm policy have been a major, factor in reducing wetland losses and realizing gains.

By themselves, the tools afforded by the Clean Water Act are not adequate to realize its goal of restoring and maintaining the physical, chemical, biological integrity of the nation's waters. The inability to strengthen them is a disappointment and a further indication of the partisan gridlock that has developed over the past dozen years in Congress and between it and the President. Recent Supreme Court decisions reducing the scope of waters which are afforded protection under the Clean Water Act represents another tough test for the leaders and staff of the U.S. Environmental Protection Agency. EPA's staff and managers, have, however, demonstrated their dedication and creativity in pursuing the goals of the Clean Water Act and the Wetlands Policy Forum, and if any group of people can find a way to make further progress, these public servants will do so.

REFERENCES

Bleichield, H. 1997. "Having a Wetland and Developing It Too," *RealtorMag*, National Association of Realtors, Washington, D.C.

Clean Water Act of 1977 (P.L. 95-217).

Coastal Wetlands Planning, Protection and Restoration Act. (16 U.S.C. 3951- 3956). Title III of P.L. 101-646.

Copeland, C. 1993. *The Clean Water Action Plan: Background and Early Implementation* Environmental Policy Resources, Science, and Industry Division, Congressional Research Service, Library of Congress. Washington D.C.

Dahl, Thomas.E. 2011. *Status and Trends of Wetlands in the Conterminous United States 2004 to 2009.* U.S. Department of the Interior, Fish and Wildlife Service, Washington, D.C.

Department of Defense, Department of the Army, Corps of Engineers. December 13, 1996. *Final Notice of Issuance, Reissuance, and Modification of Nationwide Permits* Federal Register / Vol. 61, No. 241.

Environmental News Service. *"Bush Pledges Wetlands Expansion, Restoration."* Last modified April 23, 2004. Accessed February 14, 2012. www.ens-newswire.com/ens/apr2004/2004-04-23-10.html.

Environmental Working Group. "Swamped With Cash Political campaign contributions and the assault on America's wetlands laws" Last modified March 1996. Accessed February 8, 2012. www.ewg.org/reports/wet_pac.

Food Security Act of 1985, 16 U.S.C. 3801-3862.

Federal Water Pollution Control Act Amendments of 1972 PL 92-500 (33 U.S.C. §1251 et seq).

Hanmer, Rebecca, USEPA and Page, Robert, Army. January 19, 1989. *Memorandum of Agreement Between the Department of the Army and the US Environmental Protection Agency Concerning the Determination of the Geographic Jurisdiction of the Section 404 Program and the Application of Exemptions Under Section 404(f) of the Clean Water Act.*

Horton, Tom 1993. "A Closer Look at the Case of an 'Eco-Martyr.'" *The Baltimore Sun.* Retrieved February 8, 2012, from the World Wide Web: http://articles.baltimoresun.com/1993-12-26/news/1993360081_1_wetlands-ellen-zeal.

Los Angeles Times. August 29, 1993. "Out of the Swamp of Wetland Policy: Clinton Administration wades into deep end of vital water quality issue."

The National Geographic Society and The Conservation Fund. July, 1995. *Nonpoint Water Pollution Taking A New Tack.* Washington, DC.

Natural Resources Defense Council, Inc., and National Wildlife Federation Plaintiffs, v. Howard H. Callaway, Secretary of the Army, et al., Defendants. Civ. A. No. 74-1242. United States District Court, District of Columbia.

Page, Robert W., Wilcher, LaJuana. *"Memorandum of Agreement Concerning the Determination of Mitigation Under the Clean Water Act Section 404(b)(1) Guidelines,"* Last modified February 6, 1990. Accessed February 8, 2012. http://water.epa.gov/lawsregs/guidance/wetlands/mitigate.cfm.

"Protecting america's wetlands: an action agenda." 1988. World Wildlife Foundation.

Quinlan, Paul. 2011. "WETLANDS: Regulation haters join chorus urging new Clean Water Act rules." *Greenwire.*

Seaber, Paul, Paul Kapinos, and George Knapp. 2007. *Hydrologic Unit Maps* Water *Supply Paper 2294* Department of Interior, US Geological Survey Washington, DC.

United States v. Riverside Bayview Homes, Inc., 474 U.S. 121 (1985)

US Army Corps of Engineers. January 1987. *Wetlands Delineation Manual, Waterways Experiment Station Wetlands Research Program Technical Report Y-87-1.*

US Environmental Protection Agency, "Wetland Laws, Regulations, Treaties, Policy and Guidance." Accessed February 8, 2012. http://water.epa.gov/lawsregs/lawsguidance/cwa/wetlands/index.cfm.

US Environmental Protection Agency. "Five Star Restoration Grant Program." Last modified February 2012. Accessed February 8, 2012. www.epa.gov/owow/restore/5star/.

US Environmental Protection Agency, Office of Water, Office of Wetlands, Oceans, and Watersheds. 1995. *America's Wetlands: Our Vital Link Between Land and Water.*

US Environmental Protection Agency, Office of Water, Office of Wetlands, Oceans, and Watersheds. "Chronology of Section 404(c) Actions." Accessed February 8, 2012. http://water.epa.gov/lawsregs/guidance/wetlands/404c.cfm.

US Environmental Protection Agency, Office of Wetlands, Oceans, and Watersheds. "Ski Resorts Pledge to Protect Environment," Nonpoint Source News Notes. Last modified December 2000 Accessed February 8, 2012. http://water.epa.gov/polwaste/nps/outreach/upload/2003_03_31_info_NewsNotes_pdf_63_issue.pdf.

US Environmental Protection Agency, Office of Wetlands, Oceans, and Watersheds, "Golf Courses are Getting Greener," Nonpoint Source News Notes. Last modified December 2000. Retrieved February 8, 2012. http://water.epa.gov/polwaste/nps/outreach/upload/2003_03_31_info_NewsNotes_pdf_63_issue.pdf.

US Environmental Protection Agency, Office of Wetlands, Oceans, and Watersheds. "Protecting and Restoring America's Watersheds: Status, Trends and Initiative in Watershed Management." Last modified July 2003 EPA-840-R-00-001.

US Environmental Protection Agency, and US Department of Agriculture. "Clean Water Act; Vice President's Initiatives." Last modified November 7, 1997. Accessed February 8, 2012. https://federalregister.gov/a/97-29592.

US Environmental Protection Agency, and US Department of Agriculture. February, 1998. "Clean Water Action Plan Restoring and Protecting America's Water Resources." Publication EPA-840-R-98-001.

Wayland, Robert H. III. "Testimony of Director, Office of Wetlands, Oceans, and Watersheds, U. S. Environmental Protection Agency Before the Committee on Government Reform, U.S. House of Representatives." Last Modified October 6, 2000. Accessed February 8, 2012. http://www.epa.gov/ocir/hearings/testimony/106_1999_2000/100600rw.pdf.

Wayland, Robert, Davis, Michael, "Memorandum to the Field Subject: Appropriate Level of Analysis Required for Evaluating Compliance with the Section 404(b)(1) Guidelines Alternatives Requirements." Last modified August 24, 1993. Retrieved February 8, 2012. http://water.epa.gov/lawsregs/guidance/wetlands/flexible.cfm.

White House Office on Environmental Policy. "*Protecting America's Wetlands: A Fair Flexible, and Effective Approach*". Last modified August 24, 1993.

Chapter Six

Taking the Franchising Route to Solve an Environmental Problem

Ronald Brand

"The Hatfields, an average American family, lived in Canob Park, Rhode Island, about twelve miles from Providence. In 1980, this family had a big problem—they could not use their tap water. They couldn't drink it, bathe in it, or cook with it. Their well was contaminated with gasoline that migrated from the neighborhood gas station, just a quarter of a mile from their house."

Three years later "buried gasoline tanks gained the national spotlight, when *60 Minutes* released its investigative report, "Check the Water." That report revealed that "others . . . were in the same situation—gasoline leaking from underground storage tanks was contaminating their drinking water" (U.S. EPA 2004, 5)

"That report and similar stories" led Congress to pass legislation requiring the U.S. Environmental Protection Agency (EPA) "to develop a comprehensive regulatory program for underground storage tanks storing petroleum and certain hazardous substances."

What did this mean for EPA? It had to deal with an estimated 2 million underground storage tanks (USTs). These tanks were at 750,000 sites, located in 3,000 counties and 56 states and territories (U.S. EPA 1989). These places included gas stations, convenience stores, government installations, trucking companies and military bases. It was estimated that from 5 to 35 percent of the tanks were leaking. The leaks were occurring throughout the tank system, from the pump to the piping and connectors, and from the tank itself. EPA quickly assembled a task force of about seven people from within the Office of Solid Waste and Emergency Response (OSWER). OSWER ran two major programs, Superfund and Hazardous Waste. These programs were experienced at writing regulations and had about 3,000 people to inspect polluted sites, develop clean-up plans, and enforce compliance with the requirements. They also worked with and utilized state resources for sites that did not require direct federal participation. Where and how would this new tank effort fit in? To get started the task force worked on developing regulations that would require all owners and operators of tanks to register their tanks with the states. This helped to determine where all the tanks were, and registration fees would help to fund state programs.

At that time I was asked to meet with the EPA administrator. He explained the need to create a program to deal with the USTs. After discussion, he offered me the job of developing and heading up the program. I later learned he had discussed the job earlier with two experienced EPA program chiefs. Both declined tackling it, feeling that the resources allocated were not adequate for the magnitude of the problem. They were especially concerned about the staffing proposed for the program. The allocation was forty-five positions at headquarters and about forty-five people distributed among the ten regional offices. Viewed from the traditional way EPA shaped and ran its programs they were right. Despite this, I agreed to head up the UST program.

I have been asked why I chose to accept the position of heading the program in view of the dire picture laid out by other experienced program managers. Years of reviewing and evaluating EPA programs and proposed initiatives provided me with a unique view of what approaches were effective and what management and strategy choices caused programs to have severe problems or limited their success. This gave me confidence that I could do better.

Working for the Agency's deputy administrator gave me insights into the issues involved in dealing with Congress, the Office of Management and Budget, and environmental and industry groups. I was sensitive to the way these groups frequently made the program managers veer off their main course. As a result they managed in response to incidents rather than maintaining their focus on their planned strategy for accomplishing the program's purpose.

I was also responding to a new challenge. My experience as a staff analyst and advisor to the leaders who ran the Agency and its programs led me to believe I could avoid some of their mistakes and that I would have the courage to do things differently.

In retrospect, I did not appreciate the difficulties we were to face. I had just completed two years as an assistant to the deputy administrator of EPA. Before that I was director of the Program Evaluation Division for the Agency. In those jobs I had participated in the review of most of the agency's programs. That work gave me insights into what worked and didn't work. Like most people in staff positions I had been "adviser to the king." So, of course, I had visions of how things could be done better, if I were in charge.

We then received three valuable gifts. First, the administrator said, "Don't do this like our existing programs! I don't know how to do it, but you have to do it differently."

Second, he told me, "We are going to create a separate office for you to develop and operate the UST program."

The third gift came from another senior EPA manager, who warned, "Don't take your problems to the twelfth floor (the administrator's office). If you do, they will try to solve them and you won't like the answers." Having seen many "shoot from the hip" responses from staff serving various EPA administrators over the years, I valued his advice and followed it rigorously.

As a member of the Senior Executive Service it was my job to translate a general legislative charge on USTs into an operating program to deal with the actual, physical problems of locating two million tanks, detecting leaks, cleaning up product in soils and water, and preventing future leaks. In this chapter you will find a description of some of the issues we confronted and the decisions we made within the broad mandate provided by the legislation and the EPA Administrator.

The three major efforts that shaped our program in its early years, were:

1. *Adopting the private sector franchise model for our organization.* We recognized the similarity we faced in having to effectively reach and manage a program involving a large number of local owners and operators, at thousands of locations, through field organizations in the fifty states.
2. *Building a national program.* We realized that organizations and individuals at many levels, from state programs to industry associations to tank and equipment manufacturers to individual tank owners, would have to be actively engaged in solving the problem of leaking tanks.
3. *Finding a management approach to make it work.* We had to identify and incorporate new values, methods and a common language in all our activities from regulation development to support of state programs.

In addition to describing these efforts I will demonstrate how we were constantly challenged to remain consistent in countless daily decisions so that the Office of Underground Storage Tanks (OUST) and its suppliers and customers could accomplish our program's purpose to protect the environment. My purpose here is not to persuade you to adopt franchising or some other mode of organizing for your program or to adopt Total Quality Management (discussed later in this paper) as a methodology for your work. However, the basic principles of these approaches are valid for any organization or type of work. For example, many managers face the need to provide support to their field agents. Also, managers in most organizations are confronted with arbitrary numerical targets set for their programs.

TAKING A DIFFERENT PATH—FROM MCDONALD'S TO TANKS

It was spring 1985. We were assembled in a windowless, conference room in a hotel in Rosslyn, Virginia, thirty minutes from our office in Washington, DC. Seated around the room were our ten UST regional representatives and about seven people from our headquarters staff. Facing them, in front of the room, were regional managers from McDonald's, Century 21, 7-Eleven Stores, and ServiceMaster, Inc. Although their products or services differed, each of these private sector corporations had successfully built a nationwide system for managing thousands of locations.

Our regional UST representatives were dubious. What, they wondered, could these franchise guys know that would help us in our work in EPA and the state UST programs?

At the same time the franchise representatives were curious about how their experience and knowledge could possibly be of assistance to EPA. Before the day-long meeting was over, both questions were answered.

How did we arrive at this place, at this time? Faced with the size of the job to be done and the resources available we realized that the traditional model of organizing could not be applied. During my career in public service, I learned to look at private industry for methods for carrying out programs. For example, I learned from assembly line methods in manufacturing and applied them to processing thousands of grant applications. In many cases there are private sector groups that do work similar to public sector activity (or to a portion of it), and they are pretty good at what they do. You need to be aggressive and imaginative in seeking comparable functions that may help in your government program. In the tank program, we had to develop common policies and processes, effectively communicate them, and get them incorporated into daily operations at thousands of locations. Our analysis and benchmarking showed franchise type organizations to be a good fit for the tasks we faced.

I explained to the group why we were considering using a franchise model for the UST program. EPA would serve as the franchiser, with the franchisees being the state programs. "What", I asked, "were the realities of working in this way?" In response, each franchiser rep stood up and gave a fifteen- to twenty-minute presentation of his company's system and its operation.

Our UST people, regional and headquarters, then dove right in asking:
"How do you measure performance?"
"What do you do with franchisees who perform poorly?"
"How do you train workers, managers?"
"How do you find ideas for new methods or services?"
"How do you incorporate changes in the franchises?"
"What is headquarters' role as related to the franchisees?"

An intense discussion followed. Both groups became more collaborative as they began to see the similarities between our government program and their franchise business practices. There were three major lessons that impressed us and had a lasting effect on our UST program design and execution.

Most important was the strong admonition, *"There are no cash registers at headquarters! All results occur in the field." "Your job as franchiser,"* they went on to say, *"is to support the field."* This advice made a lasting impression on all of us.

The next insight they offered surprised us, conflicting as it did with the high esteem we had for our own creativity. The franchisers all agreed that new ideas on ways to increase sales, lower costs, improve profits and create new programs flow in a continuous stream from the best franchisees. *Most innovations come from the field, not from headquarters.* They advised that the role of headquarters in the franchise is primarily to search out, identify, evaluate and disseminate the best ideas to the rest of the franchisees.

Finally, the franchisers emphasized that the key to improving the franchise is to *"constantly lift the performance of the bottom franchisees."* Poor performers drag down the results achieved by the rest of the organization. They can drastically harm the reputation of the entire franchise. So the franchisers all invest extra attention, help and support on the trailing performers. This, too, contrasted with normal practice in many of EPA's programs. It was more interesting and more fun to visit the best performing states where exciting things were going on.

PUTTING OUR FRANCHISING INTO PRACTICE.

In the weeks following the meeting with the franchisers their concepts, methods and vocabulary began to enter and permeate our organization. For example, we changed our organization chart to an inverted pyramid. We, the national UST program, were at the bottom. The regions, states, and vendors were above us. At the top were the tank owners. Our purpose was to illustrate that everyone's job was to support the people above them so as to bring about a change in behavior by the tank owners. The owners were the ultimate customers of our processes. We needed them to test their tanks, find and correct the leaks and damage to soil and water, and to purchase tanks meeting the higher standards. The owners had to decide to spend $50,000 to $100,000 or more, with no increase in their revenues from the investment.

Adopting the franchising philosophy affected what we did and how we did it. For example, up to that time, all our available work hours, dollars and effort were devoted to development of regulations. No other projects were undertaken. We felt pressured because our legislation required us to develop regulations. Our staff protested that this work needed to be done first and then we could work on building the state programs. However, our interaction with the private sector franchisees made us recognize that if the states were going to be ready to carry out the regulations, we had to work with them from the outset. So we set up a State Programs Branch with a starting staff of two people.

Building the franchiser-franchisee relationship became a major part of our work. Whenever someone proposed an idea to apply to the states, individuals would ask, "Is this going to help the franchisee or are we adding unnecessary work?"

We began to develop tools to help all of our support team and customers, from state agency personnel to vendors providing services that tank owners needed in order to comply with the regulations. We created publications like "Musts for USTs," "Dollars and Sense," and a manual on "Interim Prohibition: Guidance for Design and Installation of USTs." (Of course, this was before the Internet, Facebook, email, and YouTube were created to help in this type of work.)

Our staff began to furnish some materials for Spanish-speaking tank owners and operators not proficient in English to help them to understand and comply with the regulations. Other EPA programs also provided publications for these audiences. What was different, in my opinion, was our recognition that our job was to help everyone who was a link in the chain to achieve compliance with the law and regulations. Our communications staff insisted on making our documents or videos user friendly, not bureaucratic, jargon-laden products. They used humor in illustrations and text, and their plain English standards even affected our published regulations.

We supported the development and publication of a quarterly publication on UST issues, titled *L.U.S.T.LINE*. (LUST became an easily remembered acronym for the program, with the *L* standing for Leaking.) It was edited and published by the New England Interstate Water Pollution Control Commission (L.U.S.T.LINE 1985). Containing articles on technical, legislative, training and enforcement issues, it was widely read by state program staffs, tank owners, environmental groups and companies serving the industry. Although its content was serious, the writing and illustrations were informal and included a dose of humor. It has proven its value in that it continues to serve the field twenty-seven years later.

Borrowing an idea from the franchisers we held an annual, three-day national conference for the state programs. It focused on problems and solutions. Although we had seen similar conferences conducted by other EPA programs, those agendas were usually set by the federal program, federal officials chaired the panels, and the topics were frequently bureaucratic rather than practical.

By contrast, the CEO of Century 21 said that at similar meetings for their franchisees, "The franchisees establish the agenda because every franchisee across the country can contact his or her national representative with any question that he or she wants answered. 'Why aren't we doing this?' Why are we doing that?', and so forth." He also said, "We address every one of those questions" (Shook and Shook 1993).

We went further. To insure that the conference was directly useful to our franchisees, we had each session or panel at the meeting chaired by a state person rather than an EPA staffer. This achieved two purposes. First, the topics were those of most concern to the franchisees. Second, the discussions focused on the "real work" and not bureaucratic rules and paperwork.

DO YOU REALLY MEAN IT?

We wanted our regional representatives to visit each of their states at least once a month so that they could establish close relationships with our state franchisees. We felt this was necessary to get the franchising concepts to sink in. Other programs traditionally visited once a quarter. To back this up we provided a larger than usual travel allocation for our representatives.

However, a veteran regional program chief advised us that once the travel funds got to the region, the regional administrator (RA), who is responsible for all EPA programs in the region, decided where he would use the money. From the RA's viewpoint, we were providing too much money for travel for the UST representatives, so they allocated it to other programs they deemed more important. Obviously, they were not buying into the UST program's need to visit the states more frequently than EPA did in other programs.

We were pressing our regional representatives to travel to the states. The money to do this was not reaching them through the normal route. If we meant what we said, how would we overcome this barrier? We wanted to use headquarters travel money to enable them to do more state travel. We would not continue to send additional travel money directly to the regions. Instead, we began paying for other types of regional travel from headquarters funds. In that way the UST representatives did not have to pay for travel to national meetings, training, and technical work groups from their regional allocation.

It freed up their money for visits to the states. It also demonstrated that we *really meant it* when we said we wanted our representatives to get out to the franchisee's locations.

NO PLAN B

As we went all out developing and implementing a franchise model for working with the states, some of our own staff raised the "yellow caution flag."

They said, "What if the states don't choose to take on the federal program, or are inadequately prepared to implement it?" Our response was, *"There will be no work done on a Plan B."* This was based on a lesson I learned early in my career. *If you want to succeed, you need to burn your bridges behind you.* That way there is no alternative but to make your ideas work. To make it clear that we were serious about this approach we defined what we would *not* do. In a publication we issued, we said:

"Perhaps the best way to begin defining EPA's responsibilities is to say what the Regional Offices will not be doing:

- They won't run the UST program for the state.
- They won't dictate behavior at the state level.
- They won't second-guess individual state decisions." (U.S. EPA 1989)

This might appear a high-risk approach. But it seemed to me that we had three things going for this approach for the UST Program.

First, state agencies and fire departments had been handling these problems and would continue to do so, even if they didn't decide to become a franchisee. Second, owners and operators would press their states to take on the program so that they would be eligible for insurance or federal trust funds if clean-up was needed at their sites. Third, EPA's history revealed that it was very rare for EPA to step in to directly run programs in place of the state.

In fact, in 2010, twenty-five years later, there were still sixteen states to whom the UST program has not been officially delegated. They were not backward or poorly performing state programs since New York, California, and Oregon were among their number. They were not delegated because of differences in their technical or legal requirements. However, they were all finding and detecting leaking tanks, getting clean-ups done and applying federal regulations (and sometimes stricter state rules) to their tank owners. Through the use of cooperative agreements and other legal devices the program has continued to find a way to work with them in the franchise mode.

THE STATES COME UP WITH CREATIVE SOLUTIONS

The federal legislation limited us to regulating the owners and operators of tanks. A number of states, however, were free to regulate anywhere in the process, from tank installation to fuel leaks at the pump.

As the industry franchisers predicted, the states, like other franchisees, kept coming up with innovative ways to implement the program. For example, one state chose to regulate the fuel distributors, making it illegal to fill fuel tanks that did not carry the red tag indicating that the tank had been registered. There were a lot fewer distributors than tank owners so this helped in enforcement.

Another state created the equivalent of a traffic ticket for owners who failed to register their tanks. They could challenge the ticket in court or pay the fine. Unless they registered their tanks the owners would accumulate tickets and fines. We were surprised when one state reported using state police officers to check on whether or not tanks were registered. That certainly got the attention of the owners and operators. Another state put a program in place that required that any sale or transfer of ownership of a station or store with gas tanks had to show that the tanks were registered and that they were not leaking. These varied approaches were broadcast to the entire network of state and local agencies in a number of different ways including *L.U.S.TLines*, regional representatives in visits to states, and our annual conference. These ideas are considered normal now, but they were unusual in the mid-1980s.

GETTING THE CONGRESS AND BUDGET OFFICE TO BUY INTO THE FRANCHISING APPROACH

During this formative period, a congressional hearing was scheduled. It opened with a senator querying a state UST program director, "How is this franchising thing working out for you?" The state director gave a strong endorsement of the UST franchise approach. Program chiefs from three other states also responded positively.

The senator, somewhat skeptical, said to me, "Well, Mr. Brand, you must have selected your best supporters to be here."

"No, sir," I replied, "Your committee staff invited them. We had no idea who was to be here today."

We were heartened by the use and acceptance of the franchising frame of reference we had fostered. It also increased our credibility within EPA.

A similar event occurred at the Office of Management and Budget. Early in the program's existence we met with the senior examiner at OMB. I started by spelling out the framework we were creating, a program focus on groundwater protection, a franchise approach for dealing with the state programs, and the use of Total Quality Management (TQM) methods for doing our work.

I did not talk about numbers, such as dollars for grants or operations, or personnel. The examiner delved into the concepts, and we had a thorough discussion on our methods for tackling two million tanks at 750,000 sites. This went on for an hour. When we did get to the budget numbers, dollars, and staffing requests, they became secondary because they flowed from the program philosophy and design. When asked about how many cooperative agreements we would complete, or the number of tanks that would be registered, or the number of enforcement actions that would be taken, I said, "We don't know." We said we would track and report progress, but we could not predict what would happen. Clearly, such a response would have been unacceptable if we had not discussed our use in our management approach of Deming's principle of not setting *numerical targets, quotas, or goals* but focusing on *"continual improvement"* (Deming 1982, 36).

This meeting set the relationship with the examiner, and his subsequent queries and concerns reflected a thorough understanding of our approach. I also learned an important lesson. The examiner was concerned about explaining and defending his recommendations on the program to his bosses. So all we could do to bolster his knowledge and understanding helped him to help us.

ASSURING FIELD EXPERIENCES ARE REFLECTED IN THE REGULATIONS

While this work on building the franchises was going on, a major part of our work and staff was devoted to developing and issuing regulations. These related to quality of tanks required, leak detection methods, corrective action requirements, and use of federal trust funds. This involved in depth studies of scientific issues, such as "How do gasoline plumes from leaking tanks travel through soils and water?" and "What levels of leaks from tanks can be detected by the various leak detection devices or processes?"

This was difficult, intensive work. It involved groups from inside EPA and state, industry, environmental and standards setting groups outside the agency. But this was EPA's normal work and its strength. What was different in the Office of Underground Storage Tanks (OUST) was the early involvement of, and constant concern for, the users of the regulations from the outset of the regulation development process. We constantly learned from each other during the regulation development process. Experts from the state programs, oil companies, industry associations, standard setting groups, our regional offices, and our headquarters regulation development staff discussed, debated and considered data and experiences that went into shaping the regulations.

From my observations in the agency it often appeared that EPA followed industry practice. In a given company the designer would create a product or service, then "toss it over the wall" to manufacturing to make it, and then manufacturing would "toss it over the wall" to sales. Then sales would be told to go and sell it. All this went on with little or no contact with each other or with the direct users of the product. Then they watched sales fail.

A senior analyst with experience in other parts of EPA who then joined OUST said, "I've never seen the intense attention to making sure that the regulations are written in plain English." We were all convinced that if people could understand the regulations and guidance documents they were more likely to comply with them.

OUST's success in accomplishing this was brought home to me when I was in the St. Louis airport, returning from a conference. One of the conference attendees, a stranger to me, stopped me to say, "I want to thank you for the charts on pages 16 and 17, in MUSTS FOR USTS (U.S. EPA 1988). They are really easy to use and helpful." He was referring to was two tables that showed what you need to do and when you need to do it. I couldn't wait to get back to pass that feedback on to our communications staff who developed the publication.

Many people did not understand our franchising approach and some were critical of it. I remember vividly being approached by a veteran EPA regional program chief at a meeting of senior EPA executives in Baltimore, Maryland. He declared angrily, "You and your franchising are killing EPA." This was indicative of the suspicion and fear that others felt about the radically different approach we were taking. Our method of dealing with these obstacles was to avoid asking for permission or approval as much as possible. Also we developed our processes by first looking at the actual work to be done in the field, and only later considering any apparent constraints, such as legal, legislative or administrative limitations.

CARVING OUT A NEW WAY TO LEAD

Franchising provided us with a different organizational approach and a focus on building state programs. But how could we improve the way we did our work, daily, monthly and yearly? Serendipitously, in early 1985, I discovered

Mary Walton's book, *The Deming Management Method* (Walton 1986). Based on her description of work done at a New Hampshire company, I participated in a three-day training session in Nashua, New Hampshire. This was my first exposure to the teachings of Deming. In my previous work evaluating EPA programs I frequently observed two weak links: (1) the level of abstraction at which issues were discussed, and (2) the unchallenged acceptance of constraints—whether legal, financial, or past practice. Deming's focus on the "real work and workers" and his "war on quotas and targets" would help us move in a different direction in management.

Returning to DC, I persuaded and pushed our managers and staff into accepting that we all had to get trained in applying Deming's methods. With franchising we obviously had to operate differently than EPA had in the past. I felt that learning and using Deming's principles would help us to achieve our purpose. In a series of three-day sessions we trained all our headquarters and regional people in what I will generically refer to as Total Quality Management (TQM).

I recognize that some have given TQM a bad reputation, by taking short cuts, promoting "rah-rah" events, focusing on results instead of on improving processes, and even assigning numerical goals. When I use TQM in this paper, I am referring to Dr. Deming's basic principles as spelled out in his Fourteen Points (Deming 1986). Those principles still apply and are valid, despite misuse by some organizations.

We also invited our internal suppliers and customers to participate, including staffers from the Grants, Budget, Legal, and Assistant Administrator's Offices. We even cajoled our boss, the assistant administrator, and his staff to get exposed to the principles taught by Deming by participating in a one-day session. What did we learn in this training effort? The people doing the real work know the obstacles and barriers they face in trying to do the job right. So you have to have contact with the real workers, and you have to "drive out fear" so workers will let you know what those obstacles are. If you want tanks installed properly, talk to and observe installers and inspectors at work. As one experienced practitioner in applying quality programs puts it; "The only people who really understand the hands-on-operation of a micro-process (inputs, events, and outputs) are the ones who perform the process every day. They are usually the only ones *not* involved in coming up with solutions (Lareau 1991, 61). The next principles flowed directly from Deming's work. You must "create constancy of purpose toward improvement of product or service. Don't use numbers, numerical goals. Substitute leadership" (Deming 1986). Finally, we learned that you increase productivity by removing complexity, wasted time and effort, and rework (the need to do something over or extra because it wasn't done right the first time), and by improving the processes that make up your program. Of course, along with these principles we learned to use the tools of quality management such as flow charting processes, using Pareto charts to disclose what our priorities should be, and fishbone diagrams to identify causes of problems (Ishikawa 1985). At this stage we were not using the statistical tools needed to determine and analyze variation, although we were exposed to them. Understanding the importance of eliminating management by numbers was to prove especially valuable, as it helped us to withstand pressures to predict results and to avoid setting unrealistic goals.

One of the most striking things demonstrated to us was that organizations spend 25 percent to 50 percent of their time and resources on work that does not add value for their customers. That really shook us up. For us, 25 percent of our ninety work years meant that at least 22.5 work years of effort were going to non-value added work.

Of course, we were defensive about our own work. But focusing on the definition of "value added" work made us all constantly ask, "Does what we are doing help our customers do their work more easily, less expensively, more quickly, or with less rework?" Two early examples illustrate how these ideas invaded our existing culture. One of our section chiefs developed a route slip to accompany written materials being routed to others (this was during the ancient days, in the 1980s, when we still circulated information on paper). The terms used on the route slip and an explanation of each are shown below.

> *Value Added*—work that adds value for our customers, a clear guidance document or regulation, an answer to a problem in the field, simplifying processes
>
> *Necessary, But Not Value Added*—travel authorizations, administrative paperwork, required reports for personnel and budget
>
> *Rework*—needing to do things over again, for example, receiving and returning calls because of unclear instructions or confusing forms or regulations
>
> *Unnecessary Work*—preparing data that serve no program purpose just to meet an outside requirement
>
> *Not Working*—workers are ready to work, but system prevents them from doing so; that is, computers down, meeting room not available, a seven-person task force waiting for the boss to arrive so they can get started—(think about it—seven people x twenty minutes = two hours and twenty minutes wasted)

It was amazing how much our daily transactions changed as each one was filtered through this simple, self-screening device. People were usually honest in designating the appropriate category on the route slip.

As a management team we were put to an early test of our newly learned principles. Three analysts asked to meet with us. They started by asking for *amnesty*. This was a term we had learned in our training, meaning, "don't shoot the messenger for telling you the truth." They proceeded to demonstrate that a weekly status report they prepared for us was "unnecessary work." They went on to say "We never get feedback on the report, and it doesn't help us to get 'value added' work done." We were surprised and reacted defensively. The ensuing discussion showed that the analysts were right. Before TQM our response would have been to continue the report but to put a team on revising it. Now, our response was, "Stop doing the report, immediately. Don't waste another hour on it." As issues arose, the discussions or debates involved frequent use of flow charts, fishbone or Ishikawa diagrams and Pareto charts (Ishikawa 1985). This helped shorten meetings. Previously there were general discussions where it was difficult to understand what the problem was and to focus on a solution. With the use of the flow charts and other tools we realized exactly what part of the work was being questioned and where it fit into the total process. This resulted in elimination of much extraneous discussion.

Of course, sometimes we went overboard with our newfound methods. After one meeting to review a proposal, I asked why the team had prepared various charts. They seemed to have a specific problem and a simple, good solution. "Well, Ron," they said, "Actually we solved the problem without the charts, but we thought you would want to see charts." Egads! I was the cause of a new form of waste!

In speaking with former colleagues and industry personnel, some twenty years later, they still spoke of the constant emphasis we put on always using "plain English" to ensure that our materials were understandable. That stemmed from the realization that whenever we weren't absolutely clear on what was required or desired, we were creating lots of rework for everyone involved with our regulated population. This included our regional UST staff, state program personnel, vendors of equipment and services needed to meet our requirements, and the tank owner or operator. One vague word, phrase or illustration could create an avalanche of calls throughout the system.

ELIMINATING NUMERICAL TARGETS, GOALS, QUOTAS

An area that brought us into direct conflict with the established ways of doing business at EPA was dealing with estimates, predictions, targets and goals. We learned to avoid them if possible. More importantly we made sure not to inflict them on ourselves. This is based on Deming's admonition "to eliminate numerical goals for people" (Deming 1986, 75).

The basis for Deming's approach to targets, and so on, is that "numerical goals set for other people, without a road map to reach the goal, have effects opposite to the effects sought" (Deming 1986). Here is an example that shows how this occurs. In an environmental program they may have made a range of from fifty to seventy grants a year, for the past three years. Now that range is the level at which the system presently operates; unless the system is changed. Without change to the system, we should anticipate results in a range of about fifty to seventy items completed. But what usually happens? Congress, the Budget Office, the agency head's staff, decide they need to achieve more, and so they set a new target of ninety-five for the coming year. They don't change anything else or make only minor changes in resources. The person or group setting the new target wants, needs and hopes the new target will be achieved. Deming says, "Hopes, without a method to achieve them, will remain mere hopes." Elsewhere, he goes on to say, "I have yet to see a quota that includes any trace of a system by which to help anyone to do a better job."

Frequently a program chief or program personnel set higher numerical goals for their work because they feel it is expected of them. "Internal goals set in the management of a company, without a method, are a burlesque." Or, as Lloyd S. Nelson points out, "If they can do it next year with no plan, why didn't they do it last year? They must have been goofing off. And if one can accomplish improvement of 3 percent with no plan, why not 6 percent?" (Deming 1982, 75).

What are the usual tools used to foster achieving the new target? Well, for a start, the creators of the new target make sure to get it into the budget, the annual plan, and even into an individual's performance criteria. They also send out a memo from the boss, ordering or telling everyone to work harder. But they ignore the fact that programs are made up of processes, and significant and lasting change comes from improving those processes.

What happens when goals are set by people who don't have to do the work? Many of us are familiar with the contracts, or purchasing, or grants offices that are overloaded in the last quarter of the year. In order to meet the deadlines they work long hours, take short cuts and process 50 percent of the years totals in the last quarter. They make their numbers, but at what cost? Fatigue and pressure creates more errors. Items pushed out and counted as complete, come back to haunt them as rework in the following year. Both the supplier and the customer have rework, delays in their programs and great frustration for all. What can the individual worker do? He or she is operating within the system they have been given by management.

Another consequence of targets set without a method for achieving them is that it makes liars out of honest people. For example, a new program was established at EPA. It involved developing cooperative agreements between EPA and local government, non-profit, state or industry groups. At the start someone announced a goal of awarding fifty projects in the first year. Where this figure came from or what it was based on, no one knew. As the months passed it became clear that a variety of problems that normally arise in any new venture, were more difficult and complex than had been foreseen. More likely they were not even considered because the person setting the goal of fifty project awards did not consult with the people who had to do the work. Faced with failing to meet the target set, the target was changed, but not the number, fifty. Instead, what was being counted was changed, for example, from "projects awarded" to "projects approved" to "project applications reviewed." How did this make the people feel who were working hard to accomplish the work? They realized that the leadership was "playing games." And more importantly, all the work they did to get the program up and running was discounted because they did not meet the arbitrary numerical goal set by people without knowledge of the real work.

In another case I was asked to address a group of executives in a federal agency on the reasons for not setting numerical targets or goals without a plan or method for achieving them. The public service executives were involved in a program that had projects that took years to complete.

The projects involved calling for and getting bids, public comment periods in various communities and legal disputes over who would pay for the site evaluations and removal of toxic substances, sometimes with millions of dollars involved. The day after I explained the rationale for not setting numerical targets on hope alone, I received a call from one of the participants. He said, "I thought you would like to know the result of your talk yesterday. The boss sent out a memo today requiring that we finish sixty projects this year." Please note, that except for the number set, no other changes were made in the system. This is typical of the management solution that says the boss only has to order, "work harder, work smarter," and things will improve.

> Can you do anything about this in your organization? I believe you can.
> The thing you and your people have as an advantage is that you know the real work.

Here is an example from our UST work. In the early days of the program funds were appropriated for use in state programs. We had to develop and complete cooperative agreements to get the funds to the states. We had ninety days to get this done before the end of the fiscal year.

The system (Congress, Budget Office, Administrator's Office, etc.) pressed us to tell them how many agreements we would complete by the deadline. We never gave them a number. Why? Because we had no basis for predicting what the process of making agreements would deliver. More importantly we realized that setting a target would not help get the task accomplished and could do harm.

First, we roughly flow-charted and explained the process. States had to create a program, and then get approval from their budget, personnel, grants and legal people. In some states it required changes in their authorizing legislation. Each state differed in their processes, and their capacity to accomplish this work. On what basis would we set a target for completions, and how would the target help to accomplish this?

In addition, our regional UST representatives had a similar gauntlet to run in order to get the EPA portion of the agreements done. They had to get clearance from finance, grants, and legal specialists in the region. Since we were a small program within EPA, these reviewers felt they had more important items to work on and so our requests languished. These offices already had a plethora of numerical targets to meet, so adding another would not solve our problem.

Then, an OUST staffer started sending out a weekly progress report to the regions. It consisted of a map showing the states in each region. States where cooperative agreements had been signed were shown in color, with the other states left blank. This map was sent to the regional administrators in all ten regions without any comment or exhortation on our part.

Surprisingly, as the regional administrators saw their regions trailing their peers, they began exerting their influence to get more agreements done. In the end about two-thirds of the states completed agreements by the deadline. The question remains, how could we have determined a realistic and useful target and how would it have helped the states and regions get the job done better?

Finally, if we were forced to set a target, considering the difficulty of the process for completing cooperative agreements, we would have selected a much lower number. Once the system achieved that number we would have congratulated ourselves and relaxed. That is what Deming means when he decries numerical targets and goals as limiting. In our UST experience we saw this play out again and again, as we worked at continually improving processes which resulted in accomplishments beyond any number we would have set or predicted.

It may be that the targets and goals required to be set by the Government Performance and Results Act, in recent years, have made it more difficult to work in this way. However, discussion with a few current program managers gives me the impression that they are finding ways to keep the numerical goals from driving their programs.

FREEING YOUR ORGANIZATION FROM CONVENTIONS

"A convention may be defined as something which a number of men have agreed to accept in lieu of the truth and to pass off for the truth upon others" (Quiller-Couch 1928, 92). We kept finding conventions related to numerical standards, targets, and goals. Here are two examples. First, at EPA we were sometimes burdened by our scientific legacy. This meant that at times we invested excessive time and resources to discover or calculate a more precise figure than was needed to implement the program. This frequently involved unnecessary debates and defense of our numbers. In the UST area, a much-debated question was, "What percent of tanks were leaking or had leaked?" The fuel industry claimed that "only" 5 percent leaked, our estimates were 35 percent. After much "pulling and tugging" on the issue, I realized that for our purposes it didn't matter, and we stopped investing in prediction.

In an interview I did at the time, I explained, "We don't know how many tanks are leaking; there are all kinds of theories, guesses, and so on, but we'll find out" over time. "If it's 5 percent, then it's 100,000 tanks and if it's 20 percent—which is a mid-range guess—that's 400,000 tanks . . . and I say, 'Look, does it matter? If it's only 5 per cent, does it mean we don't have a problem? And if it's any number larger than that, *what would we do differently?* We've still got to get out there and find them and clean them up.'" (Groundwater Management Review 1987).

The other example involved setting a standard for leak-detection devices or methods. Our proposed regulation called for detection methods to be capable of detecting leaks of .05 gallons per hour (about two-thirds of a cup).

We questioned whether this could be done, consistently, in the field, testing existing tanks. Working with the EPA Research Division a test was set up involving two tanks at EPA's Edison, New Jersey laboratory. Twenty-seven companies involved in testing tanks were invited to participate in the test. We were surprised when the tests showed that none of the vendors demonstrated the ability to detect .05 gallons per hour (gph) leaks, reliably and consistently. The vendors did not challenge the findings.

Now, what were we to do? Up to that point an unspoken agreement existed among everyone involved. That is, the petroleum industry, state environmental programs, EPA, all acted as though what was desired (the ability to find leaks of .05 gph) was real.

A few weeks later, someone who ran a leak-detection company in California, called me at 8 a.m. (5 a.m. his time). In a worried tone he said, "I don't know what to do. Our state regulations require me to certify that my methods meet the .05 gph standard in order for me to contract with tank owners to install my equipment. But your tests at Edison say I don't meet that standard. What should I do?"

Since the states were finding lots of tanks that had leaked hundreds or even thousands of gallons of fuel, I knew we needed every resource possible to help locate and stop those leaks. So, I said, "We need you out there detecting all those leaks, especially the big ones. Just keep doing what you have been doing. Our test results are still being analyzed and are not an official standard yet." We acted in accord with Ishikawa's dictum that "No matter how many national standards are established, unless production can meet the quality standards these standards are rendered meaningless" (Ishikawa 1985).

We refused to go along with the conventional practice. Instead, our regulations specified leak detection to .2 gph that could be achieved. However, we committed ourselves, the lab and the vendors to working at developing improved methods to reliably and consistently achieve the desired .05 gph detection capability, through research and competition among vendors. This improvement took place over time and the standard is now .02 gph.

Because numerical targets can so shape or distort work efforts, it is an area that the leader must constantly monitor. An interesting example illustrating this comes from Howard Schultz, President of Starbucks Corporation (Schultz 2011, 90).

Schultz had two reasons for doing this. First, using comps ignored the significant revenues from sales of "packaged whole-bean coffee in grocery stores or beverage sales at . . . counters in supermarkets and bookstores and airports." This resulted in understating the company's projected earnings. More significantly, he was concerned that store managers were focusing so much on showing improved comps, that they were introducing products and practices that were counter to the basic core of their business. Finally, he says, "We will transform the company internally by being true to our coffee core and for doing what is best for our customers, not what will boost our comps."

IDENTIFYING AND IMPROVING A SYSTEM PROBLEM

Feedback from our regional representatives, franchisees, and suppliers disclosed a major problem in the system. State UST agencies and the tank owners in their states had to call on service contractors to identify, diagnose, and develop corrective action plans for leaking tanks. This involved a lot of paperwork on everyone's part. Contractors had to prepare proposals, submit action plans and progress reports, and document actions taken or completed.

We found that consultants were frequently "guessing" at what various states wanted in the work to be done at the site, and in the paperwork to initiate or complete a corrective action. This also increased the cost to the tank owner whom we were trying to get to comply. The result was rework and increased costs throughout the process. As Deming points out, everyone was just trying to do their best (Deming 1982).

A two-person team at headquarters, OUST, working in concert with our regional representatives created a "Consultants Day." When states showed an interest, we helped them plan a day when consultants and firms interested in bidding on detection or clean-up work could meet with state personnel. During this step we would work with the state personnel to identify and flow chart the steps in their processes for review and approval of various items. Often this revealed that there was no agreed upon process for different aspects of the work.

At that point we helped the state lay out the steps in the process, bring the various players together to agree on the flowchart created, and recognize the workload likely to hit them. There were times when we had to introduce the various state people to each other as the state group involved people from environmental, finance, legal and laboratory units. The more we did this the more we were able to build our expertise on the processes involved. This enabled us to fulfill our franchiser role of disseminating best practices.

As a result, states laid out their requirements, provided written forms and formats, and gave guidance so that the contractors could understand what was required before they began work. The states also explained the review process in their agency, so that the contractors would understand what happens to the work they submit to the agency as well as the timing involved. At the same time the state learned more about the contractor's processes and problems.

It is important to note that we could not simply develop a one best process and require all states to use it. We had to start with each state's existing situation and improve from there. The need to continually improve these processes is evident as more than 400,000 actions had to pass through it in subsequent years.

What Has Happened Since?

In 2009, twenty-five years after the programs inception, the OUST Program issued a brief report entitled, "25 Years of Protecting Our Land and Water" (U.S. EPA 2009). It shows that over two-thirds of 2 million tanks have closed. "This leaves about 623,000 tanks at 235,000 gas stations and other facilities."

This report goes on to say, "EPA, states, tribes, and regulated industry have been working together to protect our land and water by preventing and cleaning up releases from underground storage tanks. Because of this strong partnership, the nation's tank programs have:

- Properly closed almost 1.7 million substandard underground storage tanks;
- Reduced the annual number of UST releases from almost 67,000 in 1990 to just over 7,300 in 2008; and
- Cleaned up over 377,000 releases, more than 80 percent of all reported releases."

ADDING IT ALL UP

What can we take away from the experiences I have described in this chapter?

First, the decision to establish the Office of Underground Storage Tanks as a separate organization was a key to the success of the program. Otherwise it would have been one of many divisions reporting to an office director already burdened with other major programs. As a separate office we were able to wend our way through, around or over traditional budget, personnel, legal and administrative practices. It also allowed us to build our own relationships with various organizations, as opposed to having to go through a filter of expectations and limitations set by others, if we were within a long-established, larger organization. Almost certainly we would not have been able to use our no targets, no goals approach to implementation.

Clayton M. Christensen, in *The Innovator's Dilemma*, (1997) does a thorough job of showing that you need to place a program with a new approach, product or service outside of an already existing program, even if that program is successful. The existing organization, he shows, will always find additional things that need doing in the present program. Thus, they will starve the new effort by devouring available dollars, people and talent for their ongoing programs. He says emphatically, "[d]isruptive projects . . . can thrive only within an organizationally distinctive unit" (Christensen 1997, 120).

Second, the lesson from the franchisers was especially important. "All results occur in the field" resonated with us. It showed us that normal efforts in this regard were not enough. We learned that there is a much more intense level of supporting the field and that this must be part of every aspect of our program. They also made us realize that many of the innovations and practical insights came from the field. In my experience, headquarters personnel frequently assume that they are the "brains" and the field is the "brawn." In involving the field, early and often, we learned to respect and take advantage of their knowledge. To us, the term *field* included EPA regional representatives, state program personnel, and experts from the tank and gasoline industry, equipment vendors, as well as the EPA laboratories. The participants included everyone involved in the processes that contributed to the problem of leaking tanks or to finding solutions to those problems. These things can be done without adopting a franchise mode of organization. They can also be done from an existing program with a gradual ramping up in support to the field. Third, TQM provided a foundation for our work, in three respects. It provided us with a common vocabulary, method of working and set of values. It taught us the pitfall of setting or being entrapped by targets, goals, or quotas. This enabled us to work on the important major things and to minimize investing our resources in fighting fires and trying to make our numbers. Last, it made us recognize that every process could be continually improved.

Truly adopting these concepts and acting in accord with our words built an unusual amount of trust among ourselves and with the various players. This enabled us to work together to find solutions, whether in developing the regulations or in creating programs to implement the regulations. It is especially noteworthy that it made for a workplace in which energy and creativity was a constant and work was frequently fun.

Looking back it is interesting to note that we did not ask for permission or approval to adopt the franchising mode or to get trained in and work according to Deming's principles. This, in part, is due to the fact that EPA's original work focused on science and direct federal legal and enforcement issues— management or implementation by others was secondary. As we did not have to change EPA organization charts or boxes or legal documents to achieve our purposes, no approval was required. Changes in our culture, vocabulary, relationships and values were not immediately apparent and occurred over time. When the EPA administrator recognized OUST's achievements at an awards ceremony, he noted that OUST benefitted from benign neglect. We were so busy with problems in other areas, that we left them alone. If we knew what things Ron was doing, we probably wouldn't have let him do them (Thomas 1988).

REFERENCES

Christensen, Clayton M. 1997. *The Innovator's Dilemma: When New Technologies Cause Great Firms to Fail.* MA: Harvard Business School Press.
Deming, W. Edwards. 1986. *Out of the Crisis.* MA: Massachusetts Institute for Technology, Center for Advanced Engineering Study.
———. 1982. *Quality, Productivity, and Competitive Position.* MA: Massachusetts Institute of Technology, Center for Advanced Engineering Study.
U.S. EPA. 1987. Groundwater Management Review, Fall 1987.
Ishikawa, Kaoru 1985. *What is Total Quality Control? The Japanese Way.* NJ: Prentice-Hall, Inc.
Lareau, William 1991. *American Samurai.* NJ: New Win Publishing, Inc.
L.U.S.T.LINE. 1985. Bulletin 1. MA: New England Interstate Water Control Commission.

Quiller-Couch, Sir Arthur 1928. *On the Art of Reading.* London: Cambridge University Press.
Shook, Robert L. and Carrie Shook. 1993. *Franchising: The Business Strategy That Changed the World.* NJ: Prentice-Hall, Inc.
Thomas, Lee. 1988. (Personal communication with the author).
U.S. EPA. 2004. Building on the Past to Protect the Future. EPA 510-R-04-001.
U.S. EPA. 1989. Commitment to Cooperation: Franchising the UST Program. EPA/530/UST-89/011.
U.S. EPA. 2009. *Underground Storage Tank Program: 25 Years of Protecting Our Land and Water.* U.S. EPA-510-B-09-001, (www.epa.gov/swerust1/pubs/25annrpt.pdf.K).
Walton, Mary. 1986. *The Deming Management Method.* NY: Penguin Putnam.

Chapter Seven

Protection in a Non-Regulatory World

The Indoor Air Program

Thomas E. Kelly

In this chapter I want to share some of my own experience in leading several of EPA's premier non-regulatory programs, which I got to do as director of EPA's Indoor Environments Division (IED) over the final seven years of my forty-two-year federal career. To convey the special challenge of these programs, it may be useful to frame them against EPA's better-known regulatory activities. I know the difference first-hand, because, prior to my work with IED I had served for more than a dozen years as director of regulatory development across all of EPA's programs. Overlapping much of that time I also administered the Small Business Regulatory Enforcement and Fairness Act (SBREFA)—a 1996 statute requiring EPA to invite both OMB and the Small Business Administration into early and repeated negotiations on any rulemaking with the potential to impose a significant economic impact on a substantial number of small businesses, communities, or non-profit organizations. I was steeped in EPA's rulemaking culture, and my experience in bridging both worlds—compulsory and voluntary environmental action—speaks to the managerial flexibility required of the SES in today's government.

THE ROLE OF REGULATION

Regulations are recipes with teeth. They mandate specific new behaviors (and desirable results) to replace any number of old behaviors (with undesirable results), and they impose stern penalties in the event of non-compliance.

Of fear and greed, two emotions said by psychologists and advertisers to be among the most powerful motivators of human behavior, regulation, with its "Command and Control" philosophy, appeals principally to fear. The authoritarian nature of the tool is explicit. "I'm making you an offer you can't refuse. Do what I say or face the consequences." This is appropriate and successful when certain conditions apply, namely:

- There is a discrete actor or group of actors whose behavior creates unacceptable risk for public health and the environment;
- The body politic views these actors as polluters, provoking public outrage and instigating the demand for statutory and regulatory remedies;
- Specified new behaviors can be shown to produce desirable environmental improvements at costs judged to be acceptable under prevailing law and policy;
- There is a credible mechanism in place to validate the threat of undesirable consequences to the violator in the event of non-compliance.

With these factors in play EPA began immediately upon its formation in 1970 to carry out the newly strengthened Clean Air Act and the soon to be toughened Clean Water Act (1972). The purpose of those statutes, as well as that of other landmark legislation like the Safe Drinking Water Act and the Resource Conservation and Recovery Act (RCRA), was to empower the government to alter both private and public behavior that had turned our nation's land, skies, and waterways into pollution dumps in the unimpeded pursuit of economic development. Led initially by the brilliant and courageous William Ruckelshaus, EPA quickly set emission limits for smokestacks and tailpipes, while mandating reductions in pollution discharged to the nation's streams, all the while withstanding stiff resistance from auto makers, chemical companies, and other invested parties. With the power of regulation, EPA has made remarkable progress toward cleaner skies and fishable, swimmable waters over the forty years of its existence. Even today, a cursory review of the morning news illustrates the need for a committed national authority to regulate environmental behavior. Running battles over excess mercury emissions, ground-level ozone, contaminated aquifers and drinking wells, and oil spills, point to the need for principled compulsion to revoke the self-conferred license of a few to sacrifice our shared environment to the detriment of the many.

WHEN REGULATION IS NOT THE RIGHT TOOL

If we consider EPA's fundamental business to be behavior modification, channeling human activity to protect the environment, then regulation is only one tool among many. The Agency has historically employed a range of non-regulatory tools to modify human behavior as it affects the natural environment, including grants, loans, technical assistance, and information. Some of these mechanisms support regulatory compliance, such as assistance provided to states and municipalities to administer permit programs and build required drinking water and sewage treatment facilities (see for example Morris 1997; 1996). But in some areas EPA acts almost entirely outside the province of regulatory command. This is true in such areas as Energy Star, chemical pollution prevention, and indoor air quality, in which private action may not be compelled but must somehow be induced.

In the case of air pollution, exposure to harmful pollutants may take place not only outdoors, for which regulation is authorized by statute, but also indoors, for which it is not. Yet studies on air pollution and its health effects show that the preponderance of human exposure to noxious pollutants occurs indoors. As ambient air enters a building, it delivers whatever pollutants it may be carrying. Once inside, these newly introduced pollutants are reinforced and supplemented by contaminants arising from the building itself, or from its contents. As a consequence, indoor pollutants tend to concentrate at levels two to five times those outdoors, and in some cases many times more. Since people in developed countries tend to spend as much as 90 percent of their time in the so-called "built environment," the impact of human exposure to indoor air pollutants greatly outweighs that of exposure outdoors (USEPA 2011).

The issue for EPA in the mid-eighties was whether and how to address risk in this unconventional setting. The Agency could easily have fallen prey to Maslow's Law of the Instrument, which says in effect, "if all you've got is a hammer, everything looks like a nail" (Maslow 1969, 15). Lacking legal authority to regulate, EPA might have passed on the challenge to protect people indoors. In persuading people to change their behavior within the four walls of their own homes, EPA would need to appeal to people's willingness to alter their own behavior in order to protect their health and that of their family. So EPA built a program of scientifically-based public information that would influence the American people, not through a series of prohibitions and sanctions but through a creatively delivered set of messages on what, why, and how to reduce exposure to air pollution indoors.

CARVING OUT A PLACE

In constructing EPA's indoor air quality program EPA looked for where it could make the greatest difference. One thing was clear, that the Agency would never have enough people or dollars to tackle every significant indoor-air problem—not even close. The program would complement, but never supplant EPA's regulatory work on outdoor air, for which the intrinsic technical requirements are deepened and extended by a host of statutory and executive requirements, fortified by the expectation of vigorous litigation once the rule is issued. Major EPA rulemakings consume the efforts of numerous technical disciplines over multiple years of development and defense, commanding the great preponderance of available resources. The fact that human-health risk from airborne pollutants takes place predominantly indoors may be striking in itself, but it counts for little in the face of statutory, judicial, and constituent pressure surrounding ambient air regulation. At EPA, when the White House asks the administrator over for a chat, or a powerful committee chair schedules a contentious congressional hearing, it is nearly always about a regulatory issue, and resources necessarily flow to the point of greatest perceived urgency. Under any plausible circumstances, the indoor air program would have to think big while remaining small, and making the case continually to earn acceptance as a key contributor to the Agency's public-health mission.

When my turn came to lead the program, we followed a few simple rules. One of the fun ones was to make ourselves visible and memorable beyond our size. For that reason I opened many formal and informal business discussions with organizational superiors with a simple mantra: "Indoor Air: it's as big as all outdoors." I did this both seriously and humorously, and typically both at once. It became a smiling matter that the Indoor Air program would occasionally announce itself this way, and it stuck. Through this simple device, both political and career managers never forgot where the human health risk was, and our influence and visibility exceeded our modest size relative to the rest of the air program.

Another rule was to advertise the national cost of neglect of indoor air quality. A review of several analyses indicates that the annual economic loss due to poor IAQ is approximately $150–200 billion. This number includes premature death from exposure to environmental tobacco smoke and radon, lost productivity, and health expenses for treatment of asthma and other respiratory diseases (USEPA 1989; Fisk 2000; Mudarri 1994; Brunner and Mudarri 2004). On the other hand Americans spend approximately $12–20 billion annually to improve their indoor air quality, including outlays for duct cleaning, air cleaners and filtration, IAQ consultants, and building remediation (Levin 2005). Looking beyond the urgent atmosphere surrounding EPA's regulatory culture, indoor air quality was an important problem for public health and the economy, which EPA was well-placed to address.

Still another rule was to frame the program in terms that would appeal to the value structure of the administration in power. So, for conservative Republicans, who were intent on scaling back the reach and economic impact of environmental regulation, we emphasized our ability to produce public health benefits that were not attributable to regulation. For Democrats, who embraced the role of government in improving quality of life, we pointed out that 69 percent of human exposure to air toxics takes place indoors (Loh et al. 2007, 1164), while emphasizing that our voluntary approach to the indoor environment makes a "right fit" with the regulatory approach outdoors. Our program was delivering needed public benefits while deflecting criticism of the regulatory program as an example of EPA's choosing the appropriate means for the appropriate end. In both cases we stressed the low relative cost of producing notable outcomes through voluntary programs.

The last key rule was to cite and recite the results we were getting. For instance, through our Tools for Schools initiative we had built from scratch an impressive movement to monitor and improve indoor air quality (IAQ) in the nation's schools. Starting from a point at which few if any schools treated IAQ as an educational investment, EPA's program reached a point at which more than a third of the nation's schools reported having put a substantial and continuous IAQ-management program in place. EPA's radon control initiative was preventing hundreds of avoidable deaths annually from lung cancer. And our childhood asthma program was revolutionizing community-based asthma outreach programs in high-morbidity urban areas.

THE INDOOR ENVIRONMENTS DIVISION

The engine of this achievement was EPA's Indoor Environments Division (IED). By 2003, when I arrived to head it up, the group had built a fifteen-year history of innovation and high achievement. Its founders had correctly foreseen that even a small federal presence could have a significant effect on the indoor environment by issuing scientifically sound information and advice in EPA's name. Starting with a seminal guidance called "The Inside Story" (USEPA 2011) IED had steadily compiled an impressive record of scientific and technical guidance to the building industry and practical assistance to professionals and citizens alike on how to reduce their health risks indoors.

The division's architecture was already in place and organized around several key initiatives. There was a small but excellent staff of scientists and engineers who were writing and issuing state-of-the art technical guidance for the design, construction, and maintenance of buildings friendly to occupant health. The scientists also provided empirical grounding for several imaginative public outreach programs, covering the areas of environmental tobacco smoke (ETS), school environments, childhood asthma, and household radon. These public outreach programs relied on partnerships with an extensive group of non-governmental organizations which promoted EPA's environmental mission through their own networks of collegial and institutional relationships. IED offered grants in support of many of these organizations—including, for instance, the American Lung Association, National Association of School Nurses, and the National Center for Healthy Housing—while managing active peer-to-peer communication. The division had also invested in national media campaigns for asthma, radon, and ETS, whether through grant support of non-profits like the Ad Council with its access to top Madison Avenue firms, or by contract procurement with smaller firms geared to the non-profit market. The resulting advertising—some of it iconic—appeared on TV, radio, magazines, and billboards as a public service, often available to be viewed at peak times and high-volume places, producing public benefits that were valued at many multiples of EPA's initial investment.

As impressive as were the division's achievements, its operating style was so unconventional by EPA standards that it was viewed from above as chaotic and in need of reform. The division was proud of the high level of autonomy it offered each of its members. Unlike any government staff I had previously encountered, each employee had enormous leverage over the work to which he or she would be assigned. The principle behind this was sound. A voluntary program short on cash and long on urgency needed to unleash the entrepreneurial creativity of its staff, and especially to take advantage of serendipity when it arose, to get the most environmental benefit from a small allotment of resources.

The operating philosophy was to match each staff member with the topic area for which he or she had the greatest talent and instinctive energy. Although every staff member reported to a named supervisor, and was formally placed in a specific operating center, most work was organized into informal cross-division teams—for example, the ETS Team or the Asthma Team—without regard to the center of origin for each staff member. The science center contributed scientific analysis and product review to work across the division. A cross-program center provided administrative and technical services to the division (such as artwork, IT support, electronic meeting technology, publication expertise). But the remaining centers served mainly as "home rooms" for staff who were working almost exclusively "out on the floor" on topical teams, from which they managed partnership relationships and conducted public outreach campaigns. The team construct was intended to create flexible and informal work groups with an interchangeable mix of talent and interests so that the center structure would not create a bureaucratic barrier to the assembly of the best talent available to pursue a particular topic. Center supervisors doubled as "coaches" for the several teams, in which role their responsibilities fell somewhere between those of advisor and quality reviewer under the premise that the teams would be largely self-directing.

The major weakness of this setup was that center directors got to see and evaluate only those staff members contributing to the teams that they themselves coached. The obligation by the supervisor of record to provide real-time feedback and an annual performance assessment for each employee came to depend largely on information gained second-hand from another manager. This disrupted the staff-to-supervisor relationship, undermining both the force and immediacy of managerial feedback to staff. The system also put unfair pressure on the staff member serving as "team leader," or first among equals. The authority of that non-supervisory employee to direct work and enforce deadlines was ambiguous, the product of team consensus, which ebbed and flowed by issue and personality. The arrangement led even the highest performing staff to assume a sense of independence even beyond the wide latitude intentionally offered them.

Shortly after my arrival a staff member addressed an email to the full division announcing her "resignation" from a team on which she had been working with great distinction. She explained that her priorities had shifted and she could no longer invest in her previous work at the level of intensity it required. Even now I recognize this employee's intention as laudable. She diagnosed a conflict of duties and realized it was necessary to choose one over the other. So far, so good. But she sensed no need to address her dilemma first to her supervisor for discussion and resolution. Instead she publicly reassigned herself, explaining later that it was how things were done within the prevailing culture. With employees as self-motivated and productive as she, I had a good sense of how this situation might have taken root. But I also knew that any such convention worked against our getting the best from those employees who needed more structure and guidance to contribute what we needed from them. My challenge was to keep in place the best of what I found, while reestablishing the clarity of managerial direction in a federal workplace, all to get even more production and creativity from this remarkable staff.

The solution took tact and patience to put across without crushing the spirit that had made the place so vibrant. First, I clarified that the coach was not merely an advisor, but a managing supervisor. The staff-level team leader would coordinate work under the strategic direction of the supervisory coach.

Teams would still enjoy a great deal of latitude in setting aggressive goals and shaping novel strategies, but each member would be accountable to division management to contribute his or her part. I then realigned managers so that the teams they "coached" were staffed primarily by employees they supervised, who would thenceforth be working within their daily oversight. When division management reassigned staff from one team to another, they would also formally transfer that person to the center directed by the receiving coach so that staff-to-supervisor alignment would be upheld. I retained the division's tradition of a central "management team," comprising the division director, center directors, and key administrative staff, to plan, budget, and direct work across the division in a collaborative way. Except for discussions involving confidential matters like personnel issues, I opened the doors to management team meetings so that staff could hear what was being discussed—even many budget deliberations—and buy into the high trust relationship on which the entire approach relied. There were some turbulent times along the way, since great employees do not chafe in total silence, but things came together. We succeeded in enhancing order and accountability in the division's operations without sacrificing energy, creativity, and "ownership" by the talented people on whom we relied to work miracles.

GETTING THINGS DONE THROUGH VOLUNTARY MEANS

In my service with EPA's IAQ Program we fought to maintain an effective program despite continuous reductions in staffing and funding and in the absence of a stern statutory mandate like those underlying EPA's regulatory programs. Sometimes we lost, such as when the Agency's political leadership eliminated the ETS program on the curious rationale that second-hand tobacco smoke is not an environmental problem. Still, we achieved a lot for a little. In the scientific area, for instance, we completed the only comprehensive study of baseline air quality levels in the built environment. The *Building Assessment Survey and Evaluation Study* (BASE) measured interior air quality in one hundred public and commercial buildings nationwide, yielding the most comprehensive baseline ever produced on building pollution levels. On my watch we analyzed, prepared, and published the data for use by ourselves and other researchers worldwide. BASE data have since proved invaluable for further studies of such key indoor environment and occupant health concerns as ventilation control and the relationship between outdoor air pollution (like ozone) and indoor contamination as they affect health complaints and work absences by building occupants. These studies in turn have formed the basis for revised building design and technical specifications to allow for improved control over occupant health and comfort in the work environment (USEPA 2007).

We also collaborated with the American Society of Heating, Refrigerating, and Air-Conditioning Engineers (ASHRAE) on the most complete and useful manual for healthy building design now available to architects, engineers, and the construction sector (ASHRAE 2009). We invested similarly in guidance for the proper design and maintenance of schools to sustain healthy conditions for attendance and learning by both students and faculty. We worked with private national standards organizations like Leadership for Energy and Environmental Design (LEED) to move their criteria beyond a near-exclusive orientation toward energy efficiency and resource renewability to incorporate a more balanced consideration of occupant health. We collaborated with our EPA colleagues at Energy Star to issue standards for the "Indoor Air Plus" home—a set of specifications builders could use to build and advertise homes as meeting not only Energy Star requirements for energy efficiency, but also EPA guidelines for occupant health. With the National Academy of Sciences Institute of Medicine we explored the implications of climate change on the design and performance of indoor spaces, resulting in the recent publication of *Climate Change, The Indoor Environment, and Health*, a monograph that explores the extraordinary new pressures to which our indoor spaces will become subject as more severe climate conditions create more hostile conditions for human activity outdoors (National Academy of Sciences, 2011). Beyond the national movement for IAQ management we inspired in the U.S. education system that I mentioned earlier, IED made great strides in radon control and asthma prevention, about which I will offer more detailed discussion below.

Returning to the incident in which an employee independently "resigned" from her team duties, organizational discipline is one thing, but creative passion is too important to stifle over a fine point of procedure. Having corrected the local understanding on how staff assignments would be made, IED's management team agreed with the employee's judgment that it would serve EPA's higher interest for her to switch full time to a nascent project to introduce environmentally friendly, culturally appropriate, and cheap-to-manufacture cook stoves into traditional third-world households. Working with organizations and governments around the world, she became one half of an initially two-person team of to spearhead the development and growth of the international Partnership for Clean Indoor Air (PCIA), which grew out of the 2002 Johannesburg World Summit on Sustainable Development (USEPA 2012). Operating on a shoestring with the continuous support of their IED colleagues, these two built an international partnership organization from the ground up and kept it growing through years of parsimonious funding and broken commitments by other elements of the U.S. government.

They shepherded it to the point where the U.S. State Department and several other agencies, along with the United Nations Foundation, have now adopted aggressive new goals to expand the program. These two IED staffers were recent semi-finalists for the Service to America Award (SAMMIE), given annually to a select few federal workers who are serving their country through extraordinary initiative, dedication, and impact. Through the work of PCIA to date, tens of millions of homes around the world are newly cooking safely and cleanly, reducing a death toll that has been estimated at 1.6 million annually worldwide due to respiratory disease or open-fire accidents. It helps, too, that new cook stove technology is reducing particulate emissions from old stoves that have accelerated climate change worldwide.

Initiative and productivity at such a level is special in any setting—whether in government or private enterprise—but it emerges naturally within the flexible, collaborative, and goal-oriented culture of EPA's Indoor Air program. Some might object that the management philosophy and structures we employed are ultimately unsustainable within a political bureaucracy such as EPA—that the bureaucracy will crush it eventually. Perhaps that's true in the long run, but then again perhaps it's true that bureaucracy crushes everything in the long run. There is no good reason not to try something bold when we can, and to sustain it as long as circumstances continue to justify it. Certainly it would be a far greater gamble to offer employees so much room for individual initiative and self-organization in a regulatory program laboring under procedural prescription, the tyranny of the deadline, and suffocating scrutiny by the Congress or the courts. But EPA's regulatory programs are achieving extraordinary results under management schemes that fit their own legal and political context. Placed together, both the regulatory programs and the IED voluntary model demonstrate that government can be as flexible and creative as any other institution in designing management structures and staff incentives that invite high aspiration and exceptional achievement. In the following sections, I will explore the IED experience with two programs in more detail.

PROTECTING PUBLIC HEALTH: THE STORY OF RADON

Radon is a naturally occurring radioactive gas, atomic number 86, produced as part of the decay chain of uranium. Although it has always been present in nature, it was not formally identified until 1900, when a German physicist, Friedrich Ernst Dorn, detected a gas emanating from laboratory radium samples. Even prior to the scientific classification of radon, its effects were evident in the inexplicably high numbers of miners who contracted a fatal lung disease—called "mountain sickness"—dating back to the sixteenth century. Nineteenth-century epidemiological studies confirmed that uranium miners were contracting lung cancer at exceptionally high rates.

Radon is classified as a noble gas, meaning it is itself chemically inert. However, as it decays, it gives birth to highly unstable radioactive "progeny," which emit charged alpha and beta particles that attach themselves to dust floating in the air. When breathed this contaminated dust introduces radioactivity into the lungs, where it attacks individual cells, either destroying them or inflicting damage that can trigger a mutation. While the human immune system is usually capable of suppressing the effects of such damage, with sufficient exposure to radon over time the human subject may, and many do, eventually develop cancer of the lung.

Since uranium is widely distributed in the earth's crust, radon is constantly emanating from deep underground, seeking release to the surface. When it reaches open air it tends to dissipate harmlessly. But when allowed to concentrate—as in a closed mine or contained dwelling—its progency can attack human tissue and induce lung cancer. Paradoxically, as homes and buildings have become tighter in recent years, they have also become better magnets and containers for radon. That is because homes tend to operate at low pressure in contrast to their surroundings. Since "Nature hates a vacuum," when radon arrives at the surface, it is drawn to low-pressure areas, finding its way through the tiniest cracks or chinks into the building that attracts it.

In the United States cancer of the lung is responsible for nearly 30 percent of annual deaths due to cancer, a greater mortality rate than that of the next three types combined. As a nation we now understand and accept the conclusion of scientific investigation that tobacco smoke, both actively and passively inhaled, is the dominant cause of lung cancer. And next to that comes indoor exposure to radon. Unlike the case of tobacco, against which government and other public health experts have taken concerted action over many decades, concern over household radon has arisen only recently, despite ample evidence of the risk it posed. The battle to control tobacco was waged over whether and how much to regulate a highly profitable consumer product that was suspected of killing its customers. Resolve built gradually to control it as evidence piled up demonstrating tobacco's lethal effects and its ancillary costs to society. The tobacco industry was increasingly painted into a corner as "the bad guy" against whom public outrage could be effectively marshaled. Not so with radon. Since radon is a naturally occurring element there is no "bad guy" to be accused of the damage it causes and charged with the cost of its removal. Unlike tobacco smoke, or even artificially scented heating gas, radon is imperceptible to the senses, so there is no physical warning for the homeowner to take action. The only way to detect it is through a radon measurement device. Nor did Congress for many years have incentive to legislate against a human health problem about which their constituents were either uninformed or indifferent.

What happened to Stanley Watras changed all that. In late 1984 Watras, an engineer engaged in constructing the Limerick nuclear power plant outside Pottstown, Pennsylvania, set off the alarms on his way into the plant to start his day's work. At that point in the project radiation detectors had been installed but no radioactive material was yet on-site. Investigators traced the source to the Watras home, where radon was measured at 700 times the level EPA later identified as sufficient to trigger remedial action. The home was located above the Reading Prong, a geologic formation stretching across central Pennsylvania and into New Jersey, where high radon levels were frequently recorded. The Watras incident set off a wave of national concern and pushed EPA to consider how it might respond, despite its lack of authority to regulate.

The Congress subsequently passed the Radon Gas and Indoor Air Quality Research Act of 1986 and the Indoor Radon Abatement Act of 1988 (IRAA). The IRAA set the hortatory (and inherently unachievable) goal of reducing indoor radon to the average level in ambient air The goal translates to about 0.4 pCi/L (pico-Curies per liter), a concentration far below what even the most advanced control technology could reliably meet. In setting such an aggressive goal, Congress rose to meet a crest of public concern that homeowners were unknowingly exposing their families to a mysterious but deadly health risk. If the statutory goal was lofty, the means Congress afforded EPA to meet it were not. The act authorized research, technical assistance, grants to states (not to exceed $10 million a year), regional educational centers to train workers in radon abatement techniques, and an EPA-run program to test and certify radon measurement equipment, laboratory analysis, and home mitigators.

After the Watras incident EPA issued public guidance on radon risk and abatement and created vivid media campaigns to spur public curiosity about where to find reliable information on radon protection in the home. One of these campaigns, based on the premise of a random quiz for the "person on the street" dramatized how much the average American did not yet know about radon, and won an Emmy for best public service TV advertising. One of EPA's key guidance documents, The Citizen's Guide to Radon (USEPA 2009) set a voluntary "action level" to advise the public on when to mitigate high radon levels in the home. Most scientists hold that no level of radon is "safe." However, since existing technology could reliably reduce home radon levels only to about 2 pCi/L, EPA chose an action level at 4 pCi/L a point which would reward a homeowner's investment by substantially reducing radon levels and much of its associated risk. This was done for practical reasons, even though as many as two-thirds of radon-related lung cancers likely occur due to chronic exposure at levels below 4 pCi/L. In response to public alarm over high-risk areas like the Reading Prong, the Agency analyzed data on geologic formations and sampled geographic radon levels to produce a national map distinguishing among regions expected to have higher, medium, and lower percentages of homes testing at or above the action level.

The method of choice for radon abatement is called Active Soil Depressurization (ASD), and it acts like a drinking straw inserted into the ground beneath a home. ASD overrides the home's natural suction by creating a more powerful drawing action closer to the point where radon gas meets the earth's surface. The natural sucking action of the ASD collector pipe, frequently augmented by a constant fan, collects radon below the foundation and funnels it safely through the house, releasing it above the roof eave, where it is dispersed. Over the ensuing years EPA implemented the new radon statutes while building a modest national network for radon testing and mitigation. Central to these efforts were grants to states, whose programs educated the public about radon, and grants to regional training centers to help develop a fledgling industry of radon mitigators, private contractors who would market their skills to test and install ASD in homes. Another important component was a national proficiency program that set standards for mitigation contractors, calibrated radon measurement devices, and certified analytic laboratories to ensure radon measurements were valid and reliable.

Although the radon program began in an atmosphere of high concern and strenuous public demand for government action, numerous obstacles impeded the program's growth and effectiveness. By the time I assumed responsibility for the program in 2003, EPA's Radon Division, which at one time had comprised more than fifty headquarters staff, plus a substantial complement of regional specialists, operated with a vestige of eight dedicated but understandably discouraged headquarters employees and a smattering of equally committed colleagues sprinkled around EPA's ten regional offices. In the twenty-five years since Congress had authorized up to $10 million annually for state grants, the appropriation had averaged only about $8 million to be distributed each year among the fifty states as well as Native American tribes. Indexed for inflation, the value of this investment fell by more than 55 percent between 1988 and 2003. Authorization for the regional training centers had expired long before without renewal, a few of them struggling forward on a meager mix of public and private funding. Under budget pressures of its own, EPA had stepped away from the national certification program, deferring to two private organizations to manage the function on the basis of membership fees, even as the recruitment base of participants in the radon mitigation industry fell precipitously. In short, the program, which had always been conspicuously undersized for its task, was reduced to little more than a symbolic presence with an EPA logo. As I sized up my task a few wise heads counseled me to go with the flow—to let the radon program drift away in order to direct my new division's modest resources toward work with greater prominence and prospects. Certainly there were competing needs in childhood asthma and environmental tobacco smoke, our growing investment in the nation's schools, and the emerging "green building" movement. The advice was pragmatic and well meant. I considered it seriously.

At the same time I dug into a relatively recent report from the National Academy of Sciences. Issued in 1999, it was the sixth formal report of its committee on the Biological Effects of Ionizing Radiation and was referred to briefly as BEIR VI (National Academy of Sciences 1999). It updated an earlier report called BEIR IV (National Academy of Sciences 1988) on which EPA had based its original risk assessment on radon exposure. A credible review of the science underlying the assessment of radon risk was especially vital, since a number of critics had attacked the national radon program on just this basis. Even some within the Health Physics Society, scientists in the health effects of radiation, were skeptical of radon risk, calculations of which dwarfed the dangers posed by the medical equipment and other practical nuclear devices they designed and analyzed in their daily work. Their reservations were taken up by the home building and real estate industries, which opposed any federal action that might raise public concern about the safety of their market commodity. The nuclear energy industry, too, hoped to tamp down public fears about radiation in the community by opposing EPA's effort to publicize a form of radiation known to induce lung cancer within the presumed sanctuary of the home.

The earlier report, BEIR IV, had based its projections of domestic risk on extrapolation from epidemiological data built around the occupational exposure of uranium miners to radon. In 1998 NAS set out to reexamine that approach with respect to the criticisms lodged against it, as well as to conduct richer, deeper analysis on a much more complete set of data than was available for the earlier review. In BEIR VI, NAS concluded once again that extrapolation from miner data is scientifically valid and updated its estimates through analysis of many more data points involving numerous miner exposures at levels common to the home setting. In sum, the Academy concluded that its previous study had significantly underestimated the potency of radon risk. EPA's revised risk assessment based on BEIR VI included projections of lung cancer deaths 50 percent higher than those based on BEIR IV (central tendency of 21,000, up from 14,000), while estimates of mortal risk to never-smokers increased fourfold. Yet, in the several years between the release of BEIR VI and my arrival to lead the Indoor Air program, EPA had not acted to strengthen its radon outreach program. With such powerful risk estimates in hand, I realized we could not let the program die of our own neglect. On the contrary, we had to lift it off its knees by reinvigorating EPA's commitment to save lives with whatever tools we had at hand.

I knew the chances were slim of obtaining more horsepower for a public-health program with well-placed adversaries and virtually no discernible constituency. I knew the national goal was impossible to achieve as written. I was aware of the disadvantage inherent in our position as the only organization in government taking the radon threat seriously—that, if the medium is the message, a tiny program tucked within EPA's Air Office would struggle to overcome both skepticism and indifference to the significant health risk we were fighting. But I also knew that if we didn't make the greatest use of whatever opportunity we had, we would defeat ourselves. If greater institutional support was not on the immediate horizon, we needed to revitalize the program to keep it going until circumstances changed. If I was not internally optimistic, I nevertheless projected optimism as a principle of business. Fortunately we had excellent and deeply knowledgeable people working on radon, however few they were, and I recalled the words of Bill Ruckelshaus, who had rallied and rescued EPA upon his return to right the Agency following an era of scandal and plunging morale. He later said that it was not he who had revived the Agency's spirit and effectiveness, but EPA's people themselves. All they needed was encouragement, he said, and he had offered that. It seemed like a good approach to me, and I set out to emulate my hero, if only in a much smaller way.

One of the first things I did was to create a discrete organizational identity for the radon program. Finding it paired with asthma prevention in a group called the Center for Healthy Buildings, I pulled it out and created a Center for Radon and Air Toxics—returning radon as a named priority on EPA's official organization chart for the first time in over ten years. While that may sound like bureaucratic window trimming, it was actually a powerful signal to our disheartened field network of state and private partners that EPA was committed to the radon program now and in the future. Next, since part of the cycle of discouragement stems from a loss of pride in achievement, we took stock of what EPA had accomplished to date. Together we compiled statistics demonstrating that, in partnership with states, EPA's radon program could claim over 700,000 high-radon homes had been mitigated and over 1 million new homes built radon-resistant. Based on EPA's scientific risk assessment, that meant our program was already saving over 500 lives annually—a figure that dwarfed the benefits calculated for many high-profile environmental regulations.

Next we took our case to EPA's top management. In the first term of the George W. Bush administration, we found ready ears for our story of a program that was saving 500 lives a year without regulation. We then placed that fact in context. At that time, around 2004, we estimated there were about

6 million homes with radon levels above EPA's action level, of which only 100,000 were being mitigated after testing. And about 1.2 million new homes were being built annually, of which only 100,000 were built to be radon-resistant. As housing stock continued to rise, the gap would grow unless EPA amplified its effectiveness. Everyone who saw the numbers understood the need, and ordinarily this would have been the time to pounce—to request more people and dollars for a more powerful program. But we knew that was out of the question, so we asked instead for support to bring the rest of the "federal family" into the coalition of federal authorities acknowledging and acting on the risk of radon. Since radon risk is real, EPA should not be the only Agency publicly concerned about it. We pointed to DoD and HUD, for instance, each of which either controlled or influenced an enormous share of the nation's housing. If EPA's political leaders could convince the administration to instruct all relevant departments to test and reduce radon levels in housing under their authority, it would be the most powerful message possible to warn the public of radon risk and impel homeowners to test and mitigate their own properties. Of course we did not expect a quick and unqualified "yes" to this, but the request itself served to inform our political management of the dilemma we faced and convince them to stand behind our own bootstrap efforts to strengthen the program from within.

Our next step was to renew the commitment of non-governmental organizations (NGOs) that had helped spread the word on radon in the early years. Many of these organizations had abandoned the radon problem to concentrate on more charismatic health issues. They had two major reasons for this, and they both amounted to money. First was the decline in EPA's grant support—if they couldn't pay staff to work on it, they couldn't do much to help. And the other was continuing public indifference to radon as a health threat—if they could not attract public donations to support their advocacy for a cause, they needed to promote another cause. That's just practical thinking; it is how non-profits survive. And yet, we needed the support of these organizations to resurrect public awareness of radon, so we "beat the street," visiting dozens of NGOs with a simple message, framed something like this: "Here is your mission to protect public health. Here are the facts on radon risk and public health. What are you willing to do to fit this glaring public health need within the scope of your mission?" We called a national meeting for these organizations to create a sense of common purpose and to signal EPA's continuing commitment to the radon program. We asked them, in effect, to hang in there with us and offer what support they could. With very little in the way of grant dollars to offer, we did not expect a miraculous resurgence of energy from this sector, but we got the agreement of most to feature radon risk prominently in their public messaging.

As important as it was to line up support in Washington, the real work took place in the field, in state program offices and in mitigators' visits to individual homes across the country. To push the program forward, we needed to convey our new attitude to those sectors. If discouragement had taken a toll in Washington, it was an even more powerful factor in the field. States looked to EPA for funding to support their programs, but the Agency's support had fallen steadily in purchasing power over fifteen years. And members of the radon mitigation industry—which had sprung up from virtually nothing in response to the Indoor Radon Abatement Act and EPA's full-tilt initiation of the program in the early nineties—were frustrated and angry at the government's whiffing on its implicit promise to build and sustain public demand for the industry's services. A field that had once been bustling with test manufacturers, analytic laboratories, and home mitigators was shrinking and racked with contention.

Among the most difficult problems was continuous, disruptive friction between state program officials and mitigation contractors. This was a classic battle between opposing tribes with divergent values. There were many points of tension, but at its core the frayed relationship reflected each group's anxiety born of a sense of poverty. State programs were operating on a thread, and private contractors were desperate for work. While most participants got along reasonably well in practice, some vocal and influential operators and state officials so distrusted one another that they cultivated an atmosphere of mutual accusation, each charging the other with the deliberate mischaracterization of motive and action. There was also deep-seated conflict between the two private organizations that competed with each other for the modest prize of training and certifying radon mitigators in the field. At an annual "meeting of the tribes" I asked agreement for EPA to broker a national dialogue to resolve these disputes. We had too much work to do to waste energy on friction. Instead of forming a circle and firing in at one another, we needed to link arms, and step out as a single national movement to meet the public-health challenge that had brought us together in the first place. Not every warring party agreed to join the national conversation, but we cleared away a lot of underbrush over the next three years, even tackling the task of setting uniform quality conventions to be practiced in the field with the endorsement of state program directors. While not every point of disagreement were resolved, the atmosphere became much more positive, and key people in divergent roles found it possible to work more cohesively with greater mutual understanding and trust.

With the worst internal conflict behind us, in 2008 we took our biggest step forward, launching a national campaign to generate aggressive progress by all parties to our coalition. To do this EPA recruited two critical co-sponsors, the Conference of Radiation Control Program Directors (CRCPD, which represented public officials responsible for the state programs) and the

American Association of Radon Scientists and Technologists (AARST, the major industry group). These former combatants joined EPA in a triumvirate to direct a national campaign to accelerate progress on reducing radon risk. Called "Radon Leaders Saving Lives," we set a dramatic goal of doubling the number of lives saved annually within five years of that date. That meant preventing 1250 deaths annually by 2013. We knew that goal would prove impossible in an atmosphere of low resources and internecine dispute. We knew it was out of reach if everyone continued to do the same old things in the same old way. We set the goal knowing we might fail, but that it would force us to try different strategies, and that it would lasso all three parties together in the attempt, federal, state and industry.

In 2009 we greeted the incoming administration with news of this urgent project to save lives through a public/private partnership. The Radon Leaders Saving Lives campaign caught the imagination of our new political managers, and we continued to receive strong policy support, even if the budget picture remained bleak. Around that time, several federal agencies, including HHS, HUD, Energy, and EPA, began to collaborate on a broad Healthy Homes initiative begun with a big push by the surgeon general. Back in 2005 we at EPA had been successful in urging the surgeon general to issue a new public warning about radon risk in the home. This was a complement to previous surgeon general warnings about smoking and cancer, including the synergy between smoking and radon, even for those who were exposed only to second-hand smoke. The Healthy Homes campaign offered a breakthrough opportunity to bring other agencies into the radon fight, and we at EPA made sure that radon awareness, testing, and mitigation became prominent features of the work. We were nearing our long-term goal of getting the federal government, not just a small program within EPA, behind the need to reduce household exposure to radon.

I retired from EPA in 2010 with that 2013 goal still ahead of us. Since then my former colleagues have continued to work with and through their state and industry counterparts to direct net energy forward. They continue to work with modest budgetary support, and the nation's current economic climate suggests this funding trend will continue for some time. However, our consistent urging that other departments do their part has finally taken hold. In June 2011, EPA announced that the federal departments of Defense, Energy, Health and Human Services, Housing and Urban Development, Interior, and the Veterans Administration had agreed to a broad set of actions to test and mitigate radon in homes and facilities under their control. For the first time the federal government has taken a unified stance to protect public health against domestic radon intrusion. What seemed an impossible overreach when we first broached it in 2004 has now become daily practice for three reasons: 1) there was an administration in power willing to take dramatic action against a lethal public health threat despite the absence of intense constituent demand; 2) the Radon Leaders Saving Lives Campaign built an atmosphere in which everything possible seemed worth trying; and 3) we were successful in keeping the program internally vibrant until auspicious circumstances finally took hold. Will EPA meet its goal of double lives saved in 2013 over those saved in 2008? Knowing my former colleagues at EPA and in the radon community, I wouldn't put it past them.

THE STORY OF ASTHMA

Since 1980 asthma has grown to epidemic status in the United States, where currently nearly 18 million people suffer from the disease, 7 million of whom are children who miss 13 million school days annually on its account. Asthma is an underlying condition that may cause only minor symptoms until some exposure or other event triggers an attack. Outdoors, pollen and ozone are major culprits, and EPA has ratcheted down the National Ambient Air Quality Standard for ozone several times to reduce such impacts. Indoors there are many allergens and irritants that can trigger an attack, including tobacco smoke, dust, pollen, mold spores, animal dander, and pests like roaches and mites.

For many years the principal protocol for treating asthma has relied on prophylactic and emergency inhalers, accompanied when necessary by urgent medical attention—often a trip to the emergency room or inpatient facility. Emergency patients are often sent home with prophylactic sprays and emergency inhalers until the next attack repeats the cycle. As asthma rates climbed through the 1980s concern grew that treating attacks after the fact was not an adequate solution. In 1998 President Bill Clinton formed the multi-agency Asthma Priority Area Work Group to deal with asthma's rise and peel it back. EPA joined the National Institutes of Health (NIH), the Centers for Disease Control and Prevention (CDC), and other agencies as money poured in to fuel the fight. For EPA's Indoor Environments Division this ultimately meant a budget increase of 180 percent, from $5 million annually to $14 million.

In the division of labor among participating agencies, EPA took the lead on controlling the environmental triggers of asthma. This required a multimedia information campaign mounted both centrally by the agency and through such partners as the American Lung Association, the American College of Preventative Medicine, and the National Association of School Nurses. EPA also collaborated with the Ad Council to create memorable advertising campaigns, some of the most effective based on the image of a goldfish gasping for oxygen as the bowl slowly empties of water. A little boy voices over the action, "I don't want to feel like a fish with no water." Public appeals like this drove home the misery of asthma attacks and brought parents to EPA publications and, increasingly, our website to learn how to prevent asthma in the home.

EPA's goal was simple. Help parents realize their children could avoid asthma attacks through a number of best practices in the home that merged environmental prevention with medical management of the condition. To do this EPA trained numerous health-care professionals on asthma triggers and their control, and carried the message to parents and caregivers of children most subject to the attacks When I arrived in 2003 this approach was well underway, and by that time the program estimated that 3 million people were taking essential actions at home to prevent asthma attacks, with the result that more than 40,000 emergency room visits were being avoided annually.

As good as that was, the program was increasingly hampered by a continuing erosion of funding after the initial bump. Since the big infusion had come in the last year of the Clinton administration, it became an inviting target for reduction as the Bush administration went to work. Just as important was EPA's cultural isolation from the medical agencies. While there was ample anecdotal and observational corroboration that reducing exposure to environmental triggers would reduce asthma morbidity and, to a lesser extent, mortality, agencies like NIH and CDC were bound by the "evidence-based" standard that held they could not actively promote any method for which there was not ample peer-reviewed empirical evidence of safety and effectiveness. As a voluntary program based on public information, our ethic in IED was to put new learning on asthma prevention to work as soon as possible. Our own environmental scientists carefully vetted our public-education materials, so we were confident in their integrity. CDC was responsible for medical management of asthma, and EPA for environmental prevention, so the standards of evidence differed between agencies. While our staffs worked closely to share information and insights, there were few legitimate ways institutionally to jointly sponsor programs, or for CDC to pick up some of the funding slack as our own resources declined.

The key to closer cooperation came wrapped as a grant proposal from the University of Michigan School of Public Health. The director of Michigan's Center for Managing Chronic Disease, Noreen Clark, was just as concerned as we were about completing the circle of validation for the environmental management of asthma triggers. Under her leadership, the school requested EPA support for a project that would examine the record of community asthma outreach programs reporting positive health outcomes from a combined environmental and medical approach to asthma management. Called the Asthma Health Outcomes Project (AHOP) the study proposed to examine the factual basis for those reports and, where evidence supported claims of positive outcomes, identify program characteristics most closely associated with that success. We supported the project as a cooperative agreement, which meant EPA could collaborate with the university in the design and conduct of the study (University of Michigan 2007).

Michigan began by scouring the literature and reaching out to a network of more than 2500 experts worldwide to identify asthma programs that combine environmental prevention with medical management. The study team uncovered more than 400 programs that met the initial criteria—many more than had been anticipated. Of these, more than 200 had undergone substantive evaluation, and more than 100 had published results. Even better, of those programs with published results, sixty-five had evaluated their outcomes on the basis of randomized control trials, meaning their reported health outcomes would prove relevant and persuasive to our colleagues in the medically-based agencies. The AHOP study showed there were programs operating in American communities that could document reductions as high as 80 percent in unplanned provider visits, and step-downs in the classification of asthma severity for 50 percent of patients presenting with moderate to severe asthma. We found programs that were achieving 60 percent to 75 percent reductions in emergency room visits and an 80 percent decrease in hospitalizations for their sickest clients. There were even suggestions of savings as high as $800 in health costs annually per child with asthma. In short, the findings were astounding and moved us quickly into action.

Although not all health outcomes were as dramatic as these highlights, all programs meeting the study criteria reported positive outcomes and they shared many features of what we recognized as a spontaneous, peer-developed model for community-based asthma management that really worked. We understood that, if we could isolate those elements of a successful program, we could propagate them and improve health outcomes nationally. Abstracting the key factors for success proved to be quite easy, as nearly all the most successful programs shared the same traits in one way or another. While they required creative energy and dogged persistence to achieve in practice, they were deceptively simple to state:

- Organize around a committed champion, often a physician with high community prestige and strong professional credentials;
- Create strong ties to the community, including neighborhood-based planning, locally hired staff, and accessible walk-in clinics;
- Invest in high-performing collaborations; reach out to import all available resources; recruit partners and be a partner in return;
- Integrate health-care services—rely on proven best practices, maintain patient contact beyond the clinic, facilitate communication across the care network;

- Tailor interventions to the individual, the setting, and the community—recognize and plan to reduce exposure to triggers in all environments in which patients may customarily find themselves.

We developed a plan to make these principles contagious and to spread the success of the top programs among the rest. We were determined to "infect" all community programs with a vision and plan for effective community outreach. First we identified some of the most effective leaders of well-performing programs and invited them to serve as "faculty" for peer-to-peer learning. We developed materials that we called a "Change Package" that laid out the five core principles of success with numerous examples of how they applied in actual community settings. Then we initiated an annual national meeting, EPA's National Asthma Forum, to which we invited more than 200 community practitioners, funders, insurers, and other key parties. We built the agenda around the Change Package and its five core elements and put the doctors, nurses, and administrators with the most experience not only at the lecture dais, but at each table to serve as collegial experts. We structured the forum not simply as an information exchange, but as a catapult for action at which every participant was challenged to identify specific workable plans for introducing new practices to which they would commit even before leaving the meeting. The Asthma Forum created excitement, spread knowledge, built peer networks, and fostered determination that accelerated the adoption of proven methods for reducing asthma attacks around the country. We went on to repeat the process for an increasingly large group of practitioners in each of the last several years of my EPA career.

As we moved forward, we added new features to build value for our program. One was a series of annual awards to care providers to "catch them in the act" of being successful, and to credit the authors of singularly effective approaches that we could then hold up as models for others to follow. Among the first to receive this award was Children's Mercy Hospital of Kansas City. Children's Mercy had an intriguing structure. As a hospital, they had beds to fill, and emergency asthma care was a money maker for them. As an insurer and public-health advocate, they had equivalent incentives to keep costs down and community health up. They resolved the implicit conflict resoundingly in favor of preventing childhood asthma in Kansas City. They set up clinics in high-morbidity neighborhoods and created partnerships with other providers, training treatment staff and outreach workers in asthma management. They developed an asthma education program for the more serious cases and taught partners how to train caregivers in the recognition and management of asthma triggers and symptoms at home. Finally, they developed a triage system to identify "frequent flyers," children with the most serious cases, and set up a system of home visits to identify and eliminate asthma triggers in the patient's home environment. Over several years Children's Mercy reduced emergency room visits by 80 percent and hospitalizations by 50 percent. EPA celebrated this success by awarding the 2005 National Environmental Leadership Award to Dr. Jay Portnoy and his staff. In subsequent years, Dr. Portnoy returned to the Asthma Forum as faculty, and, when he later became president of the American College of Allergy, Asthma and Immunology, he opened further opportunities for collaboration between EPA and the medical community. Throughout this period, our collaboration with CDC deepened and became increasingly productive, not simply because our goals were congruent, but because the AHOP study adhered to the evidence-based model to which CDC was committed. EPA continued to lead on managing the environmental management of asthma, while CDC approached the same goal through the redesign of medical intervention, with the energy of both agencies redoubling each other at a central point.

In all of this we were deeply aware that EPA's role was not so much that of expert as impresario. The real genius, the most courageous creativity, was to be found in community asthma clinics across the country. The opportunity we recognized for EPA was to identify their great work, figure out why it was successful, and erect a national stage on which they could perform for others to see. To extend the energy and learning beyond the limits of an annual forum, we later developed a campaign called Communities in Action for Asthma-Friendly Environments, aimed at growing the number of community-based programs using best practices (now nearing 600). The work takes place in a virtual meeting place (www.asthmacommunitynetwork.org) where practitioners swap methods and inspire one another on a daily basis. To complement the emphasis on health care itself, we also reached out to America's Health Insurance Plans to collaborate on model business cases that community programs could adapt to attract reimbursement for environmental interventions that improve health outcomes. At the same time we expanded the award program to recognize insurers that offer benefits for environmental trigger management. Since then EPA has been tracking demonstrations of improved health outcomes at a cost acceptable to insurers through managing environmental triggers. While this is the steepest hill to climb, several community-based programs have already made the case and are now being reimbursed, not only for emergency treatment of asthma, but also for disease prevention through management of environmental triggers.

CONCLUSION

The difference between regulatory and voluntary programs is profound. Both aim to change public behavior in environmentally appropriate ways, but one does it by command appealing to fear, the other by suggestion appealing to "greed," or, more precisely, people's desire to improve their lives. Voluntary programs lack the regulatory program's thump of authority. They can recommend, but neither prescribe nor proscribe. They can counsel, but not enforce. But within that designed powerlessness there are advantages and opportunities frequently denied to EPA's more puissant programs. Here are a few:

EPA's Bully Pulpit: EPA's public standing brings to mind what used to be said of E.F. Hutton—When EPA talks, people listen. Public awareness of the Agency's authority and expertise arises primarily through familiarity with its regulatory actions. Voluntary programs benefit from that established "brand awareness," with the result that advisory messages are more readily heard and heeded than they might otherwise be. And voluntary programs are not nearly so embattled in civic contention as their regulatory cousins.

Greater Freedom of Association: There used to be a saying around EPA, "Never hug a polluter." That came about, I am told, due to incidents early on when EPA managers were photographed at public events beaming happily with corporate executives who would later become targets of enforcement. These days EPA regulatory programs often enter into practical partnerships with industry groups, but they must be extremely cautious in doing so. For voluntary programs, like Energy Star and those addressing radon and asthma, EPA-industry partnerships are a prime way of doing business, and we get to hug each other all the time.

Greater Freedom to Change Course: Most regulatory programs are subject to strict standards and procedural limitations prescribed by statute or judicial decree. This is right and necessary to protect private interests from unconstrained government action. However, authorizing statutes are often inflexible in the face of real-world realities that might argue for timely program adjustments in everyone's best interest. Moreover, courts sometimes impose deadlines that make little sense outside the scope of a successful appellant's narrow interest—throwing program priorities, staffing, and resource allocations into prolonged chaos. Managers of voluntary programs are typically free to design sensible actions that meet real-world needs, and to adjust them flexibly in response to changing conditions.

Greater Freedom from Hostile Oversight: As one corner of the Iron Triangle, members of Congress frequently seek to influence, if not actually intimidate federal executives on the provisions of regulatory actions important to their constituents. Regulatory managers are commonly called upon to testify before Congress, often under strained circumstances. As appropriate as this may be in a representative democracy, it draws a lot of time and attention away from the job at hand, and regulatory managers must stay very tough indeed to keep from developing a Pavlovian sense of caution about their work. By comparison, managers of voluntary programs enjoy considerably more freedom to work creatively within the law, outside an atmosphere of threat, criticism, and manufactured political hurdles.

As noted in chapter 1, an essential purpose of the SES is to deploy exceptional managerial competence across government through a corps of senior executives who can adapt flexibly to a wide variety of presenting situations. EPA's mix of regulatory and voluntary programs illustrates the range of contrasting situations to which SES executives must address themselves.

REFERENCES

ASHRAE (American Society of Heating, Refrigerating, and Air Conditioning Engineers). 2009 *The Indoor Air Quality Guide: Best Practices for Construction and Commissioning.* http://www.ashrae.org/publications/page/IAQGuide.

Brunner, Greg and David Mudarri. 2004. US EPA, unpublished document.

Fisk, William J. 2000. *Health and Productivity Gains from Better Indoor Environments and Their Relationship with Building Energy Efficiency,* Annual Review of Energy Environments, 2000, 25:537-66.

Levin, H. 2005, *Annual Expenditures for Indoor Air Quality Prevention or Mitigation,* Lawrence Berkeley National Laboratory, Berkeley CA, June 2005.

Loh, Miranda M. et al. 2007. *Ranking Cancer Risk of Organic Hazardous Air Pollutants in the United States.* Environmental Health Perspectives, Aug; 115 (8)1160-66.

Maslow, Abraham. 1969. *A Psychology of Science.* Washington: Regnery Gateway Editions.

Morris, John C. 1997. The Distributional Impacts of Privatization in National Water-Quality Policy. *Journal of Politics* 59,1: 56-72.

———.1996. Institutional Arrangements in an Age of New Federalism. *Public Works Management & Policy* 1,2: 145-157.

Mudarri, David H. 1994. *The Costs and Benefits of Smoking Restrictions,* US EPA, prepared for Chairman Henry Waxman, Subcommittee on Health and the Environment, US House of Representatives.

National Academy of Sciences. 2011. *Climate Change, the Indoor Environment, and Health.* Washington: National Academies Press.

———.1999. *Health Effects of Exposure to Radon: BEIR VI.* Washington: National Academies Press.

———.1988. *Health Risks of Radiation and Other Internally Deposited Alpha Emitters: BEIR IV.* Washington: National Academies Press.

USEPA (United States Environmental Protection Agency). 2012. *Partnership for Clean Indoor Air.* www.pciaonline.org/.

———.2011. *The Inside Story: A Guide to Indoor Air Quality,* Washington. www.epa.gov/iaq/pubs/insidestory.html.

———.2009. *Citizen's Guide to Radon.* www.epa.gov/radon/pdfs/citizensguide.pdf.

———.2008. *Indoor Air Plus Construction Specifications.* http://epa.gov/indoorairplus/.

———.2007. *Building Assessment Survey and Evaluation Study.* www.epa.gov/iaq/base/.

———.1989. Report to Congress on Indoor Air Quality, Volume II: *Assessment and Control of Indoor Air Pollution.* Washington.

———.1987. *Unfinished Business: A Comparative Assessment of Environmental Problems*, Washington.
University of Michigan Center for Managing Chronic Disease. 2007. *Asthma Health Outcomes Project.* http://asthma.umich.edu/media/ahop_autogen/AHOP_2-21-08.pdf.

Chapter Eight

Formal Systems for Planning and Management

David Ziegele

> The principal challenge facing public managers is to understand the impor-
> tance of carefully defining the core tasks of the organization and to find both
> pecuniary and nonpecuniary incentives that will induce operators to perform
> those tasks as defined (Wilson 1989, 174).

That sounds very straightforward. Why is it so challenging to do in practice? This chapter will explore the reality of establishing and operating planning and management systems under a government-wide framework in a complex, decentralized agency with many non-federal partners. It will examine the forces that support or reinforce the development and use of these systems at the Environmental Protection Agency (EPA), the many factors that complicate or impede it, and the lessons that can be learned from EPA's experience in results-based management. It will not be a detailed history of the Agency's planning and management systems, nor will it address, except perhaps in a cursory way, the developments of the last few years.

Like all major federal agencies and departments, the Environmental Protection Agency was required to implement the Government Performance and Results Act (GPRA). The law, passed in 1993, was simple compared to most federal laws. It required the development of five-year strategic plans every three years, annual performance plans, and annual performance reports (GPRA 1993). Although the law was passed in 1993, the first deadlines did not hit agencies until 1997. EPA had developed strategic plans before 1997, had committed to specific activities as part of previous annual budget requests, and at different times in its history had internal accountability systems to track progress against commitments. However, GPRA set up a more rigorous and integrated structure for these activities and products and subjected them to the external scrutiny of the White House Office of Management and Budget, congressional appropriations committee staff, and the interested public. It also allowed external groups to examine and "grade" EPA's planning and management efforts against those of other agencies and departments. As will be seen, EPA chose to go beyond the basic requirements of GPRA to pursue much more fundamental and far-reaching results-based management reforms.

WHY FORMAL PLANNING AND MANAGEMENT SYSTEMS?

Fundamentally, strategic planning and performance management are about (1) making choices on what the agency will do (and at least implicitly, what it will not do) and how it will do it, (2) implementing the plan, (3) gathering data to assess progress, and (4) using performance data to change policies and programs, as needed, toward better results or more cost-effective strategies.

Formal planning and management systems are designed to help policy makers make their agencies more effective by asking and answering several key questions:

- What business are we in? What mission has the American public, via its elected officials, charged us to carry out?
- What are the most important problems or opportunities for us to address in fulfilling that mission?
- What can we commit to achieve in the long-term (what are our five-year goals and strategic objectives) and what activities and tools (strategies) will we use to make long-term progress?
- How should we align our dollar resources and the work of our employees with our strategic goals and objectives and ensure sufficient funding to carry out our strategies?
- What specific activities and results can we commit to achieve next year if we're given the funding we are requesting?
- Looking back at the end of each year, did we spend the funding as we committed, did we achieve our performance commitments, and are we making expected progress toward our long-term goals and objectives?
- What did we learn from our progress or lack of progress? What adjustments should we make in our funding, day-to-day activities, strategies, or long-term objectives in order to best achieve our long-term goals? Are our strategic goals still viable?

Some have linked results-based management in the public sector with the concepts of Total Quality Management developed by W. Edwards Deming (Gabor 1990) and Kaoru Ishikawa (Ishikawa 1985) for use in the private manufacturing sector. It is often described as the "Plan, Do, Check, Act" Cycle or PDCA Cycle. The concept is that for manufacturing companies to continuously increase product quality and for public organizations to improve their results, they shouldn't just "do" their work—they should plan for the long term, focus their resources on achieving long-term goals, measure performance, act on what they learn from performance data, and factor that into improved goals, strategies, and processes.

Beyond getting better results, why else would public managers direct and support the implementation of formal planning and management systems?

Control/Compliance

There may be a rare federal political appointee who comes on board as a caretaker and does not want to make his or her mark on the agency's policies or adjust its strategies and approaches. For the majority who come on board with an agenda for change, formal management systems can provide mechanisms to establish new directions and align resources and activities with them. Put more bluntly, senior leadership wants to gain control of the organization and ensure that employees at all levels, as well as implementation partners like states, tribes, and local governments, are aligned with the stated directions. Inertia is a powerful force in large bureaucracies and implementing even marginal changes in policies and practices can be challenging. As Peter Drucker recounted:

> When General Eisenhower was elected president, his predecessor, Harry S. Truman, said, "Poor Ike; when he was a general, he gave an order and it was carried out. Now he is going to sit in that big office and he'll give an order and not a damn thing will happen." (Drucker 2001, 250)

Drucker's lesson was that orders got executed in the military because everyone knew that officers personally verified that their directions were being followed. Drucker advised executives to follow the military officers' example to observe firsthand what is happening in the field. A broader lesson is that a policy direction or order amounts to little unless there is management follow-up, execution, and accountability. Since much of what large federal agencies and their partners do cannot be directly observed in a meaningful way, management systems can help serve as the executives' "eyes and ears" in the organization, providing at least some amount of control and compliance through performance commitments, performance measurements, and review of performance results for follow-up action.

Gain Internal/External Support for Program Direction

Everything a federal political appointee does is potentially open to scrutiny by a public that is likely organized into factions with varying views on key issues of the day. A formal planning system may not gain universal support for the strategic directions contained in a strategic plan, but a robust process for engaging with stakeholders may at least give interested parties the sense that the agency understands their points of view. Similarly, a participative planning process within the agency can help build in the ideas and concerns of the managers and staff who will eventually be charged with implementing the goals and strategies. And finally, a well-written strategic plan and annual plan can help an agency communicate what it is doing, why it is doing it, and what results it expects to achieve.

THE POLITICAL, LEGAL, AND ORGANIZATIONAL SETTING FOR PLANNING AND MANAGEMENT

Since its founding in the 1970s, EPA has operated in a difficult political, legal, and organizational environment that is often a reflection of the American public's diverse and often conflicting views on environmental protection and cleanup. This can have a profound impact on the Agency's ability to plan strategically and focus its resources on the highest-priority problems.

EPA is the frequent focus of criticism from both houses of Congress, made more difficult for the Agency by the large number of committees and sub-committees that have jurisdiction over different parts of its work. The last twenty years, including the several years before EPA created its first GPRA strategic and annual plans, have seen escalated partisan divides over environmental issues in general and EPA's role in particular. No major piece of environmental law has been passed since the 1990 Clean Air Act Amendments (proposed to a Democratic-controlled House and Senate and signed by Republican President George H.W. Bush). However, members have used information requests, oversight hearings, special investigations, legislative riders, procedural legislation, and other tools to make the Agency's work more difficult.

Additionally, the most readily apparent environmental problems, such as severe and visible smog, rivers polluted to the point of catching fire, and open chemical dumps, have been mitigated by the efforts of EPA, state and local agencies, and responsible companies and municipalities. The public and politicians are more divided about the need for government to address the remaining problems, which while significant, are less visible and require a more diverse set of tools than issuing and enforcing permits. EPA's efforts to use compliance promotion, regulatory flexibility in exchange for exemplary environmental performance, voluntary programs, public education, and technical assistance have not been consistently or broadly supported by members of Congress and the general public, many of whom wish to see the Agency's role limited to actions specifically required by law. Others would prefer that the Agency focus its resources on more aggressive traditional "command and control" strategies centered on permitting and enforcement. Even within the Agency, there have been varying views on the extent to which EPA should rely on its traditional tools and authorities versus alternative methods that may, in some cases, be more effective in addressing a problem.

EPA also operates in a very litigious setting. It is routinely sued by industry groups and environmental groups for its actions and perceived inactions. Many of the national standards issued by the Agency were done so under court-ordered deadlines, which limit EPA senior leadership's ability to use resources flexibly. Essentially, significant amounts of the Agency's priorities are dictated to it by statute and the courts.

Unlike in EPA's earliest years, much of the environmental protection work in the United States is delegated to state, tribal, and local authorities. While most of these partners' work is exemplary, it sometimes is not, and EPA usually lacks the resources and political will to step in and take over the work of a laggard state agency. States, for their part, have accepted the responsibility to run environmental programs using their own authorities or delegated federal authority, yet do not usually get sufficient federal grant support to cover the full workload associated with implementing federal law. This can add to tensions and further limit EPA's ability to influence in a "top-down" way state and local performance. EPA has been very motivated in recent years to consult in a more meaningful way with state, tribal, and local program managers and, to the extent possible, work in partnership with them on joint priorities and accountability. The National Environmental Performance Partnership System (NEPPS) has been used as the framework for setting joint priorities, agreeing on how work should be divided up, and providing flexibility where possible for local situations to be addressed. Under the NEPPS framework, states can work with their regional office counterparts to establish Performance Partnership Agreements that identify joint priorities and strategies. They may also combine federal grant funds in Performance Partnership Grants, allowing the states to redirect federal resources to high-priority problems or implement non-traditional approaches to solving problems.

Also, EPA's programs operate under multiple statutes, with diverse authorities and tools for the Agency and its partners to use, depending on the pollutant, chemical, waste product, industry practice, or receiving medium (air, water, etc.) being addressed. The statutes present a bewildering array of things that the Agency must do, could do, and cannot do under different circumstances. This, again, can limit senior managers' ability to shift resources or priorities across programs or within programs. Prescriptive and proscriptive authorities can also force EPA to "look for its keys under the lamppost," that is, conduct the activities it is authorized to do, and ignore what may be more fruitful opportunities that are outside its authorities.

Finally, EPA headquarters is organized by large offices, headed by assistant administrators, which largely follow EPA's statutory authorities (e.g., Office of Air and Radiation, Office of Water, etc.). Assistant administrators are political appointees who typically have substantive experience and expertise in the program areas they lead and usually bring to the job their own agendas for advancing those programs. Assistant administrators understand that their legacies will likely rest on their program-specific accomplishments and not the extent to which they advance or support cross-program efforts. Despite dozens of admirable efforts over the years to foster more cross-office or "multi-media" approaches to environmental problems, it has proven difficult for top management to move most of the Agency's work out of a single-office or single-program perspective. Cross-office coordination is further hampered by the common knowledge that Agency budget decisions are most often part of a zero-sum game (at best), in which competition, even when subtly pursued, can be a sounder strategy than cooperation.

Earlier Planning and Management Efforts at EPA

EPA's implementation of GPRA in the late 1990s was not the first time that the Agency produced strategic plans or ran formal performance tracking systems. Previous administrators had commissioned both.

For example, during the Carter administration, the agency operated a system that tracked "Planned Program Accomplishments." Based on accounts from managers and staff in the agency at the time, the system died from the weight of too many tracked elements and more detail than senior managers were willing or able to use.

In the early Reagan administration, Administrator Ann Gorsuch Burford set up an accountability system, called the "Administrator's Management Accountability System," to track progress against commitments, with a focus on reducing backlogs of key programmatic outputs, such as issuance of water pollution permits and the setting of statutorily mandated national pollution standards.

When the scandal-ridden Burford team left EPA in 1983, newly appointed and returning Administrator William Ruckelshaus and his Deputy Administrator, Alvin L. Alm, also an Agency veteran, adapted the accountability system to capture a broader set of program elements. The perception in the Agency was that Administrator Burford's purpose for the system had been to "show that we are doing what is required by statutes" (and not necessarily more than that). Ruckelshaus and Alm wanted both to galvanize

Agency managers and staff to "get the environmental cop back on the beat," particularly in enforcement, and to show the public that they were doing so. Deputy Administrator Alm, as the Agency's *de facto* chief operating officer, used the system's quarterly reports as the focus for individual discussions with headquarters program office chiefs and with regional managers on his visits to the Agency's ten regional offices. He reviewed the performance reports in detail and held managers accountable for performance.

The system was managed by managers and staff in the Agency's policy office. They strove to keep the number of tracked items to a manageable number and to have the quarterly reports and management discussions be about meaningful performance and more than "bean counts." This was a daunting task for a number of reasons:

1. The seriousness with which the Deputy Administrator was using the system made Headquarters program managers want to have their programs tracked in the system (counter to the stereotype that career bureaucrats want to be left alone to operate their programs without scrutiny from top management or the public). It was clearly the way to get management attention, to get managers and staff to perform energetically, and potentially to maintain or increase program resources. These factors put the policy office in the position of constantly grappling with programs to keep the system focused on a manageable number of measures, and not to track and count everything that could be tracked and counted.

2. There were few program elements beyond pure outputs/activities (rather than outcomes or results) that could be tracked on a quarterly basis. This inevitably led to the appearance that the system was less about environmental results and more about "how many widgets you could produce."

3. When it was possible to track only activities rather than results, senior management sought to steer staff toward the activities that are most clearly linked to results. In most programs, there was no simple way to distinguish the more consequential actions from the less consequential and to provide incentives for people to focus more attention on the former where possible. This led to the perception that managers and staff would gravitate toward completion of the "easy beans" that would "get the numbers up" and avoid the risk of missing a performance commitment. A joke around the Agency was that "every sewage treatment plant within twenty miles of the regional office was inspected five times this year."

The system continued to be used for several years after Ruckelshaus's and Alm's departure, but generally with less top management time and attention than in its early years. It was eventually dropped in the early 1990s.

Similarly, the Agency produced strategic plans in the years before GPRA went into effect. However, the purpose of these plans was primarily to identify and reinforce the administration's policy and management themes rather than to develop and communicate long-term programmatic goals and objectives. For example, the Agency's 1995–1999 Strategic Plan, known informally as "the orange book" from its cover color, was framed around seven "Guiding Principles":

- ecosystem protection
- environmental justice
- pollution prevention
- strong science and data
- partnerships
- reinventing EPA management
- environmental accountability

The plan described each of the guiding principles and outlined objectives and strategies for each. The objectives and strategies varied in their level of detail and were generally not expressed in terms that could be measured or related to expected environmental results. Nonetheless, the plan reflected serious thought about the Clinton administration's priorities for how EPA's work should be done and had some degree of influence in the Agency.

Although the 1995–1999 Strategic Plan did not identify measurable long-term environmental goals, the Agency was undertaking a parallel effort that was designed to do just that. The National Environmental Goals Project marshaled the efforts of dozens of managers and staff around the agency to identify a set of environmental problems or programs and determine the measurable outcomes the Agency would commit to in the coming years. In December 1996, the Agency published a draft document, "Environmental Goals for America," for review by its government partners (EPA 1996). For each of the twelve environmental goals identified in the report, it characterized the progress to date and the challenges remaining, identified the parties responsible for taking action, proposed specific environmental milestones to be achieved by 2005, and briefly outlined the approaches or strategies EPA and its partners would take to achieve the 2005 milestones.

Given that the "Environmental Goals for America" draft document presented a limited number of goals, measurable long-term milestones, and organizational strategies, it was in many ways a strategic plan (and arguably a better one than the Agency's more thematic and rhetorical 1995–1999 Strategic Plan). The goals report unfortunately suffered from several problems unrelated to the quality of its content:

- The participative process the Agency used to develop it took a very long time, during which some of the initial energy behind it began to dissipate.
- It then ran into philosophical and policy roadblocks at the Office of Management and Budget (OMB), which had to approve the document before it could be made final.
- Finally, the last stages of its long development process overlapped with the beginning of EPA's process for developing its first strategic plan under GPRA.

The draft Goals report was released for what became a multi-month review starting in December of 1996. EPA's GPRA Strategic Plan was due to Congress by September 30, 1997. OMB managers raised a serious concern about the substantive relationship between the two documents and potential public confusion if they were published as separate products during the same time period. OMB's concern was communicated succinctly by a senior OMB official in the summer of 1997 in a phone conversation with a senior OCFO manager, "If the goals and objectives in the two documents are identical, why do we need both documents? And if they're different, how do we explain that to Congress and the public?" Because the GPRA plan was required by law and the National Goals report was a voluntary effort (about which OMB had always been skeptical if not overtly negative), EPA withdrew the draft goals report from government review and ended the project as a standalone effort.

Despite its never having resulted in a final product, the goals project ended up making a huge contribution to the Agency's planning and performance management efforts, as much of the content of the draft report was incorporated into the Agency's September 1997–2002 Strategic Plan, released in September of 1997.

Another tremendously important precursor to the Agency's implementation of GPRA was the report by a group of high-level career managers charged in 1995 with examining how the Agency carried out its planning, budgeting, and accountability processes. Administrator Carol Browner and Deputy Administrator Fred Hansen created the Planning, Budgeting and Accountability Task Force in response to an influential study conducted by the National Academy of Public Administration in 1995 at the request of the Senate Appropriations Committee (National Academy of Public Administration 1995). Among other important findings, the task force noted that the Agency had, up to that point, failed to develop a substantive link between its stated goals and its budget requests, nor had it provided a meaningful "feedback loop" to assess the extent to which it was achieving desired results and adjusting accordingly. As the group stated in its February 1996 report, "It is time for EPA to link its budget to clear policy goals and measurable environmental results. Only then will we be able to tell the public what we are going to do to protect communities' health and the environment, how we will do it, how much it will cost, and when we will deliver results" (EPA 1996).

In 1997, the Agency summarized its intentions as follows:

1. To develop a clearly articulated mission and a set of goals and objectives for accomplishing the mission as well as a set of guiding principles by which these goals can be translated into our day-to-day activities and programs.
2. To make better use of scientific information related to human health and environmental risks in setting priorities.
3. To improve the link between long-term, outcome-based, customer-focused, environmental planning and yearly resource allocation.
4. To develop a new management system that allows EPA's leadership and the American public to assess our accomplishments accurately and provide useful feedback for making future decisions. (Environmental Protection Agency 1997)

As part of the broader effort to improve the Agency's management for results and in response to a specific recommendation from the Planning, Budgeting and Accountability Task Force, Administrator Browner directed that the Agency undertake a reorganization to form a new office to integrate these important functions. The Office of the Chief Financial Officer (OCFO), formed in July of 1997, consisted of two offices. The Office of the Comptroller, with responsibility for budgeting, financial management, and financial services, was moved in its entirety from the Office of Administration and Resources Management to OCFO. The Office of Planning, Analysis, and Accountability was a newly created entity that pulled the largely moribund strategic planning functions from the Agency's policy office (Office of Policy, Planning, and Evaluation) and added staffs focused on accountability and analysis related to priority-setting and performance measurement.

The reorganization was intended to ameliorate the longstanding divide between planning and budgeting by bringing the planning and budgeting staffs under a common political appointee (the CFO) charged with integrating the functions. It was also expected that the analysis staff of the newly formed Office of Planning, Analysis, and Accountability would bring together information on the relative risks of the environmental problems on the Agency's plate with economic analyses of the costs of reducing those risks, thus allowing senior managers to set strategic goals and priorities on a more rational basis than may have been possible in the past. Because of the large amount of work necessary to develop the Agency's first GPRA strategic plan, annual performance plan, and goals-based budget structure, detailees from around the Agency were brought in to get the work underway, rather than waiting for the formal reorganization to be complete.

Implementing the New Vision for Planning, Budgeting, Analysis, and Accountability and GPRA

The Government Performance and Results Act of 1993 requires government agencies to do a small number of relatively simple-sounding things (GPRA 1993):

1. Develop a five-year strategic plan every three years
2. Develop an annual performance plan, with performance goals and measures, to accompany the agency's annual budget request
3. At the end of the fiscal year, develop an annual performance report that identifies which annual performance goals and measures the agency met and failed to meet.

In the wake of the reports from the National Academy of Public Administration and its internal Planning, Budgeting and Accountability Task Force, the Agency launched an aggressive approach that went well beyond the basic requirements of GPRA.

1. Organizationally integrating the planning, budgeting, and accountability functions—most other agencies assigned to an individual or small staff the job of writing the agency strategic plan, annual plan, and performance report.
2. Capturing 100 percent of agency goals and activities in the strategic plan—other agencies developed strategic plans that "cherry picked" strategic goals from among the agencies' activities or presented broad overlays of goals, rather than developing specific strategic goals and objectives for the entire array of the agencies' work.
3. Integrating the Annual Performance Plan and President's Budget— other agencies sent separate documents to Congress to fulfill the GPRA requirement for an Annual Performance Plan and to submit their agencies' portion of the President's Budget. Starting with its Fiscal Year 1999 budget request, EPA submitted its GPRA Annual Performance Plan and budget as a single document—the money requested and performance targets to be achieved.

4. Restructuring the Agency's budget and its accounting structure to mirror the goal and objective structure of the strategic plan. This was a massive undertaking that involved moving every dollar and workyear previously grouped by "program element" into the new goals-based budget architecture.
5. Conducting analyses to portray the relative risks presented by environmental problems and the costs of mitigating those risks.
6. Upgrading and integrating the functions related to tracking Agency performance and improving how performance data informed Agency decisions. The accountability staff in the Office of Planning, Analysis, and Accountability brought together responsibility for the GPRA Performance Report, EPA's implementation of the Federal Managers' Financial Integrity Act, and coordination of the Agency's response to audits by the Inspector General.

To maintain a participative process and to secure Agency "buy in" on the new directions underway, the CFO set up and chaired a Planning, Budgeting, Analysis, and Accountability Advisory Board. The board was made up of senior career officials who met monthly to offer helpful advice and assistance to OCFO. And to the extent that some mid-level planning and budgeting staffs in the programs and regions were resistant to the new approaches, the engagement of the Advisory Board helped communicate that these were Agency decisions and not solely OCFO's initiatives.

SUPPORTING AND IMPEDING FORCES AND LESSONS LEARNED

The preceding sections provide a factual backdrop of the history and context for EPA's efforts to revamp its planning, budgeting, analysis, and accountability systems. In each of the following sections, I will present my assessment of the factors that can help advance and impede those efforts in the "real world" of environmental agency management and lessons learned from experience. I served in the newly created Office of the Chief Financial Officer from its inception in 1997 until early 2005, briefly as Deputy Comptroller, then as the first Director of the Office of Planning, Analysis, and Accountability. In the latter capacity, I was responsible for the Agency's strategic plan, the planning portions of the annual planning and budgeting process, and the Agency's annual performance report, among other duties.

Planning Strategically

Ideally, strategic planning in a regulatory agency would entail identifying the nature of the problems to be addressed, the most important contributors to the problems, and strategies for addressing those contributors. It would also allow top managers to consider shifting priorities and resources across programs or problem areas based on expected public value.

In my experience, EPA program managers and their staffs typically have the desire and ability to gain a clear strategic view of the problems they are trying to mitigate or prevent and the biggest contributors to those problems. They also use different factors to set priorities within their areas of responsibility. And finally, when authorized to do so by Agency or administration leaders, they do develop multi-year and sometimes multi-agency strategies to set new direction for action and to galvanize support for it. If and when the new initiatives are approved by the administration, these strategies then get reflected in Agency planning and budgeting documents.

However, many factors constrain or impede EPA from truly planning strategically. A simple one is that OMB guidance typically directs agencies to develop their GPRA strategic plans based on currently expected resource levels and current legislative authorities. As stated in the August 2011 version of OMB Circular A-11, the primary directive governing planning, budgeting, and performance reporting: "A strategic plan is not a budget request; the projected levels of goal achievement must be commensurate with anticipated resource levels. The strategic plan should not bind the Administration to new budget or legislative commitments" (Executive Office of the President 2011, Section 210 page 3). In other words, agencies might quietly contemplate what additional strategic results they could achieve with increased resources and new authorities, but they are not to make that planning public via their GPRA strategic plans.

As mentioned above, EPA offices are often constrained by prescriptive statutes, lawsuits, the threat of lawsuits, pressure from interest groups, intense scrutiny from members of Congress and their staffs, etc. Also, EPA's major programs can be considered to be "mature," as the statutes they have been operating under have been in place, without major amendments, for at least fifteen years and in most cases, many more. Currently, a typical EPA program's mix of activities and resource allocation likely reflect an equilibrium state borne of the external and internal forces brought to bear on it over many years. The activities they carry out as a result may or may not be those that will most effectively meet long-term goals—they are likely the ones that will get reasonable results, will keep supporters at least minimally happy, and keep detractors' concerns at bay. Thus, a program's ability to apply a rational, results-based strategic planning process to its mission and to make major changes as a result, is severely constrained. The same is obviously true for making major shifts in priorities or resources across programs as a result of planning strategically.

With regard to lessons learned, the largest is that development of a strategic plan does not mean that program managers and staff will (or necessarily should in all cases) truly plan strategically. It is possible to develop a useful strategic plan that is a description of what will be accomplished if programs are implemented for the next five years as they are being implemented today. However, that straight extrapolation may not meet the expectations of internal and external stakeholders. Thus, senior leaders responsible for the planning process need to be clear about the assumptions and constraints that will guide program managers as they develop their portions of the strategic plan (e.g., assume current authorities and resources or instead, explore and propose broader and more ambitious potential strategies).

Goal-Based Budget Structure

EPA senior managers made the courageous decision to restructure EPA's budget and accounting systems to mirror the Agency's GPRA goals, objectives, and "sub-objectives." Thus, a five-year target for reducing ozone pollution by a certain amount became not only a public commitment of intended results, but also a designated bundle of resources (contract money, workyears, and grant money) that would be a line item in annual budgets and end-of-year financial statements. This contrasted with the previous approach of budgeting by office and program, unaccompanied by a commitment to achieve specific long-term results.

The traditional budget structure generally separated the budgets of program offices that may well have been working toward the same broad goals or objectives. In contrast, the new structure brought together in the budget (as well as the strategic plan) all offices working on the same goals and objectives. Thus the performance commitments and budget for the Office of Research and Development's applied research on wetlands accompanied those of the Offices of Water's wetlands program office and its regional and state components. As important, as part of the annual planning process, OCFO facilitated "goal team" meetings, in which program managers with resources and strategic objectives in a given goal would coordinate a group meeting with the deputy administrator to discuss their program directions for the upcoming budget year.

In the Government Accountability Office's review of agencies' GPRA implementation, it noted that EPA was one of only two agencies to link planning structure and budget accounts, and one of only three agencies that made substantial changes to program activity structures within their budgets (EPA 1999).

The factors reinforcing this new direction were primarily a desire on the part of senior management to move fully in the direction of "managing for results" and to embrace the recommendations of the Planning, Budgeting and Accountability Task Force. It was also responsive to the findings and recommendations of the earlier National Academy of Public Administration report, which had been supported and closely followed by staff on the Senate appropriations sub-committee with jurisdiction over EPA. EPA senior managers likely also understood, at least intuitively, that program offices and regional offices would invest more fully in the substance of strategic planning and performance measurement if they were integral to the budget structure and process for getting funds, rather than more loosely "linked."

The factors potentially resisting or impeding the goal-structured budget and accounting system were numerous and strong. First, it required an extraordinary amount of work by OCFO and budget and accounting staffs around the Agency. Fortunately, earlier investments in budget and financial management automation made the work easier than it would have been otherwise, but by no means easy.

To the surprise of some, the new budget structure was received in a lukewarm and sometimes hostile manner by budget professionals outside of EPA who had to make sense of and make decisions about EPA's budget. Their problems were less philosophical than practical—OMB staff and congressional appropriations staffs have relatively little time to review budgets, understand them, develop questions for the Agency, and develop options and recommendations for their bosses on where and how the budgets should be changed. Their starting point for examining a new budget is typically incremental: "What has changed from previous years' budgets?" That is, which programs have proposed increases from "the base," which have proposed decreases, what new initiatives have been included, and where did the funding come from for them? Obviously, a budget that shows up in a completely different structure from those of all previous years is going to complicate the lives of reviewers on a tight deadline. To at least partially ease this problem, EPA budget staffs prepared "crosswalks" to show where the elements of the new budget were in previous years' budgets.

EPA made one major mid-course correction to the planning architecture in its 2003–2008 Strategic Plan, released in 2003. The two previous GPRA strategic plans had ten strategic goals. With those ten goals, every EPA program, dollar, and workyear had a "home" somewhere in the ten goals and underlying objectives. Given the nature of an organization as large as EPA, this necessarily meant that the ten goals were a mix of "ends" (e.g., Clean Air, Clean and Safe Water, etc.) and what many regarded as "means" for achieving those ends (e.g., effective management, quality environmental information, etc.).

Input from internal and external stakeholders and OCFO's own experience in managing the goal-based planning and budgeting process had shown that 1) ten goals, no matter how important each may be, were more than senior managers or the public could be expected to focus on, understand, or care about and 2) given top management's limited time for and interest in the processes for priority setting and budgeting, time and attention on "means" goals could take focus away from the environmental goals that were at the core of EPA's mission. In 2001 and 2002, at the request of Deputy Administrator Linda Fisher, OCFO led a major mid-course review of the Agency's results-based management practices. The many recommendations from that effort included one to make the Agency strategic plan more useful by focusing the goals on the environmental goals of the Agency (EPA 2002). Thus, OCFO recommended and the acting administrator agreed in July of 2002 that the Agency's strategic architecture should have five strategic goals. Resources and results for support functions could be captured elsewhere in the Agency's strategic and annual plans and budgets, and could be allocated across the five goals in the Agency's cost accounting system.

A similar, long-simmering debate has occurred within the Agency and between the Agency and some stakeholders about whether the enforcement and compliance-promotion functions of the Office of Enforcement and Compliance Assurance should have their own goal or should be integrated with the air, water, land, and communities/ecosystems goals to which environmental compliance presumably contributes. This is a case where political considerations trump "planning and management purity" and likely will for the foreseeable future. Among the diverse public and stakeholder views on the expected role of EPA, one of the strongest is that EPA is an enforcement agency—the environmental cop on the beat when market forces fail and when other government entities might falter. In this view, for a regulatory agency, high-profile enforcement presence and compliance with the law are important ends in themselves. Thus, every confirmed and acting administrator since 1997 has opted to include in the strategic plan a goal focused on enforcement and compliance promotion.

With regard to lessons learned from goal-based budgeting, I believe that EPA made the right decision to restructure its budget to mirror its strategic goals. A more incremental shift to results-based management, while having lower transaction costs, would not have galvanized the program offices to focus sufficient attention on the relationship between results and funding. In most respects, OCFO and its counterparts in the program offices and regions did an admirable job implementing the monumental change.

I also believe that the initial establishment of a comprehensive ten-goal structure was a reasonable one. Given the revolutionary nature of the 1997 shift to a goal-based budget, I don't believe that senior managers in support office functions would have agreed that their omission from the 1997 Strategic Plan's goal architecture was fair or workable. By 2003, with several years' experience trying (and largely failing) to put the support functions' planning sessions on the same level of top-management interest and importance as those of the line program offices, there was a sounder basis (though definitely not unanimity) for excluding them from the formal strategic architecture and limiting the strategic goals to the environmental program goals. The more streamlined five-goal structure proved to be a much more workable framework for strategic and annual planning, budgeting, and performance reporting.

Cross-Program, Goal-Based Planning and Budgeting

Bringing related programs together for internal planning and budgeting processes and in external documents presented both benefits and challenges for EPA. Forces supporting it included the fact that it allowed senior managers to get a feel for the strategic directions of related functions in single settings. Using the example cited above, it was efficient and useful to have in the room the representative from the Office of Research and Development whose applied research work would be supporting the environmental goal under discussion. In some cases, these forums, such as goal team meetings with the Deputy Administrator in advance of budget discussions for the coming year, fostered cross-program coordination and communication that would likely not have occurred otherwise. No program manager would want to risk appearing to work at cross purposes or in an uncoordinated way with another program manager during a meeting with the Deputy Administrator.

In other cases, these meetings were a vehicle for communicating cross-office, coordinated planning and implementation that was part of business as usual. A good example of this was the teamwork between the managers and staff in the Superfund program in the Office of Solid Waste and Emergency Response and those in the site remediation enforcement office in the Office of Enforcement and Compliance Assurance (which enforced the requirement that parties that contributed to pollution at Superfund sites pay for the clean-up). This cross-office coordination pre-dated GPRA and Agency Goal Teams and was easily integrated into the Agency's goal-based planning and budgeting.

Similarly, presenting strategic objectives for related programs linked by a common goal in the Agency's strategic plans provided the public with the opportunity to see the mix of the programs that contribute to environmental outcomes.

There were also several forces working against the multi-office, goal-based approach to planning and budgeting. The most notable was the traditional autonomy senior managers had to make budget proposals for their own offices rather than doing it collaboratively with offices doing related work.

Although EPA is perceived to be an agency in which nothing major gets done unless all affected offices are fully involved and get "a say," if not veto power, over the outcome, priority setting and budgeting were traditionally areas in which decisions were made within program offices and generally not vetted with others before submission to the budget office. Indeed, while Goal Teams would join together to discuss past performance, upcoming priorities, and resource needs in general terms in their meetings with the Deputy Administrator, Goal Teams did not make decisions on specific resource levels that individual offices within the goal would request. This remained within the purview of the individual "National Program Managers" or NPMs (usually assistant administrators) in whose offices the programs were carried out.

Another variable that potentially limits the effectiveness of goal-based, performance-based priority-setting and budgeting is the extent to which political leaders (in EPA's case, usually the Deputy Administrator as chief operating officer) focus on goals, strategies, and performance data as they interact with other senior leaders and career managers and staff on budget decisions. In purely performance-based decision making, resources would flow to the programs that are addressing serious environmental or public health problems, that have articulated strategies for how they will make progress, and that are consistently delivering measurable results in a cost-effective way. Resources would flow from programs that do not have a handle on the nature and severity of the problems they are addressing, have not devised clear strategies for making progress, and do not have in place outcome-based performance measures to judge how past or future activities relate to longer-term results.

The extent to which senior leaders use every opportunity to scrutinize programs' problem assessments, goals, strategies, and past and expected future results will dictate how seriously Agency managers and staff will invest in performance management—clear goals, sound multi-year strategies, and outcome-based measures. Managing for results is hard work. If it is not rewarded with positive feedback and favorable resource decisions where appropriate, savvy managers will gravitate toward the practices that do seem to garner positive feedback and resources—predicting dire environmental consequences if resources are cut, invoking the threat of interest group lawsuits, delivering entertaining but substance-free presentations at planning and budgeting forums, or perennially promising improved performance measures without actually doing anything to develop and deliver them.

Finally, another constraint or disincentive for the use of goal-based planning and budgeting is that Congressional decisions on agencies' budgets sometimes bear no relation to the magnitude of the risks being addressed or the expected programmatic results. External groups often pressure EPA and Congress to maintain or increase funding for politically popular programs that, dollar for dollar, may not necessarily deliver the same magnitude of results as other programs. For example, grant programs to fund the construction of wastewater treatment plants push federal money out to municipalities across the country and support jobs in the transport, construction, and construction materials sectors. EPA's attempts over the years to trim this program in order to marginally increase funding for higher-priority initiatives have usually been rebuffed by Congress.

Regarding lessons learned about cross-program planning processes, central planning and budget offices need to build processes that will have inherent value to the participants, so that they will invest time and effort to do meaningful planning and performance measurement in order to benefit and not out of the bureaucratic necessity to "feed the beast" (the planning and budgeting office's processes). Program participants shouldn't feel that the investment in planning and budgeting reaches the point that "planning is our most important product" (as one EPA senior manager jokingly described his own office's internal planning systems). Reducing the transaction costs of setting performance targets and reporting on results, as EPA has done in recent years with new data systems, will help keep the cost-to-benefit ratio of results-based management reasonable. Another necessary ingredient for program managers to value planning and results-based management is their seeing that planning products and processes are influencing decisions by the Agency's most senior managers. Since those senior appointees often don't stay more than a few years, this means being ready to adapt planning processes to fit the management style and temperament of the person at the top. Some senior leaders are less interested in Agency management than policy issues or managing political firefights. While it may be tempting to think that they will undergo a sudden conversion when presented with an elegant and involved planning process (i.e., the "build it and they will come" model), it is more likely to reinforce his or her current preferences and aversions. It would be better to scale back the process closer to the level of the senior leader's level of interest and willingness to invest than to risk putting his or her indifference on display for all to see.

Developing and Using Outcome-Based Performance Measures and Data for Decision-Making

True results-based management requires that programs have in place measures for judging progress or lack of progress toward long-term results, have performance data of adequate quality and frequency to feed the measures, and use the results from analysis of the measurement data to make adjustments in their program strategies or goals.

Factors reinforcing the development and use of performance measures and information have largely come from outside of EPA's programs. OCFO has done an admirable job over the years of encouraging, cajoling, and assisting programs in improving their measures. In the early years of GPRA implementation, OCFO helped make net improvements in the Agency's annual performance goals and measures by getting programs to cut back on the total number of measures and focus where possible on those that were more outcome based rather than pure activity counts. As likely happens in all management systems that appear to be important, programs' early bias was to include one or more (sometimes many more) performance goals and measures for every program in their portfolio, under the assumption that goals and measures would provide the program with visibility and internal and external support.

OMB became a driving force for performance measurement improvements during the Bush administration through the Program Assessment Rating Tool (PART), a largely subjective process by which OMB analysts judged the extent to which programs had outcome-based measures in place and were achieving results. The threat of low PART scores and the possibility of subsequent budget cuts motivated many programs at EPA and across government to invest in improving their performance measures.

There are many forces constraining the Agency's ability to uniformly report on the environmental and public-health outcomes of its activities across all programs. People outside EPA have often wondered why the Agency faced (and to a large extent still faces) such difficulty in doing this.

The program structures outlined in EPA's authorizing statutes greatly affect its ability to collect data to support outcome-based measures. The programs with the best performance data are those whose authorizing statutes set up a performance-based regulatory scheme. The largest and most notable is the Clean Air Act criteria air pollutant program for regulating sulfur dioxide, ozone, and other ubiquitous man-made pollutants. The statute requires EPA to set a health-based standard for the pollutant in the ambient air, to manage the development of state and local implementation plans for achieving the standard, and to monitor the ambient air to judge progress. This statutory framework has driven the spending of hundreds of millions of dollars to develop reliable monitoring equipment, deploy it widely, collect and analyze the data, manage the data, and make far-reaching decisions on which regions are adequately addressing their pollution problems and which are not. As a result of this and related authorities (such as the ability to require facilities to report on their pollutant emissions), EPA has reasonably good data on ambient air quality for these pollutants.

In contrast, while EPA has an indoor air program, it does not have the authority to regulate indoor air quality. It therefore cannot direct other governmental entities, citizens, or companies to monitor pollutants in the indoor air. To track indoor air quality trends over time, EPA would have to undertake or commission special studies, which would require getting permission from OMB to collect information from non-government entities.

Similarly, EPA tends to have relatively poor results data when the focus of the program is on management practices rather than pollution reduction. Regulation of hazardous waste, for example, involves (among other things) getting companies to identify whether they are generating or handling a hazardous waste, to apply for a permit to do so, and to comply with the conditions of the permit for record-keeping and dealing with the waste safely. It is not an explicit goal of the program to reduce the amount of waste each company produces or to track and reduce citizens' exposure to hazardous waste (though there is a presumption that safe handling of the waste will reduce the risk to workers and others). Therefore, EPA's data on citizens' exposure to hazardous wastes is miniscule compared to its data on air quality and air pollution emissions and ambient air quality in relation to affected populations.

Other constraining factors on developing and using outcome-based performance measures are limited resources at the federal and state level to put monitoring in place and to gather, analyze, and manage additional data; technical limitations of monitoring equipment; incomplete scientific knowledge on the exposures and risks (to both human health and ecosystems) of some pollutants; unclear relationships between environmental outcomes and EPA activities; and data lags that result in performance not being available for many months or years after the end of the fiscal year in which the work was done.

A major lesson learned about performance measurement is that, despite the admonitions of OMB, the National Academy of Public Administration, the Government Accountability Office, and others who believed that EPA should be able to make dramatic leaps in the outcome orientation of its annual performance measures, there appears to be no substitute for steady, incremental progress toward better measures. Better measures require different and better data, which EPA and its partners must have the authority, resources, and technology to collect, manage, and analyze. They also require agreement among EPA and partners on what the most useful and scientifically sound measures will be and they must agree to collect and submit the data in a consistent way and on fixed schedules. All of this takes hard work, time, and a great deal of focus by senior management and staff.

Nonetheless, it is possible and necessary to make real progress over time. As outlined by EPA senior career manager Michael Stahl in his Spring 2009 article in *The Public Manager*, measures of intermediate outcomes, such as pollutant loadings to be reduced by an agency action, help bridge the gap between activity counts and measures of ultimate results. Among other benefits of intermediate outcome measures, data are more readily available for intermediate than for final outcomes, they provide some insights into the extent to which agency activities will lead toward final outcomes, and they have a direct cause-and-effect relationship with agency activities (whereas final outcomes may be influenced by many factors in addition to agency activities) (Stahl 2009, 7).

Another promising opportunity not pursued by the Agency during the early years of GPRA implementation is selective sampling of program activities to estimate the intermediate outcomes. For example, if it is not feasible to estimate or directly track the expected pollutant loading reduction from every water pollution permit, statistical sampling of a relatively small number of permits may give the Agency a timely indicator of the effectiveness of the permitting program in contributing to longer-term outcomes.

In any case, as programs make progress in improving the quality of their performance measures, they expand their opportunities to actually use the performance information to inform planning, budgeting and day-to-day management decisions, in ways not afforded them by pure activity or output measures.

Central Planning and Management in a Decentralized Intergovernmental System

A strength of central planning and management, as mentioned above, is that it can help secure senior management's control of a large bureaucracy and counter the natural tendency of people wanting to pursue their own approaches to achieving the agency's general mission. A downside is that players close to the center of the centrally managed system might use it to exert top-down control over others in the implementation chain at the expense of bottom-up input on priorities or flexibility to adapt programs to regional or local conditions.

An early reality of EPA's GPRA implementation was that National Program Managers (NPMs) established program-wide performance targets for a given fiscal year as much as fifteen months before that fiscal year began. These targets were then reflected in NPMs' national program guidance. Regional offices needed to begin translating those targets into region- and state-specific targets, but lacked the flexibility to deviate greatly from the mix of activities reflected in the NPMs' already established national targets (since by that point they were public commitments). To the extent regional managers and staff agreed with the NPMs' strategies and mix of activities, this offered them an attractive negotiating tool in working with state agencies on grant agreements (i.e., "I'd like to accommodate your needs, but headquarters insists that we do more of X and less of Y"). To the extent they didn't agree with the strategies and activity mixes, their flexibility to deviate from them was limited.

EPA headquarters offices, regional offices, and states and tribes with the delegated authority to manage EPA programs have wrestled for decades with issues of flexibility and accountability. (Regions, for better or worse, face both sides of the issue, since their work is overseen by headquarters and they oversee the work of states and delegated tribes.) Unfortunately, too often the two concepts are portrayed as being mutually exclusive—"If you're to be accountable (for doing what I need you to do), there can't be much flexibility, if any." And from the other side, "you want me to perform and be accountable for activities that aren't relevant to my environmental situation. You should give me flexibility to do what works here."

Through its internal evaluations and extensive consultation with states and tribes, EPA learned lessons about working with partners to implement results-based management and put in place many reforms to better align national, regional, state, and tribal priorities and programs. The middle ground that EPA and its partners gradually shifted toward was built on two concepts: (1) regions, states, and tribes should engage earlier and more meaningfully with headquarters on national-level planning and priority-setting, so that national program priorities might better reflect their needs and interests; and (2) regions and states should make a strategic case for the need for flexibility to deviate from national priorities, but should be held accountable for getting results from the work that they do as an alternative to national priorities.

As part of the Managing for Improved Results Steering Group effort mentioned earlier, senior career managers recommended reforms to get more meaningful early input from regions and states on national goals, objectives, and strategies, as well as the priorities for the upcoming fiscal year. In turn, regions agreed to do more early planning, in consultation with states and tribes, so that they could make a strategic case for their priorities, either by trying to influence national priorities or to request flexibility to deviate from national priorities in order to address unique situations (EPA 2002).

In a later effort conducted jointly by EPA and the Strategic Planning Committee of the Environmental Council of the States (ECOS), states and EPA agreed on farther-reaching reforms to improve the way that state and EPA programs could improve their joint long-term planning and priority-setting and find ways to provide flexibility to meet local conditions while aggressively pursuing broader environmental goals. While there will always be tensions in decentralized programs in which public expectations for government action outstrip the available resources, these reforms and others have helped EPA and States manage their programs

Using Comparative Risk and Cost Data to Inform Priority-Setting and Decision Making

Part of EPA's initial mid-1990s vision for planning, budgeting, analysis, and accountability was that the Agency would move toward priority setting and budgeting based on comparison of the risks presented across EPA's programs and comparison of the costs of mitigating them. There were and are forces supporting EPA planning and priority-setting that would rely on a more formal system for considering relative risk and the costs of reducing that risk. Members of Congress and their staffs have periodically pushed the Agency in this direction and were vocal about it in the mid-1990s. It was the subject of key recommendations in the National Academy of Public Administration's (NAPA) 1995 study on EPA cited above, as well as a 1997 NAPA study on the Agency (NAPA 1997), and was raised in reports by the Government Accountability Office (GAO 1991) and EPA's own Science Advisory Board (EPA 1990).

There was some internal support for enhancing the Agency's tools for doing comparative analysis of risks and risk reduction across and within programs, as reflected in the recommendations of the 1996 Planning, Budgeting and Accountability Task Force mentioned earlier. OCFO was authorized to hire a small staff of scientists and economists to begin work on it. Despite getting this charge and having bright, energetic, and creative staff assigned to the work, OCFO did not succeed in getting comparative analysis for planning, budgeting, and priority-setting off the ground. Several factors came into play, and they illustrate the constraints that EPA and likely other public health agencies would face in attempting to do the same things today.

The idea of formally comparing environmental risks and costs and using the comparative analysis as the basis for priority-setting and budgeting had always been controversial. For example, despite the reality that government and society cannot work on all problems with equal speed and rigor, many environmentalists are philosophically opposed to the concept of ranking or rating existing human health and ecological risks in order to choose to deliver unequal protection or mitigation. Even some advocates for more consideration of risk and costs in priority setting and budgeting have felt that data and analytical limitations would make it unworkable.

Personnel changes in top Agency management lessened some of the support for comparative analysis for planning and budgeting. For example, Deputy Administrator Fred Hansen, who had been the primary internal customer for the Planning, Budgeting and Accountability Task Force's recommendations, left the Agency in mid-1998 and CFO Sallyanne Harper, responsible for day-to-day implementation of the new results-based management direction, left in early 2000. Administrator Carol Browner had not been an advocate for risk-based priority-setting and budgeting, nor were Mr. Hansen's and

Ms. Harper's replacements. With other crucial issues needing their and the Administrator's time, attention, and support, they were not inclined to push a controversial (and discretionary) initiative to an unreceptive boss.

Discussions that OCFO managers and staff had, via private interviews, with senior career managers around the Agency also illustrated some of the forces constraining the use of comparative analysis in priority-setting and budgeting. These were some of the opinions expressed by the interviewees:

- The results would be misused if (when) leaked outside the Agency.
- Data and analytical methods do not yet allow for apples-to-apples comparisons of environmental risks and risk-reduction efforts.
- Comparative analyses would be more useful for broader strategic planning and priority-setting than for annual planning and budgeting.
- Assistant administrators already consider risk when setting priorities within major offices and programs, so more finely-tuned, cross-Agency analyses aren't needed.

Regarding lessons learned from this experience, senior managers took a calculated chance that the Agency would support expanded use of comparative cost and risk data for planning and budgeting. In hindsight, they underestimated the technical challenges that would require this to be a long-term effort as well as the level of internal resistance that would keep program offices from providing necessary support to sustain the work in either the short or long term.

CONCLUSIONS

EPA admirably adapted the government-wide GPRA framework into an aggressive, tailored effort for results-based management that went well beyond the requirements of GPRA. In the face of many legal, political, technical, and organizational constraints, it put an ambitious system in place and then worked with its partners to evaluate it and make improvements and reforms that would have been difficult to imagine in 1997.

These are some of the overarching lessons learned from EPA's experience with results-based planning, budgeting, analysis, and accountability, and which may be applicable to other public organizations:

1. Dramatic organizational and infrastructure changes help facilitate dramatic changes in management practices. Reorganizing to bring together EPA's planning, budgeting, analysis, and accountability staff into a

single office and restructuring the budget to mirror the Agency's goals and objectives were challenging but ultimately crucial steps in making a shift to results-based management.

2. Lower the transaction costs and reporting burden associated with planning, budgeting, and performance management. Automated data systems and process streamlining can help achieve this. Similarly, streamlining the structure and content of plans, budgets, and reports, as EPA did in shifting from ten goals to five goals, will help ensure that the benefits of results-based management aren't overwhelmed by the costs of implementing it.

3. Assign dedicated staff to planning and management functions. While these processes and systems can be operated by staff doing it part-time as "other duties as assigned," central planning and budgeting offices as well as program and regional offices benefit from having core teams that can focus a critical mass of time and attention on activities such as improving performance measures, integrating performance targets and budgets, and analyzing performance data.

4. Engage senior agency leadership in long-term planning, goal-based budgeting, and review of performance data. Adjust systems to fit senior leaders' management styles and to help them achieve their policy goals.

5. Engage with partners and stakeholders to evaluate planning and management systems and make continuous improvements to them.

6. While excellent written plans and performance reports are important, the primary purpose of results-based management is for senior managers and staff to *use* performance data to make priority-setting and budget decisions and improve their programs to get better results for the American people.

REFERENCES

Drucker, Peter. 1996. The Effective Executive. As reproduced in T*he Essential Drucker*. 2001. New York, NY: HarperBusiness.

Environmental Protection Agency Science Advisory Board. 1990. *Reducing Risk: Setting Priorities and Strategies for Environmental Protection*. Washington, DC: EPA.

Environmental Protection Agency. 1996. *Managing for Results*. Planning, Budgeting and Accountability Task Force Report. Washington, DC: EPA.

———. 1996. *Environmental Goals for America With Milestones for 2005: Draft for Full Government Review*. Washington, DC: EPA.

———. 1997. *EPA Strategic Plan for 1997–2002*. Washington, DC: EPA.

———. 1999. *Testimony of Sallyanne Harper, EPA CFO, before the Subcommittee on Government Management, Information, and Technology, Committee on Government Reform, U.S. House of Representatives*. Washington, DC: EPA.

———. 2002. *Managing for Improved Results: Report to the EPA Deputy Administrator and CFO by the Managing for Improved Results Steering Group*. Washington, DC: EPA.

Executive Office of the President. 2011. *OMB Circular No. A-11: Preparation, Submission, and Execution of the Budget*. Washington, DC: OMB.

Gabor, Andrea. 1990. *The Man Who Discovered Quality: How W. Edwards Deming Brought the Quality Revolution to America*. New York: NY Times Books.

Government Performance and Results Act. 1993. http://thomas.loc.gov/cgi-bin/query/z?c103:S.20.ENR:=.

Ishikawa, Kaoru. 1985. *What is Total Quality Control? The Japanese Way*. NJ: Prentice-Hall, Inc.

National Academy of Public Administration. 1995. *Setting Priorities, Getting Results: A New Direction for EPA*. Washington, DC: NAPA.

———. 1997. *Resolving the Paradox of Environmental Protection: An Agenda for Congress, EPA, and the States*. Washington, DC: NAPA.

Stahl, Michael. 2009. New Imperatives for Public Managers. *The Public Manager* 38/1:5–8.

United States Government Accountability Office. 1991. *Meeting Public Expectations With Limited Resources*. Washington, DC: GAO.

Wilson, James Q. 1989. *Bureacracy: What Government Agencies Do and Why They Do It*. New York, NY: Basic Books.

Chapter Nine

Lessons for Leadership in Environmental Management

John Charles Morris and Gerald Andrews Emison

The preceding chapters describe a variety of executive behaviors applied to a range of national environmental problems. Two attributes stand out: First, each chapter demonstrates a steady commitment to advancing environmental protection even as venues, problems and tools to solve those problems vary. This is a commitment to be true green and thereby fundamentally improve the nation's environmental conditions. Second, the actions profiled in each of the chapters transcend environmental matters and offer a window into effective executive behavior at the federal level, regardless of the policy subject matter. The actions represent a dedication to general public service. We see behavior that is beyond doctrine but is nevertheless exceptionally principled. The foundational principles revealed concern protecting the environment, thereby displaying a commitment to true green outcomes. And these foundational principles also concern leading various large organizations in ways that display effectiveness, efficiency and professionalism; these show civil service that seeks to advance the public interest. This chapter reviews lessons that we can draw from both environmental management and more general effective executive behavior in the federal sector that are the core of the preceding chapters.

TRUE GREEN: EFFECTIVELY PROTECTING THE ENVIRONMENT

The lessons the preceding chapters display for environmental management fall into three categories: those that embrace novelty and innovation, those that engage multi-faceted complexity, and those of pragmatic purposes and methods. All of these are realized through large-scale public institutions in complex and turbulent conditions.

Embracing Novelty and Innovation

Whether managing pesticides, coordinating state and federal activities or budgeting that advances strategic purposes, innovation in environmental management is essential and perpetual. Novel circumstances are constantly appearing. New advances in science, new insight from economic and management analyses and even new interests in politics continuously appear. Past problems and the effective responses to these problems can yield insight, but new conditions bring unique challenges. Responding effectively to these challenges requires environmental executives to be constantly on the lookout for innovative ways to approach environmental management.

Such innovation requires executives to consider all tools that are available to advance environmental protection. Environmental regulation represents a major tool for advancing environmental protection during the period of time this book covers. But regulation is by no means the only tool available or employed. Use of economic incentives, such as market-based solutions for acid rain, information, such as that in the pesticides labeling activities, as well as persuasion to achieve objectives in the indoor air and underground storage tank programs demonstrate the importance of considering every policy implementation tool as new conditions emerge.

We have seen that effective environmental executives must be prepared to move toward unexpected opportunities and apply novel approaches to new challenges. Science, as well as the other features of environmental policy, does not stand still. New discoveries are constantly being made. Effective environmental executives recognize that there really is no such thing as a final decision, but a decision that suits the conditions at that time and must be reconsidered should conditions change.

Multi-Faceted Complexity

The second category of lessons for effective environmental management concerns the sheer complexity of environmental policy decisions. Environmental management occurs at the intersection of science, engineering, technology, organizational behavior, intergovernmental affairs, politics, and economics.

As a result of such a complicated landscape, effective executives must act with simultaneity always in mind. To do so requires an organizing, overarching principle or purpose. One theme across the chapters has been adherence to a set of principles or objectives that focus executive action. We know that environmental pollution has a highly cross-linked nature. Acting on one pollutant invariably has consequences beyond the straightforward control of the target pollutant. There are externalities that must be considered (both positive and negative). For example, controlling particulate matter in air pollution often results in the reduction of air toxic compounds not previously targeted. Environmental executives who are effective regularly take into account such conditions.

This complicated setting affects resources as well. We have seen that money certainly matters, but so do a lot of other things: local support, vision, execution of programs are some others. The environmental executives writing in this book demonstrate the value of an adequate budget; however, they also illustrate the inadequacy of focusing solely on financial matters as the pathway to in protecting the environment. It is important to accept institutional messiness and incompleteness as the basic matrix within which environmental protection takes place.

We have seen in these chapters that while environmental policy is complicated, the solutions must be simple in order to gain support from staff, stakeholders and politicians. The management of purpose as a simplifying approach is a constant recurring theme. Many chapters show that it is important to be clear with all stakeholders about purpose, goals, methods, and limits which are acceptable and appropriate. Ambiguity allows the involved parties to stray from achieving the program's purpose. In both wetlands and indoor air experiences, logical and understandable program objectives became essential to build and retain support.

Managing Purpose and Methods Pragmatically

These chapters, and the experiences that they describe, reveal executives carefully attentive to managing the purpose of their program. And they do so in a pragmatic, results driven manner. Practicality, rather than purity, characterizes effectiveness in these settings. As a result, these executives never lose sight of the ultimate purpose of their activities: protect the environment. These executives focus on the particulars of an environmental situation. Rarely do general, conceptual approaches succeed. It is actions, not theories, that are the touchstone of these executives' practices.

We see that knowledge of environmental processes must be matched with knowledge of administrative and regulatory processes, personnel management and human relations. Superficiality will not suffice. That said, this knowledge should only go to a certain depth. Complete exhaustion and mastery of a subject can lead to over attention and harmful behavior that neglects other important aspects of in environmental decision.

Since results are the ultimate metric for these executives, a willingness to ask for help from other stakeholders reinforces the practical orientation of achieving outcomes irrespective of purity of processes. It is important to look for convergence of interests among all stakeholders, those inside and outside of government. To do so effectively requires a reputation for integrity and competence. Personal character matters, especially during times of difficulty.

These effective executives are constantly appraising politics of interests and power; however when politics are based solely upon symbolic needs, such as we have seen in the pesticides, indoor air and wetlands programs, they can hinder environmental protection. As a result, it is important to not let mischaracterizations and half-truths gain traction, but to refute them quickly.

TRUE BLUE: EXECUTIVE PROFESSIONALISM IN CIVIL SERVICE

The lessons by professional administrators illustrated in this volume provide keen insight into the challenges and opportunities of environmental management. They also offer important insights into the component elements of successful executive professionalism more general in large-scale public organizations in complex conditions. In an era in which public service is maligned by both elected officials and the general public (Goodsell 1994), tens of thousands of dedicated public servants at all levels of government strive daily to provide services in an efficient and effective manner. They remain true to the ideals of public service: competence, public interest and steadfast purpose.

The environment in which this activity takes place is, at best, turbulent, complex, and shifting. Staying true to the ideals of public service is especially noteworthy because of the highly complex and unstable context in which the authors act. Against a backdrop of increasing demands for government goods and services, several factors are worth noting. First, resources are increasingly scarce. As anti-tax and small-government elements in society grow more strident and more powerful, additional pressure is placed on government managers to "do more with less." Second, calls to reduce the size and scope of government regulatory activity require managers fundamentally to rethink how mandates can be accomplished. Finally, the political divisiveness and turmoil of the past decade have served to supercharge interest groups, political parties, and citizens. The net result of this turmoil is that public managers are placed under significantly greater pressure from different stakeholders in the policy domain.

Competing Philosophical Models for Executive Management

Additionally, senior public managers must navigate this turbulent environment while balancing several philosophical interests as well. We have seen this accomplished by the authors of the preceding chapters as they blend and apply a number of philosophical frameworks. Across all these chapters we see executives striving for effectiveness and using various viewpoints based on their pragmatic application rather than any single doctrine.

On the one hand, we value a neutral, competent civil service, free from political pressures and political strife. In the words of Woodrow Wilson, "[a]dministration is a field of business. It is removed from the hurry and strife of politics" (Wilson 1887, 209). In this philosophy, professional competence and neutrality replace political responsiveness, and the job of a civil servant is to implement the policy decisions arrived at by elected officials as efficiently and effectively as possible. Politics, values (whether personal or societal), and interests are not important. Public administrators are guided by their professional skills and abilities.

On the other hand, the Constitution serves as the guiding framework for both the structure and values of American governance (Rohr 1986). The Constitution's centrality in society provides a widely-accepted, stable, and well-known touchstone against which to measure and evaluate administrative activity. In this view, the job of administrators is to act in a manner consistent with the Constitution; to do so provides unassailable legitimacy for administrative activity.

A third philosophical view suggests that government agencies should reflect the ethnic, gender, racial, and socioeconomic diversity present in society. The notion of agencies as microcosms of the broader society they serve is predicated on the notion that public servants best serve citizens when there is immediate empathy between public servants and citizens. In this view, the job of the public administrator is to serve their fellow citizens (see Marini 1971).

A fourth philosophy suggests that public administrators should be responsive to the desires of elected officials. This notion, common in the United States in the mid-nineteenth century (see Mosher 1982), places the legitimacy of the agency directly in the hands of democratically-elected representatives of the people; the job of government is thus to satisfy the whims of the electorate. In this model, public administrators are subservient to elected officials, and their positions as public servants are tied to their ability to keep elected officials satisfied.

Finally, we can conceive of a philosophical model that treats citizens as customers, much the way a private sector business interacts with the recipients of its goods and services. Popularized in the 1990s by Osborne and Gaebler (1992), this philosophical view effectively bypasses the "middleman" of the elected official in the previous philosophy. As customers, citizens are always right, and it is the job of public administrators to keep customers happy. The net effect of this model is that the loudest citizen voices (often interest groups) define the age-old question of politics—who gets what, when, where, and how (see Lasswell 1950; c1936).

Elements of all five of these philosophical approaches are reflected in the vignettes offered in this volume. Indeed, one of the more obvious observations one might draw from this volume is that senior public managers are caught squarely in a multi-sided vise. The competing underpinnings of each of these philosophies are rarely congruent, and are often directly incongruent. Moreover, the adherents of these philosophies are generally not shy in espousing their vision of the "right" way; the net result is that public managers are seemingly left with no single central philosophical touchstone to guide their actions, but choose approaches with an eye to what works.

Navigating Complexity

We have seen in these chapters executives who have navigated turbulent conditions. It is an important truism of the sea that the prudent mariner never relies on a single source of information for successful navigation (USCGA 2002). Indeed, the metaphor of nautical navigation is apropos for application to senior executive management. The lessons of nautical navigation are the result of literally thousands of years of trial-and-error. Senior professional management in the United States is somewhat less ancient; while we know much about the Senior Executive Service, we can learn much by analyzing the real-world experiences of senior managers who have "been there and done that."

These chapters show senior executives operating in complex and turbulent conditions. Lessons from other fields shed light on what works, and how senior managers can safely navigate the often complex and turbulent waters of the political world. Although early scholars of public administration sought to draw a clear distinction between the political and administrative functions (see Wilson 1887), the chapters in this volume clearly illustrate the inherent difficulties with this dichotomy. The metaphor of the navigator is apropos because, like the senior executive in government, the navigator operates in ever-changing conditions—calm seas and fair weather can quickly become rough seas and nasty weather. However, both the navigator and the senior executive must be able to negotiate all conditions and operate successfully *regardless* of the conditions. Varied experiences of people who have moved successfully through turbulent waters—sometimes shallow, sometimes rough—can provide valuable lessons to those seeking similar careers.

The United States Coast Guard Auxiliary's textbook for their Advanced Coastal Navigation course (USCGA 2002, 12–2) lists key principles for professional navigation. In the following part of this chapter, we will apply these principles to the challenges faced by professional senior managers navigating their way through the turbulent environment of modern American governance:

- *Pay attention to detail.* Successful senior managers, like navigators, sweat the small stuff. Seemingly minor errors can quickly compound into major miscalculations. The more accurate the measurements, the more precisely the position fix will be. This is often a difficult task: like a navigator trying to take star sights on the pitching deck of a ship, the environment of a senior manager is a rolling, shifting, unstable platform. However, by paying close attention to the small nuances of that environment, both the navigator and the senior manager can accomplish their tasks.
- *Practice is essential.* Executive management, like navigation, is an acquired skill. In both cases, the path to proficiency lies in the practice of the craft. Senior managers are not born into their positions, and new navigators are not turned loose on long-distance voyages without demonstrating their competence. Competence in each case is achieved through years of practice and application, coupled with a continuous re-evaluation of knowledge. As knowledge is gained through practice, that knowledge can be applied in newly confronted situations. The senior managers contributing to this volume have not only had many years' service, they have all learned useful and important lessons they have been able to apply as they were learned. None of these lessons would have been confronted but for ongoing practice and learning.
- *Do not rely on any one technique for determining one's position.* Novice navigators learn an important truism early in their careers: sources of information on which they rely can sometimes provide spurious or inaccurate information. The magnetic compass, a staple of navigation for hundreds of years, is susceptible to deviation in the earth's magnetic field, large ferrous structures on the ship, and variation (drifting) of the earth's magnetic poles. Likewise, as reliable as the GPS system is, signal quality is dependent on magnetic and radio interference, solar flare activity, and the constant availability of the satellite signals. Senior managers can receive (or not receive) signals from co-workers, employees, political leaders, or stakeholders; all of these signals are subject to inaccuracies. An executive who relies on a single source of information may suffer from spurious information; if there is no other source of information against

which to compare, the executive may never know whether the information is accurate or not. Just as a navigator checks her compass reading against a GPS signal and sight bearings, the prudent executive seeks different sources of information to determine her situation. A manager who relies alone on secondary reports to assess the effectiveness of a program will likely not have an accurate picture of reality.

- *Be alert to anomalies.* Anomalies are unexpected or unexplained events or circumstances. A navigator who notices a change in the color of the water (typically associated with a change in water depth) would be wise to alert the captain, even if the charts suggest there is no shallow water nearby. Anomalies will always exist for the senior manager, but recognizing an anomaly for what it is can help separate the known from the unknown. More importantly, recognizing anomalies can help the executive search for explanation to make sense of the anomalies.

- *Emphasize routines in times of stress.* Organizations, large and small, run on routines. Naval aviators regularly engage in one of the most stressful jobs in the world: landing on the deck of an aircraft carrier at night. One way they combat this stress is to make the process as routine as possible— a continual scan of the important instruments and indicators in the cockpit, in the same order; following checklists; and maintaining situational awareness. A navigator in a storm may worry about the ship being cast on a shoal, but this is precisely the time when knowing one's position, course, and speed is most critical. Following a routine of gathering position data and plotting that position on a chart (routine tasks) can help ensure the ship stays clear of the shoal.

    One may argue that the nature of the job for senior public executives is one of constant stress. The lesson for senior executives is that stress can be managed. First, to paraphrase an old saying, no manager is an island. By definition, managers supervise others, and the point of the work is to accomplish a goal. A successful manager does not operate as a solitary figure, but acts as a catalyst to raise the level of performance of those around him. Complex tasks in organizational settings are not accomplished alone; they are accomplished when groups of people interact in productive ways. The vignettes in this volume provide ample evidence of group efforts to achieve worthy goals. Individual and group stress can be reduced by following established routines. Just as a pilot reduces stress by employing routines, organizational routines can be an effective method of stress reduction.

- *Slow down or stop the vessel if necessary and circumstances permit.* Perhaps one of the most important lessons from the sinking of the *Titanic* in 1912 is that an unwillingness to heed danger, and to continue both course and speed, is a recipe for disaster. A navigator sailing into an unfamiliar port and unsure of the location of the safe channel slows the ship down in order to provide time to confirm the relative positions of the ship and the channel, and ensure that the course is appropriate for a safe voyage. The job of the senior manager is much the same—to assess whether the course and pace of activity is appropriate for the conditions at hand, and if not, to slow the pace until the parameters of the situation are clear.

- *Preplan as much as possible.* An old saying the naval aviation community is "to fail to plan is to plan to fail." Successful navigation has a destination in mind. Knowing what lies between the starting point and desired location is critical to safe navigation. Is there shallow water that must be avoided? Will the tides and currents push the vessel off course, or slow the vessel? Senior managers are also well-advised to plan as much as possible. What is the goal (destination)? Are there known obstacles (political, technical, organizational) that must be accounted for and negotiated? Are there forces that can aid our progress, or that will oppose us? Like an unexpected squall on the water, some events cannot be foreseen. However, having a plan to know what to do in unexpected circumstances can be the difference between success and failure.

- *Be open to data or information at variance with your understanding of the situation.* One lesson every beginning navigation student learns is the tragedy on the coast of California in 1923 when nine destroyers ran aground and were sunk (see USCGA 2002, 12.12–12.14). Sailing in a line down the coast in foggy conditions, the navigator in the lead ship believed his position, as reflected in his dead reckoning navigation plot, was well south of his actual position. Although there were several pieces of evidence to the contrary (including newly developed technology producing radio bearings, and the pleas of navigators on the trailing ships), the navigator stuck to his belief that the ships were safe, a belief he presumably held right up to the point his ship ran on the rocks at the Devil's Jaw, with eight other ships in the squadron dutifully following suit.

The object lesson here is that humans tend to seek information that reinforces preconceived notions, and information to the contrary is often dismissed. A failure to be alert to apparently anomalous information is potentially dangerous, and can lead to tragedy. Senior executives are no less susceptible to this phenomenon than other people. However, senior executives are also surrounded by competent people who may well spot anomalies (or problems) first; a good manager will consider such information, whether or not it is congruent with deeply-held beliefs.

- *Know and operate within your limits.* People tend to rise to positions of executive management because they have a proven record of success, and are judged by others to be capable of increasing levels of leadership and responsibility. However, even the most competent people have limitations. A navigator who has sailed within sight of land his entire career would be ill-advised to cross an ocean with nothing more than a sextant to determine their position. Likewise, a manager who lacks the requisite skills, or who tries to stretch farther than their skills, risks danger for themselves and their organization. While new skills and abilities can (and should be) acquired, one does not undertake a voyage knowing the skills are beyond one's current capabilities.

An effective executive can build a team in which the skills and abilities of other team members can help compensate for limitations of the executive. Just as the CEO of a software company lacks the up-to-date programming skills of the new hires, the goals of the senior executive are achieved through the efforts of others. The ability to trust in the performance of others, and to create conditions that allow others to produce good work, are essential skills for the senior manager. As seen in the vignettes in this book, productive human relations are a critical part of the task of executive management.

The larger lesson for this volume is that executive leadership, like navigation, requires both a specific set of skills and the knowledge of when and how to apply, or adapt, those skills. Whether the executive leadership is found in the environmental domain or any other policy domain, competent executives are the key to converting policy directives into successful policy outcomes. The job requires not only the ability to manage people in the organization, but to operate in a turbulent, complex, and uncertain environment in an effective, creative manner. Successful executive leadership not only requires a vision of a better world and a plan to achieve that vision, it also requires the executive to act as a buffer between the turbulence and uncertainty of the environment and the "technical core" of the organization—the men and women charged with the day-to-day tasks required to achieve the desired outcomes (see Thompson 1967).

Our examination of the activities of senior executives in the U.S. Environmental Protection Agency exemplifies the world of the senior executive in national government. While particular circumstances vary from agency to agency, the larger lessons offered by these remarkable people are transferrable to many settings. Their combination of skill, experience, knowledge, and dedication to the ideals of public service are object lessons not just in grace under fire, but of the ideals exemplified in the concept of the Senior Executive Service. They are "true green" in their dedication to effective environmentalism, but they are "true blue" in their dedication to service to their fellow citizens.

REFERENCES

Goodsell, Charles E. 1994. *The Case for Bureaucracy: A Public Administration Polemic*, 3rd ed. Chatham, NJ: Chatham House.

Lasswell, Harold. 1950 (c1936). *Politics: Who Gets What, When, How*. New York: P. Smith Publishers.

Marini, Frank, ed. 1971. *Toward a New Public Administration*. Scranton, PA: Chandler.

Mosher, Frederick C. 1982. *Democracy and The Public Service*, 2nd ed. New York: Oxford University Press.

Osborne, David, and Ted Gaebler. 1992. *Reinventing Government: How the Entrepreneurial Spirit Is Transforming the Public Sector*. New York: Plume Books.

Rohr, John. 1986. *To Run a Constitution: The Legitimacy of the Administrative State*. Lawrence, KS: University of Kansas Press.

Thompson, James D. 1967. *Organizations in Action: Social Science Bases of Administrative Theory*. New York: McGraw Hill.

United States Coast Guard Auxiliary. 2002. *Advanced Coastal Navigation*, 4th ed. Washington, DC: Coast Guard Auxiliary Association, Inc. (Publication AN-1).

Wilson, Woodrow. 1887. The Study of Administration. *Political Science Quarterly* 2: 197–222.

About the Contributors

Ronald Brand served as director of the Office of Underground Storage Tanks at the U.S. Environmental Protection Agency (EPA) (1985–1991). He was recognized for outstanding accomplishments in setting up a unique state-federal organizational arrangement with the award of the Presidential Rank Award (1988). He also received the EPA Gold Medal for his demonstrated leadership in Total Quality Management (1990). Prior to that he led the EPA Program Evaluation Division in examining programs throughout the Agency. As a member of the SES he then served as Assistant to the Deputy Administrator, EPA, focusing on management and financial issues affecting program performance. From 1958 to 1970 Brand served in a number of management positions in programs of the U.S. Department of Health, Education, and Welfare (now HHS), finally being named to the position of deputy assistant secretary for management. Brand received a B.A. degree (1954) in public administration from New York University. He was also selected as a National Institute of Public Affairs Fellow at Princeton University (1965). He coauthored *Total Quality Management in Government: A practical guide for the real world,* 1993, Jossey-Bass Publishers.

Gerald Andrews Emison is a professor of political science and public administration at Mississippi State University. Prior to joining MSU Jerry served in a number of senior executive positions with the U.S. Environmental Protection Agency as the director of the Office of Air Quality Planning and Standards, as the deputy regional administrator in Seattle and as the director of the Program Evaluation Division. Among his activities he was an architect of the Clean Air Act of 1990, supervised EPA's cleanup responsibilities at the Hanford Nuclear Reservation and managed the spotted owl controversy for EPA. As a result of his work at EPA he received the presidential rank designation for meritorious senior executive service. He is the author of *Practical Program Evaluations: Getting from Ideas to Outcomes*, which was published by CQ Press in 2006 and the coeditor (with John C. Morris) of *Speaking Green with a Southern Accent*, which was published by Lexington Books, 2010. In addition he has authored over seventy professional journal articles, book chapters and academic conference papers. He was chosen by students to be the departmental professor of the year in 2006 and 2008. He received his Ph.D. in city and regional planning from the University of North Carolina at Chapel Hill. He also holds additional graduate degrees in political science and engineering management. His undergraduate work was in civil engineering at Vanderbilt University. He is a registered professional engineer, a board-certified environmental engineer of the American Academy of Environmental Engineers and a member of the American Institute of Certified Planners.

Thomas E. Kelly retired in 2010 from a forty-two-year federal career, thirty-two years of which he served at EPA. Beginning in 1978 he helped design and organize EPA's original program evaluation function, which he proposed would operate as an internal management consulting firm. In 1987 he entered the SES as EPA's director of Standards and Regulations, responsible to manage EPA's regulatory development process as well as statistical, economic, and ecological analysis in support of Agency rulemaking. In 1996 he was appointed EPA's first statutory chair to administer the Small Business Regulatory Fairness Act (SBREFA), conducting intense regulatory negotiations among EPA programs, the Office of Management and Budget, and the Small Business Administration. From 2003 through 2010 he led EPA's science and outreach program to protect public health from air pollution indoors, also acting for a significant period as director of EPA's Radiation Protection program. He is a recipient of EPA's Gold Medal for Exceptional Service and the Agency's Distinguished Career Award. He entered federal service in 1968 as a management intern with the Department of Health, Education, and Welfare, where he concentrated on program evaluation for public mental health programs. From 1976 to 1978 he served as a program evaluator for the Department of Commerce. He holds a BA in English literature from Wesleyan University (CT) and an MA in sociology from American University (DC).

A. Stanley Meiburg is the deputy regional administrator of EPA Region 4 in Atlanta, Georgia, a position he has held since 1996. He began his career with EPA in 1977 and has served in a variety of positions with the Agency. Dr. Meiburg holds a B.A. degree from Wake Forest University and M.A. and Ph.D. degrees in political science from The Johns Hopkins University.

John Charles Morris is a professor of public policy and serves as the Ph.D. Graduate Program Director in the Department of Urban Studies and Public Administration, at Old Dominion University in Norfolk, Virginia. He is a noted scholar in fields of public-private partnerships and environmental policy. He has published more than fifty scholarly papers in journals such as *Public Administration Review*, *Journal of Politics*, *Policy Studies Journal*, *American Review of Politics*, *Review of Public Personnel Administration*, *State and Local Government Review*, *Politics and Policy*, and *Public Works Management & Policy*, among many others. He is coeditor of five books, including *Building the Local Economy: Cases in Economic Development* (2008, with Douglas J. Watson); *Speaking Green with a Southern Accent: Environmental Management and Innovation in the South* (2010, with Gerald A. Emison); and *Prison Privatization: The Many Facets of a Controversial Industry* (3 volumes; forthcoming 2012, with Byron E. Price). He is also lead author of *Cleaning the Waters: Grassroots Environmental Collaborations, Social Capital, and Ecosystem Restoration in Hampton Roads* (forthcoming 2013). He teaches courses in public policy theory, governance, policy evaluation, public-private partnerships, collaboration, and intergovernmental relations, among others. He is the recipient of several teaching and mentoring awards. He received his Ph.D. from Auburn University, and served as an associate professor at Mississippi State University prior to his arrival at Old Dominion University. He has also served as an evaluator and research coordinator for Policy Studies Associates, Inc., and the City of Auburn, Alabama; and as a research associate for the Center for Governmental Services, Auburn University, and the John C. Stennis Institute of Government, Mississippi State University.

Lee M. Thomas retired as chairman and CEO of Rayonier, a diversified forest products company headquartered in Jacksonville, Florida. Prior to this position he was president and chief operating officer of Georgia Pacific, a global manufacturer and marketer of tissue, packaging, paper, building products and related chemicals in Atlanta, Georgia. He worked with the company for thirteen years managing several of their businesses prior to becoming president in 2002. From 1989 to 1993 he was chief executive officer of Law Environmental Group, a national environmental engineering firm. Prior to his twenty-three-year business career, Thomas spent twenty-one years working for local, state, and federal government agencies. His final eight years were in Washington with the Reagan administration. He was associate director and executive deputy director of FEMA for two years and then at EPA for six years. He served as assistant administrator for solid waste and emergency response from 1983 to 1985 and as administrator from 1985 to 1989. Thomas has a BA from the University of the South in Sewanee, Tennessee and a M.Ed. from the University of South Carolina.

Robert Wayland served in many positions at the Environmental Protection Agency during his twenty-eight-year career including deputy assistant administrator for policy, planning, and evaluation and deputy assistant administrator for water. He was director of EPA's Office of Wetlands, Oceans, and Watersheds (OWOW) from 1991 until 2003. In this position, he led EPA's efforts to encourage the management of water resources on a watershed basis. Innovations to which he made significant contributions included establishment of the Clean Water Action Plan, Watershed Assistance Grants, 5-Star Restoration grants, the first national Coastal Condition Report, development of a Federal-State-Tribal Action Plan to curb the "Dead Zone" in the Gulf of Mexico, and the 1993 Interagency Wetlands Plan. He was awarded the Elizabeth Fellows Partnership award by the association of state water quality agencies, the President's Award of the Wildlife Habitat Council, and was presented with EPA Distinguished Career Award by Administrator Christie Todd Whitman. Presidents Bill Clinton and President George W. Bush each awarded Wayland the Presidential Rank of Meritorious Executive. Prior to joining EPA, Bob worked for a U.S. Senator, a California Congressman, and the National Transportation Safety Board. Since retiring from EPA he has served as vice chair of the Virginia Water Control Board, board chair of the Southeast Watershed Forum, and served on the board of the Environmental Protection Agency Alumni Association.

Susan Wayland served in many key senior executive positions at the Environmental Protection Agency during her tenure from 1972 to 2003. Her career culminated as the acting assistant administrator for the Office of Prevention, Pesticides and Toxic Substances (currently the Office of Chemical Safety and Prevention) during the last two years of the Clinton administration. Prior to that, as deputy assistant administrator, she took the lead on a wide range of management responsibilities and served on numerous cross-agency and cross-government budgetary and policy, planning, and implementation endeavors, including food safety, agricultural policy, and international chemical harmonization. For the majority of her career, she worked on national pesticide policy and operational issues, including the implementation of the Food Quality Protection Act of 1996, pesticide reregistration, ground water and endangered species protection, and strategic planning. As deputy and acting assistant administrator, she also oversaw policies directed toward industrial chemicals and pollution prevention, including lead standards, green chemistry, and chemical testing. She was awarded the Rank of Meritorious Executive by President George H.W. Bush, the Rank of Distinguished Executive, the highest honor available to members of the Senior Executive Service, by President William Clinton, and the EPA Distinguished

Career Award. Since retiring, she has continued to be active in local environmental issues, and enjoys watching bald eagles soar outside her kitchen window.

David Ziegele is a management consultant who supports government agencies in the areas of program evaluation, performance measurement, and strategic planning. Prior to his retirement from federal service in 2005, he served in several senior positions at the Environmental Protection Agency (EPA), including director of the Office of Planning, Analysis, and Accountability; deputy comptroller; director of the Office of Underground Storage Tanks; special assistant to the administrator; and director of the Program Evaluation Division. In recognition of his contributions at EPA, he received the presidential rank award for meritorious service, the Senior Executive Service distinguished career award, and an EPA gold medal. Before joining EPA, he worked at Peace Corps Headquarters and served as a Peace Corps Volunteer in Togo/West Africa. He received a liberal arts degree from the University of Iowa and a master of public administration degree from the University of Southern California.

Index

CPSIA information can be obtained at www.ICGtesting.com
Printed in the USA
BVOW032240240213

314000BV00003B/8/P